# SUMMERS *of* FIRE

# LINDA STRADER

# SUMMERS *of* FIRE

## A MEMOIR OF ADVENTURE, LOVE AND COURAGE

*Bink Books*
Bedazzled Ink Publishing Company • Fairfield, California

978-1-945805-66-0 paperback

Cover Design
by

DESIGNS

Bink Books
a division of
Bedazzled Ink Publishing Company
Fairfield, California
http://www.bedazzledink.com

*For my mom, who always believed in me.*

# AUTHOR'S NOTE

This memoir is based on journals I kept during my seven summers working for the U.S. Forest Service and Bureau of Land Management from 1976 to 1982. Most of the names in my story have been changed. Conversations in this book are based on memory or from entries in my journals.

# ACKNOWLEDGMENTS

Thank you to all of those who supported and helped me throughout the writing of my story: Denise Roessle (who sadly passed away before the book was published), Lise Hicks, Duke Southard, Colin Treworgy, Wendy Cohan and Cheryl Eriksen.

I also want to give a special thank you to Joanne Burch, without whom this story probably would have never been completed. Thank you, Joanne, for being my friend, advisor and writing coach.

*August 15th, 1974*

*I wish I could stand on a mountain and touch a star.*

*I wish I could run and run down a beautiful snow-covered hill and never stop until I wanted to.*

*I wish I could find peace outside me, and most of all, inside me.*

*I wish for once in my life I could be at ease with things around me—sincerely content.*

# ONE

## Summer of 1976: Florida Ranger Station,
## Santa Rita Mountains, Southern Arizona

*Monday, May 31st*

"UH-OH," MY CREWMATE Joe said, staring behind us. "There go our packs."

My Pulaski froze mid-swing. I lowered it to my side, momentarily forgetting the wildfire in front of me. Smoke swirled between the two of us. I leaned around Joe and saw nothing but pine trees on fire, which, all things considered, made sense. *Where did our packs go? Was an animal dragging them away?* Then it hit me. Our packs were up in flames. The forest fire had jumped our line—the narrow defensive belt of raw earth we'd feverishly clawed through the woods. All of our gear. Gone. Including our canteens of precious water.

This was my first fire; but not Joe's. When he said we'd just rebuild the line, I thought, *okay, no big deal.* He seemed calm and not too concerned about when we'd get more water, so I didn't worry about that either. Even with our gear a pile of ashes, we'd no choice but to continue to build line. In my hands I clutched a Pulaski, invented by a forest ranger for just this kind of work. A combination ax and hoe, it made building line easier. Easier, but still brutal, hard work. With flames a mere foot away, I removed fuel from the fire's path, down to bare mineral soil, our fireline. My arm muscles burned from swinging the ax end at small trees, my back pinched from scraping pine needles and the duff underneath them with the hoe. Intense heat from the fire and exertion made me thirsty. *A drink of water would be really good right now.* The gum in my pack, which might have helped, had turned into a melted glob. As I chopped and scraped everything to bare earth, I mentally inventoried what I'd lost besides my canteen: headlamp, socks, my Levi jacket. *Damn, I really liked that jacket.*

While we were focused on our work, the sun rose higher in the sky. Temperatures had climbed over ninety, I figured. My mouth felt like the dry, dusty, desert below. I so wanted a drink of water. I really needed a drink of water. An abrupt shift in the wind funneled smoke into the draw like water pouring from an overflowing dam. My eyes stung, teared, my vision blurred. I tried holding my breath, but couldn't for long, and smoke filled my lungs.

My chest seized, hurt, and I exploded into a coughing fit. Remembering the bandana around my neck, I retied it bandito style over my face.

"Over here!" Joe said, waving me on. "Get down low."

Crawling, choking, with tears streaming down my face, I followed him. Instead of my heart pounding from the hard work, it thumped with the fear that we'd be overcome by smoke. At the edge of a ridge, I yanked down my bandana to suck in fresh air, terrified it wouldn't be enough, terrified that I'd inhaled too much smoke. Soon oxygen filled my lungs, and I breathed easier.

I turned to Joe, who was also recovering . . .

"We'll wait till the smoke clears," he said hoarsely.

I nodded, grateful he knew what to do. We sat for a few minutes, clearing out our lungs, blinking to regain our vision. If I had any moisture left in my body, I would have needed to wipe sweat from my brow, but I didn't. My tongue felt swollen, glued to the roof of my dry mouth. My teeth were gritty, but I didn't have enough spit to lick them clean. *Don't think about how thirsty you are, it will only make it worse.* Thinking that made it worse.

The drone of plane engines rose above the crackling of the nearby fire.

Overhead, a huge, slow-moving C-47 carried fire retardant, slurry. The silver bird gave me a twinge of hope. Slurry, a mixture of water and fertilizer, would knock-down the fire. The plane circled, making a second pass. I watched in awe as the hatch doors on the bottom opened, releasing a plume of dark pink, which rained through the forest canopy, dampening flames. With its nose turned up, the plane disappeared from view.

"C'mon," Joe said, "now's our chance."

I nodded. We left our fresh air zone and returned to the fire, where pine sap boiled, snapped, and sputtered.

Despite intense, nagging thirst, I kept scraping, digging.

"Make the line four feet wide," Joe said.

Again I just nodded, afraid if I opened my mouth to say something I'd dry it out even more. Somehow we managed to reach the lower edge of the blaze, although I had no idea if we were catching the fire or not, or if Scott, the third member of our crew, had made any progress. There'd been no sign of Scott since he'd vanished across the rockslide hours ago. He had the only two-way radio, so we couldn't check in.

As the sun climbed higher, I noticed a rise in the temperature and a wind shift. Instead of fire burning slowly downhill, it picked up spead and headed uphill. This was not good. On autopilot, mouth clamped tight to conserve moisture, I pushed myself to scrape more line clear of flammable pine needles, chopping overhanging branches that could breech our clearing. I'd no idea how long we'd been working, and wondered when we'd get some help.

Distant voices made me pause. Through tall ponderosas I caught a glimpse of bright yellow fire shirts. *Finally!* Leading the group: a firefighter from the Nogales crew carrying multiple canteens strapped across his stout frame—a walking canteen shop. "Anybody need water?"

I uttered the first word to come out of my mouth in hours. "Me!" I accepted one, fumbled to unscrew the cap, and took a swig, resisting the temptation to drink too much too fast, which could make me sick. I savored the wetness, swishing the water around my teeth, tongue, and gums before swallowing. Water never, ever tasted, or felt, so good.

After quenching my thirst, I realized that behind him stood the Catalina Hotshots. *Hey, I know these guys!* I broke into a big grin, hoping they'd recognize me.

"Hey, Linda," one said, smiling. "I heard you made it to a fire crew."

My grin expanded. *Oh, yeah I did.* Too bad we couldn't talk, I was dying to tell them all about my new job, but we had work to do. We had to get this fire under control.

# TWO

WHAT A MAD, crazy day. I'd only been on the job two weeks and barely managed to get fire training under my belt when that five a.m. fire call came in.

Glenn was the first person I met when I arrived at Florida Ranger Station in mid-May to work on a fire crew. The lean, darkly tanned man wore a Forest Service uniform, his lined, weathered face alluding to many years in the sun. Sweat stains radiated around the band of his gray Stetson. He extended his hand, and in a deep, commanding voice, said, "Hello, I'm Glenn."

He supervised all the fire personnel at Florida, including the ten-person fire suppression crew, of which I was the one and only woman. After we shook hands, he grasped my hand a moment longer and turned it over to study my palm. When he let it go, he squeezed my upper arm and raised his eyebrows, a corner of his mouth lifting. I offered a tentative smile. *Is he teasing, or does he think I can't handle the job?* After an awkward moment, he released my arm.

Then Glenn introduced me to Opie Taylor. Not the one from TV's *Mayberry RFD*, although he resembled him enough to have earned the nickname. Glenn asked him to escort me to my quarters. Later Opie offered me a ride to Green Valley to buy groceries. After unloading, he hung around my kitchen, in no hurry to leave.

"Um, well, I'm beat, so . . . thanks again for the ride," I said, putting the last of the groceries away.

Still he stood there, leaning against the door frame, legs crossed at the ankle.

"Do you want to go to bed?" he asked, leering.

*Are you kidding me?*

I found him more amusing than offensive.

"Uh, no, we've only just met," I said, suppressing laughter. "You need to go."

Still, he wouldn't leave, trying to get me to change my mind. Finally, I placed my hands on his back and shoved him over the threshold, saying, "Get. Out!" and slammed the door shut.

I stood there for a moment in disbelief. Opie's proposition was so outrageous, I laughed it and him off. Aside from the fact that casual sex didn't interest me, after two painful breakups over the past year, I'd concluded that keeping guys for now as "friends only" would give me time to regroup. I did not want, or need, a serious relationship.

The next Monday, everyone except Mark and me went to train in Nogales, leaving me to a fate unknown. I never knew what to think of Mark. Over the past week, I'd overheard him talk incessantly about gorgeous college coeds and complain about his miserable marriage. A huge turnoff despite his good looks. Would I have to listen to endless blabbering all day long about sexy blonds with perfect legs?

Inside the fire cache, Mark gave me a box of headlamps to test while he inventoried gear. In no time he'd charmed me with his affable nature. I enjoyed his easy, contagious laugh. Mark was also sophisticated, educated— unlike anyone I'd ever met. This attracted me, but remembering his annoying comments, I didn't understand why. *He can only cause trouble*, I thought. *Don't get involved.*

Two days later, Mark asked if I'd like to go running.

Pleased, I said, "Sure, I like to run."

Jogging down the station's dirt road, he turned to smile at me. "I can run better if I think about something really nice."

Short of breath, I simply smiled back. Out of the corner of my eye, I noticed he watched me—and continued to do so for a while. I wondered: *Was I "something really nice"?* A warm glow spread through me to think maybe I was. When we finished our run, Mark asked me to his quarters for dinner. *Not a big deal*, I thought, knowing we wouldn't be alone or anything. Those of us living at Florida often shared meals.

The next evening, Mark and I hit the Florida Trail to test out our fire packs before we'd need them. Virtually effervescent from our nonstop talking and laughing, the feeling continued into the next day . . . until late afternoon, out of nowhere, his attention waned. Was I now invisible and insignificant? Confused, I went for a walk that night, feeling rejected and wondering what I'd done. Plus, I'd drifted from my "don't get involved" stance already, which infuriated me.

Still ruminating in the morning, I took an arduous, solo hike up to Florida Saddle, tackling the loose rock and tight switchbacks of the first two miles to reach pines—the whole point of going. Water gurgled inside a trailside pipe, the station's water source. Maybe I could fill my canteen at the spring. A Steller's jay scolded me for daring to enter his territory. *Intruder alert!* he squawked. Once in the forest of Douglas fir and ponderosa, I perched on a rock to sort my thoughts. Was I too ugly for Mark? *Or maybe he is just full of shit.*

Confusion unresolved, too soon I needed to slide and skid down to beat sunset. I returned to find the guys drinking at Mark's quarters. They invited me to join them. I figured, *why not?* Maybe it would improve my mood. I sat on the couch between Mark and Scott, one of our fire prevention technicians whom I'd talked with often. Mark rested his arm on the couch behind me, fingers touching my shoulder, giving me pleasant tingles. Then Scott discretely took my hand, doubling the sensation. To make it even more surreal, when Mark left, Tom, our tanker crew foreman and someone I also enjoyed talking to, took his place *and* my hand. Not only was all of this attention overwhelming, but mind-boggling. What in the world did they see in *me?*

However, their flirting delighted my soul, and like a cactus in a brief summer rain, I soaked up every solitary drop.


THAT LAST DAY of May had started out as usual. I woke early, listening to the wistful calls of mourning doves, bed springs squeaking as I shifted onto my back to get comfortable. Dusky daylight filtered into the bedroom of my U.S. Forest Service living quarters. A new sound, footsteps crunching gravel, approached my open bedroom window.

Glenn spoke through the screen. "Linda? We've got a fire."

*OhmyGodOhmyGod!* I sat up straight. "Okay! Be right there!"

Hands trembling with nervous excitement, I marathon dressed in my Levi's, chambray workshirt, and added a yellow Nomex fire shirt. Red Wing boots tied, hardhat snatched off the kitchen table, I dashed over to the office located behind my quarters, raring to go.

"We're the only ones here," Glenn said, his mouth tight in a flat line. "Don't these guys know it's fire season?"

As the assistant Fire Control Officer, he was annoyed by their absence. He picked up the phone and dialed Scott at home in Tucson. Next he called crewmate Joe, who lived in nearby Madera Canyon.

After hanging up, Glenn strode over to an old wooden dresser which served as the coffee station. He filled a mug, plopped two sugar cubes into the dark liquid, and took a sip. Steel-blue eyes glanced over at me from beneath a weathered gray Stetson. "Might as well take a seat. It'll be 'bout hour 'till they get here."

*What? Why weren't we gone already?* This made no sense. Wasn't a fire supposed to be some kind of emergency?

With no other choice, I sat, anxious, waiting to go to my first fire. Good thing I'd trained with my crew of ten just last week. We'd even had a mock fire drill, complete with smoke bombs, which fooled everyone but me. I saw through the charade. But would that be enough? A nugget of self-doubt crept in.

A long fifty-five minutes later, two pickup trucks roared into the complex. Packs loaded into our truck, Scott, Joe, and I sped out of the complex, dust clouds billowing in our wake. Two miles later, Scott hit the paved road to Madera Canyon, his foot heavy on the accelerator. A column of smoke rose beneath the rocky bluffs of Mt. Wrightson, the Santa Rita Mountains' highest peak at over nine thousand feet. My stomach fluttered—this smoke was the real thing.

We turned off the pavement and started up a rough four-wheel-drive fire access road, my seat belt cinching tighter with every bump. I struggled to readjust, only to have it squeeze me again the next time we hit a rock. The next jolt I narrowly missed bashing my head on the roof—saved by my hardhat. Sunlight slanted through tree tops, warning of the impending heat. With Tucson's predicted high near one hundred degrees, it'd be hot up there, even at six thousand feet, but all I thought about was tackling that forest fire.

The road ended, and we jumped out of the truck. Pack shifted into position, Pulaski in hand, I followed Scott and Joe as they scrambled up and over a ridge toward our blaze.

Emerging at the top of a lichen-covered rockslide, I got my first look at my first fire. Stiff downslope breezes pushed the heavy sweet-smelling smoke to a canyon of sycamores and cottonwoods. Wind-fanned flames crackled and popped as they consumed brush and lower limbs of ponderosa pines. I stood mesmerized and apprehensive, but unafraid. Time to go to work. I turned to Scott for instructions.

"Joe. Take Linda and flank the fire, then pinch it off at the bottom. I'll tackle the head, then move to the other side and meet up with you guys. Let's see if we can catch this sucker before the winds switch."

Fire training had taught me that winds flow downhill at night and uphill during the day. Fire burns much faster upslope, pre-heating the vegetation ahead of it. Faster than anyone can run. Dangerous. Deadly. We sure wanted to stop this fire before it made an uphill run, when there might be no stopping it.

Scott disappeared across the rockslide, while Joe and I began building line. Fire snapped through tawny grasses, creeping steadily in its search for more fuel. Adrenaline pumped through every vein, pushing me to dig faster. My fire pack bumped my elbow. I shoved it back. Another bump. Joe suggested we ditch our packs on the opposite side of our newly built line, where they'd be safe.

Back to work, digging, chopping, moving debris away from the flames to keep them from advancing. Extreme heat prickled my face, stinging like needles. Sweat burned my eyes. I looked up to see Joe had stopped working and was staring behind us. "Uh oh . . ."

# THREE

SO MUCH FOR our fire gear.

Now, rehydrated, Joe and I joined the twenty hotshots and the rest of our crew to finish containing the ten-acre Kent Fire with a line around the perimeter. It didn't take long with so many hands.

"Okay, guys, let's take a break," Scott said. "Helicopter flew in some C-rations."

I sat, but felt guilty—as though I should keep working until I'd personally snuffed out every flame. Sitting did feel good, though. Almost too good. What if I couldn't get up again? But I rejoiced in sips of spectacular, wonderful, and oh-so-wet water. I couldn't get enough.

Tom fished through the stack of cardboard boxes containing our meals. "Oh, goody. C-rats. Good enough for Vietnam platoons, good enough for us. What's your pleasure? We've got spaghetti with meatballs, beef stew, tuna . . ."

"I'll take a tuna," I said, unable to imagine eating cold spaghetti, or beef stew, no matter how starving I was. A tiny P-38 can opener had the lid off in seconds. I forked a mouthful and chewed. What else hid inside the box? Kind of like delving into a Christmas stocking: A one-inch tall bottle of Tabasco sauce, rock-hard Chicklets gum, fruit cocktail, and canned crackers. That amused me; I'd never heard of canned crackers. What else? Waterproof matches and a package of toilet paper the size of a cigarette lighter. *Seriously?*

I recognized a familiar voice from the hotshot group. "So, Linda, how was your first fire?"

I'd met the hotshots the previous summer at Palisades Ranger Station, in the Santa Catalina Mountains, north of Tucson, Arizona. In my fire crew timekeeper role, I'd kept track of this elite firefighting crew's hours as they'd battled fires all over the west. An impressionable nineteen-year-old, I was captivated by their flirting, camaraderie, travels, and fire adventure stories. I'd even dated a few, including the one who just spoke to me. By the end of the summer, I never wanted a desk job again.

Sidestepping the awkward moment (I'd just recently broken up with that hotshot), I smiled and addressed everyone.

"Great! I saw a slurry drop. And Joe and I were nearly overcome by smoke."

Heads nodded enthusiastically. Only a true firefighter would brag about a near miss. I'd just been indoctrinated into the world of fire, and couldn't stop my insides from dancing.

"So how was your first fire?" Mark asked Joe.

My head jerked up hard. *What? First fire?*

"Hot," Joe said, generating laughter.

I scrambled to come up with reasons why I'd assumed he'd fought fires before, but couldn't think of a single one.

The laughter died down, and Mark smiled at me. We held each other's gaze for a moment, and glanced away. Pleasant tingles filled my chest.


RESTED, WE NOW had to mop-up the fire, extinguishing every single hotspot so it wouldn't restart later. Hard to get motivated now that the excitement was over. My legs were heavy, leaden; not surprising since I'd already slaved for nine hours.

Between charcoal-covered trees, over blackened rocks and scorched earth, I trudged through the aftermath, skidding and sliding on rough terrain. It didn't help that on my back I carried what the guys called a "piss-pump," a bag of water with a spray nozzle on the bottom. Quite handy for putting out hotspots, but a royal pain to carry. The weight of five gallons followed gravity, pulling me downhill. To compensate, I leaned uphill, even on a side slope. When the water started sloshing, I nearly fell over. Annoyed, I hiked back to the staging area and traded the now-empty bag for a shovel. Throwing dirt on a fire put it out by both cooling and smothering. Travel light and upright: My new motto.

Fourteen hours after dispatch, we were released. I dozed in the back seat, vaguely aware of the drive, waking fully when we rattled over the cattle guard rails at the entry of the complex. Giant oaks hung over the road, filtering moonlight through their canopies, creating mottled purple shadows. Florida (Flor-ee-da) Ranger Station, in the Santa Rita Mountains of Southern Arizona, my summer home and workplace. Built over thirty years ago by the Civilian Conservation Corps (CCC), it had all the charm and character one could imagine: Quaint buildings, over a dozen of them, nestled in a canyon of giant white oaks. More white oaks and a few sycamores lined the ephemeral Florida Creek, which only flowed after snow melt or heavy summer rains.

"Report tomorrow at four o'clock," Glenn said as we stumbled out of crew-cabs.

*Four?* I didn't even want to think about it.

My summer quarters, one of those quaint buildings painted soft yellow with a green-shingled roof, looked better than ever. I sat on the edge of my swayback mattress and pulled off my boots. I placed them up high to keep scorpions from crawling inside and summoned up the energy to shower. When I pulled back the curtain, a scorpion, tail held high and ready to strike, attempted to climb up the slick tub.

"Eek!" I grabbed the nearest weapon, a boot, and smashed it to pieces. I'd never *been* stung, and had no desire to *be* stung. How did it get in there anyway?

Underneath the spray of warm water, I lathered up and rinsed. My long blond hair, filthy and matted with sweat, took two shampoos to get squeaky clean. I stepped out, snatched my towel off the rack, and dried off, only to see soot speckles remained on my calves. Too tired to do anything about it, I fell into bed and fell into a dream-filled sleep.

Dreamland: smoke, fire, flames, and planes—interrupted by a rude clanging. I rolled over and smacked the button on my wind-up alarm clock. Outside my window, light had barely begun to edge out dark. How could it possibly be time to get up? I threw back the covers and stood up. *Ow.* My quads let me know I'd overdone it. I shuffled to the bathroom and flipped on the light. Numerous blisters on my palms stung, with several open and bleeding. Wincing, I peeled away loose skin. Not much I could do about those.

Dressed in Nomex fire-resistant clothes, I went to fix breakfast. After pulling down the door handle of the 1950s fridge, I reached for the milk. Inside, the shoe-box freezer held two ice-cube trays encrusted with frost. I frowned. *Must defrost that one of these days.* After cereal and toast, I walked to the office, ready to report for firefighting, day two.

The office screen door creaked on its rusty hinges when I entered, and the evaporative cooler, perched in a window, blew moist air into the room, enhancing the telltale musty odor of old building. Standard government issue furnishings here, collected for function, not aesthetics. I stiffly took a seat in one of the gray metal chairs.

Glenn half-smiled. "You know, the best cure for aching muscles is to work out the soreness." He winked at Eric, our crew foreman, who grinned widely at me.

How could more hard work make me hurt less? That didn't seem possible.

"We've got the Safford Prison crew coming to help mop-up today," Eric said as he drove us out of the station.

*Prisoners? We're working with prisoners?* Would I be safe? After all, these men were in prison for a reason. Plus, they hadn't seen a woman . . . in what, years? Would they try to escape? Nervous, I made plans to keep my distance.

The mop-up process couldn't be rushed and required great patience. I scanned the charred forest, searching for wisps of smoke or red embers, listening for whistling, popping. Across a wide rockslide, a burning stump required my attention. Before stepping onto the slide, I tested it with the weight of one leg. *Seems okay.* I ventured out. The slide gave way, carrying me downslope, as I struggled to balance as though on a surfboard. Frightened,

I worried I'd face-plant a tree at the bottom if I couldn't stop. But the rocks quit moving, and I took a calming deep breath. Venturing farther caused more sliding, until I made it to the other side. Cursing under my breath, I used saplings to pull myself back up the slope, praying they wouldn't rip out of the ground.

Upon reaching the smoldering stump, I next scraped around for dirt. One foot felt a little warm. Then very warm. Then downright hot. I leapt to one side, nearly losing my balance. Where I'd stood glowed red-hot. No wonder we weren't allowed to wear steel-toed boots. I could only imagine how catastrophic that could be. For the rest of the shift and until the fire was declared out, I carefully checked where I put my feet before doing a darned thing.

Hours of hard, gritty work later, I sat with my crew on a break. Sweaty, ash-smudged prisoners joined us. Glancing at my crew, I noticed I wasn't the only one a little apprehensive about these men. Everyone sat quietly, except for one prisoner, who introduced himself, offered cigarettes, and after lighting one for himself, quipped, "Man, these aren't the Santa Ritas, these are the Steep-a-ritas!"

I laughed with everyone else and relaxed. These prisoners were simply men with a sense of humor and an amazing work ethic, just like us.

# FOUR

AFTER WORKING TEN days straight, I finally had a day off. Mark and Scott came over at lunchtime to visit, and as Mark was leaving, he said I should get with him later so I could assemble a new fire pack to replace the one that got torched. Late that afternoon, I met him in the fire cache.

"Let's get you squared away," he said.

As I repacked my gear, he stood close by and watched. "You know, I'd come over to see you, but you've always got someone there."

Surprised me for a moment. *I do?* Then I realized, I did.

Mark then said, "You're quite the influence on everyone here. Plus, you're so damn cute." A warm smile crossed his face.

Self-conscious but flattered, I tucked a strand of stray hair behind my ear and continued packing. Most everyone teased and flirted with me—harmless fun which I didn't take seriously. Why would I? I never thought I was pretty, but Mark made me feel that way. He had a way with words. I liked that. However, my radar went up. I thought he could be handing me a line.

"You think I'm bullshitting you, don't you?" he asked.

I admitted it had crossed my mind.

"Well, I'm not."

Could I believe him? I wanted to. His attention felt good. Really good.

At six that evening, Mark asked if I'd like to see the old Florida dam. The thought of being alone with him sent my heart fluttering. Maybe he'd say more wonderful things to me. A cool, woodsy-scented breeze drifted down canyon. Florida Creek trickled with the last of snow melt, a hatchery for the clouds of gnats floating around our heads. I waved my hand to disperse them.

"We used to come swim here last year," Mark said. "Now it's silted in. We should get the crew up here to dig it out."

I gave him my best smile. "We'd need lots of beer!"

We laughed heartily at the odds of that happening, beer or no beer. Our laughter died down—a sudden moment of shyness settled between us.

"To tell you the truth, I'm a little afraid of you," he said.

My heartbeat skipped. *Of me?* My hands trembled, and I lowered my eyes. *Will he kiss me?* He scooted closer, pulled me to him, and pressed his lips to mine for the most fantastic kiss ever. I melted into his arms, oblivious to everything around me. Our kiss ended, and he held my hand during the walk back. "I'd do a lot more for you than you think I would, Linda."

I lay awake for hours that night, thinking about what his comment might mean.

Next day, an enthusiastic group filled the office for our morning meeting. "I hear it'll be a busy fire season," Eric said.

Mark's eyes caught mine for a moment, and my heart rate doubled. He filled a cup with coffee. "Catalina District already had two."

Sounded great to me. The hard work? Forgotten. Sore muscles? Gone. When would we go to another fire?

The screen door creaked open, slammed shut. Glenn hung his Stetson on the coat rack and sat at his desk. "From now on you guys from Tucson need to stay at the station overnight. Stick around on the weekends, too. It's fire season, you know."

I kept my eyes lowered, grateful he wasn't speaking to me.


NOW INTO MY fourth week, I discovered working on a fire crew didn't mean that's all I'd do. Which was fine by me—I liked the variety of projects we did.

Madera Canyon Road didn't belong to the federal government, but Glenn still took pride in its upkeep. When the County bladed the bar ditches, overturning trees in the process, he sent us to drag them out of sight. On the way, Eric noticed trash on the side of the road and pulled over. I leapt out and tossed a soda can and beer bottle into the back. *People are such slobs*, I thought, when we found more trash just up the road.

We parked and piled out of the crew-cabs. Cicadas buzzed in this open rangeland which native mesquites and tawny grasses called home. A herd of cattle turned our way and then moseyed off to their watering hole. I removed a bandana from its storage place under my hardhat webbing and folded it into a sweatband. Leather gloves protected my hands. Grasping a half-buried mesquite limb, I tugged hard. It refused to budge. I tugged harder. It broke free, delivering me a face full of thorny branches and dirt. This would not be easy.

At lunchtime, I crawled under a scraggly mesquite, the only shade available, and removed my hardhat to dry out my sweaty hair. Flies buzzed around me, landing on my moist skin for a drink. I sipped some hot canteen water, which took care of dehydration, but didn't quench my true thirst. Inside my lunch bag, cheese and crackers had morphed into a cheese melt; my apple had baked one degree from turning into applesauce. When lunch hour was over, no one had the motivation to start working. Shimmering heat waves rose from the sand, the air motionless and stifling. We sat, drained of energy, silent. Glenn's truck swung in behind our vehicles. *Uh-oh.* Caught sitting on the job. Guilty, I jumped up.

Glenn brought over six-packs of soda. Many hands reached out to accept one, but I hesitated. I never touched regular soda. Calories, you know. But I couldn't turn it down, the cans were so cold, they perspired. Just holding the can cooled my body by two degrees; or at least it seemed that way. The lid popped with a *fizztz*. After three deep swallows, I shook the can. *Rats, empty.*

Reenergized from the sugar rush, I reached for a branch to drag. That's when I noticed a half-buried bottle glinting green in the stark afternoon sun. Tempted to ignore it, my conscious chastised me for not picking up trash. I plucked it out, and brushed off the dirt. *Coca Cola.* I looked at the bottom. *1929!* From that moment on, my boring, hot job became a treasure hunt, which sure made the day fly.

A few days later, Glenn switched us to a new project.

"You're working the Old Baldy Trail today," he said. He squished his second cigarette of the morning into a Smokey the Bear ashtray. *Only You Can Prevent Forest Fires*, it read.

My first trail duty day. Excited, I tucked a brown-bag lunch into my pack along with a poncho and jacket, in case it turned wet or chilly. Since the Kent Fire incident, I carried a gallon canteen, plus two extra quarts of water—more than anyone else. Heavy as heck, but for sure I'd never be thirsty again. I chose a Pulaski, just as good for trail maintenance as it was for building line. With my eyes on the boot heels in front of me, I marched up the trail. A few guys sang, "Heigh-ho, heigh-ho, it's off to work we go . . ." Too self-conscious to sing along, I instead rolled my eyes at their off-key crooning.

Deep in this ponderosa pine forest, I inhaled the heady, sun-warmed scent. Every bit as wonderful as the forest around my home in Prescott, a small community in Northern Arizona. Not that I always felt that way. My parents moved our family from Syracuse, New York to Prescott in the middle of my senior year of high school. It took me a while to forgive them, but I did, and I grew to love living with a forest all around.

My job hunt began right after graduation. I'm guessing I must have known I needed something unconventional. I only lasted two days as a waitress, a month as a receptionist. I applied at the phone company and was tremendously relieved when they didn't hire me. One job, where I made "authentic" Indian jewelry, had potential— but it ended when my employer was thrown in jail for tax evasion. Then last year I got in with the Coronado National Forest. Although I worked indoors, the Forest Service ranger station sat up high in the Santa Catalina Mountains. At first, it seemed perfect. Then I decided I wanted to work outdoors.

The call came in late April from the Coronado's Nogales District Ranger. "I've got a firefighter position open in the Santa Rita Mountains, thirty miles north of Nogales."

*Firefighter! But in Nogales? Are there forests in Nogales?* I had no idea. I didn't want to fight brush fires like the ones they had in Southern California.

I hesitated, then asked, "Are there any trees?"

With suppressed laughter, he replied, "Oh, yes, there are trees."

*Maybe I should be more specific.* "I mean, are there *pine* trees?"

He outright laughed. "Yes, there are pine trees."

South of Tucson, I stared out the bus window at several mountain ranges in the distance. Not one of them appeared to have *any* trees, much less pines. Anxiety rose in my throat. Had he lied to get me to take a job no one else wanted?

THE OLD BALDY trail shot straight up to Mt. Wrightson, at least that's how it felt to my leg muscles. Glenn scoffed at the Forest Service's requirement for physical training (P.T.s), saying that if we did our jobs we wouldn't need P.T.s. Panting and breathless, I had to agree.

At the end of the trail, we spread out. A few guys cut overhanging branches so a rider on horseback wouldn't get whacked in the face and dragged trimmings out of sight. I worked with the rest, chopping grass and shrubs growing into the trail, removing those annoying "toe-trippers," pointed rocks and protruding roots, from the tread.

A short ways down, I recognized a drainage problem. I'd need to build a water bar. Collecting the right rocks took some time. I scouted uphill first, using gravity to help move them. Soon I formed a pile, and started assembly of the angled diversion channel to steer water aside, and keep it from running down the middle of the trail. My activity disturbed an ant den, which emitted an unpleasant, pungent odor. I monitored the swarming ants carefully. Their bites hurt like heck. Rocks tamped in tight, I stood back and admired my handiwork. Way more fun than cutting branches.

"C'mon," Mark said after work. "I'll take you to dinner in Tucson."

Thrilled by the invite, after I showered I stood in front of my closet. Easy to decide what to wear—I'd only brought one dress. I eyed myself in the bathroom mirror. Did I look okay? I frowned and twisted my hair into a bun. A deeper frown. I let my hair fall, brushed it smooth, and called it good enough.

After a lovely dinner filled with great conversation, Mark pulled off on a side road below the station and parked. "You're all I can think about," he said, running his hands through my hair, pulling me close, and kissing me deeply. All my reservations about him flew out the window, my stance on not getting involved right behind them.

Back home before dawn, I lay awake, worried that Mark and I were heading into trouble. I didn't want to be responsible for his marriage falling into ruin, even though he'd made it clear the marriage was already failing. I told myself that in time, I would know the right thing to do. But I really needed to know what to do at that very moment, and I didn't.

We tackled another steep trail the next week. Trained into a higher fitness level, I could enjoy the hike without gasping for breath. Nothing beat working outside, but hiking into wilderness to repair trails . . . what could be better? They even paid me to do this. I'd do it for free! Okay, maybe not. But I didn't mind swinging a tool for what I considered a privilege.

On lunch break, we stretched out in the shade of pines.

"I still say the Forest 'Circus' needs to replace those ancient C-rats," Mark said, referencing an inside joke about the agency. "I puked my guts out after eating the spaghetti."

"Wusses," Opie said. "Can't you take a little food poisoning?"

Tom pitched a pinecone at me. "What've you got for lunch?"

I laughed. "Nothing you'd like!" I tossed the pinecone back.

Propped up against the bark of a ponderosa, contented, I listened as Mark and Tom discussed how to make our fire packs lighter. Amidst the pine needles, I found a blue jay feather and attached it to my hardhat. I'd read feathers brought good luck. I slid down on my back, closed my eyes, and positioned my hardhat as a fly deterrent over my face. A beautiful day. Not too warm, the sky a perfect solid blue. I sure couldn't imagine being stuck in an office. On top of it all, I fit in with these guys. It felt good, filling one of those empty spaces inside you that you don't know you have until it's brimming.

Late afternoon, we got a call to return to the station, but no fire as we'd hoped. Then another call came in, which turned out to be another false alarm. This time we hung out at the office, in case the third time was the charm.

Joe sat next to me on the office steps, the first time we'd talked since the Kent Fire. Not surprising; he didn't say much to anyone. Always clean shaven, with hair cropped short, shirt and even his Levi's pressed, he sat in the corner of the office during the morning meeting while everyone else bantered. His deep-set green eyes were always observing, taking it all in. Texas John teased Joe, calling him "Josephine," making Joe blush. What was that all about? Who hid underneath the shyness? He had me curious.

Our friendly conversation didn't last anywhere near long enough for me—there was much more I wanted to know. Impulsively I said, "I'm hungry. Want to come over for dinner?"

"Sure," he said. "Let me go home and clean up."

When Joe arrived a couple hours later, he looked so sharp it threw me off kilter. My earlier thinking of "friends only" faltered. Now I wished I knew what he thought of me. He was often shy; but tonight, not so much. Earlier,

Texas John had mentioned that Joe never had a girlfriend. Curious, I wanted to ask Joe why not, but couldn't drum up the nerve.

STATION MAINTENANCE WAS on tap today. Mark, Texas John, and I drove down to the horse corrals below the station to treat the wood with creosote. I'd worked with Texas John a few times. Twenty years my senior, he treated me like a helpless little girl, which could be why I volunteered to go first—to prove him wrong.

Creosote is a vile, caustic wood preservative—something I'd never encountered before. I secured the cuffs of my workshirt, tied a bandana over my nose, and pulled on leather gloves. To protect my eyes, I wore cheap, oversized plastic goggles. They slid down my nose. I pushed them back up. Meanwhile, John filled the sprayer. The sharp chemical odor of tar pierced my nose, giving me an instant headache. I'd have to work fast. Texas John pumped the handle to pressurize the tank. "Here ya go, sweet thang."

He and Mark sat on a rail to wait their turn.

Tank in one hand, wand in the other, I squeezed the trigger to coat a post with the fine mist, making sure to stand upwind.

Moments later, Texas John startled me by leaping off the fence. "Shit! Look out! It's gonna blow!"

*What?* I glanced down just in time to see that the hose had expanded in the middle like a snake swallowing a rat. It exploded, spraying me with the nasty chemical. Overcome by fumes, I watched the corral spin, and then everything went dark. Voices filtered into my subconscious sounding like they came from underwater.

"She's out!"

"We need to get her to a shower and fast."

Someone picked me up and set me on the front seat. Driving up to my house, Mark asked, "You okay over there? Geez you gave me a scare."

"I guess . . ." Darned world wouldn't stop spinning.

"Damn. You need to wash that stuff off."

Mark supported me as I wobbled inside. "Can you manage?"

I nodded. After stripping off my chemical-soaked clothes, I stepped into the steady spray. Still dizzy, I leaned against the stall.

"You okay in there?" Mark asked from outside the bathroom door. "You stay in there at least fifteen minutes."

I thought of asking Mark for help, but I managed, washing and rinsing until the water ran cool. After the long shower, I studied my reflection in the mirror. Anywhere not protected by bandana or goggles was fiery-red. A light finger-touch hurt, like a bad sunburn. *Not too bad, I'll be fine.*

I dressed in clean clothes and walked back to the office where Glenn insisted that I take the day off. I refused. I wanted to go back to work.

"Well, okay. You can tidy up the office," he said.

Not exactly what I had in mind.

"She fainted because of the fright," I overheard Texas John say as I entered the office the next morning.

Clark, another fire prevention tech, stood with John by the aluminum coffee percolator. John glanced at me, smirked, and filled a stained ceramic mug.

My jaw clenched tight. "Bullshit, John."

Texas John winked at Clark. "If you say so."

Infuriated, I recognized he would never have said that if I'd been a guy. I didn't see the point in defending myself either, what good would that do?

Later that morning, stuck with John digging a trench for a new water line, he insisted on showing me how to make shoveling easier. Still mad, I folded my arms and glared at him. Okay, so it did make shoveling easier, but I resented him speaking to me as though I had the IQ of a turnip.

"I don't get why you'd want a job like this," he said, pitching a shovelful of dirt. "Seems unlikely for a girl."

"So what kind of job would you like me to have?" I asked, my voice laden with sarcasm.

He hopped out of the trench and extracted a cigarette from his pocket. "I like my women barefoot, pregnant, and in the kitchen."

I rolled my eyes and frowned, thrusting my shovel into the rocky soil. *Well, isn't this is going to be fun.*

Early next morning, I sat in the office, wondering what we'd do that day. Part of me worried something might come up that I couldn't handle. Then what? I stuffed those thoughts aside. If I could fight a fire, I could do most anything.

An hour later, I stood at the helipad below the Florida complex, pacing, hands tucked in pants pockets so no one could see my jitters. Helispot maintenance was on tap today. I'd never flown in a helicopter before. I did sit in one with a guy from the Helitack crew in the Catalinas last summer, probably breaking all kinds of rules by doing so, but that didn't count. We'd never left the ground.

The *swoop, swoop, swoop* echoed ahead of the helicopter's arrival. Above the landing pad the Hughes Bell made a half circle and settled down, sending out a whirlwind of debris. The pilot shut down the engine; the long blades revolved slower and slower, coming to a stop. I squinted to get a better look at the man who hopped out: handsome, trim, gray at the temples, wearing

Army fatigue coveralls. After a moment of conversation with Glenn, he stepped back to wait.

"Today you guys are going to clear brush from our remote helispots we use for emergencies. Before we get started, we need to talk about helicopter safety," Glenn said in a serious tone.

When Glenn spoke, we listened. He commanded our respect.

"Always, even when the engine is not running, even when the blades are not turning, approach the chopper in a crouched position." He demonstrated. "Remember: Blades lower when they slow down, so always stoop lower than you think you need to. Better safe than sorry." He made a slicing motion across his throat. "Decapitation, folks. Not a pretty picture."

My mouth went cotton-dry. What if I forgot and stood up? No, I wouldn't forget. Would I?

"Second—like with a horse, stay away from the rear. Tail rotor will do more than kick you—if you get my drift. You have no business being anywhere near the rear of a helicopter, ever. *Always* approach from the front."

You could've heard an oak leaf hit the ground in the silence that followed. Eric nudged Joe. Tom and I exchanged glances. I thought about the training movie where a guy got hacked into pieces. I shivered to rid my thoughts of the gory picture. Hopefully, none of us would do the unthinkable.

Our pilot selected the correct combination of passengers to equalize weight distribution. He pointed at me. "You—up front." Then to Joe. "You—backseat." The cockpit shifted when I climbed in. Joe hoisted himself into the back, sitting next to our gear.

When I fished for the seat belt, the pilot appeared by my side, leaned over, and buckled me in. He winked and skirted around the front to hop in. I started to say something about closing the door, but there *were* no doors. Only my seat belt prevented me from falling out. The lack of doors was bad enough, but the windshield wrapped underneath my feet. I could see out through the floor. Flying in a fish bowl.

No, I didn't like this. My uneasy smile reflected in the pilot's dark Ray-Bans. He grinned at me, donned his helmet, and fastened the chin-strap. After positioning the microphone, he radioed dispatch for take-off. He flipped switches on the console and others above him on the ceiling. The engine began a high-pitched whine, craft shuddering, blades building up momentum. A sensation of weightlessness accompanied the upward lift. Higher and higher we rose, my stomach refusing to stay in sync with the rest of me. I tried to control the weird feeling by holding my breath, but it didn't help. Below, onlookers bowed their heads, holding onto their hardhats to keep them from blowing off.

Tilting toward the mountains, we soon picked up elevation, flying parallel to the steep terrain, amazingly close to tree tops. A sudden drop in altitude made my stomach lurch. *Oh my God, we're going to fall out of the sky!* Wide-eyed, I turned to the pilot for reassurance.

He grinned broadly. "Mountain air currents. Play havoc with stability."

That was not reassuring. Another dip, another stomach flip. I pressed a hand on my stomach to prevent it from happening again. That didn't work, either. We continued our ascent with less turbulence, so I relaxed a little, cataloging sensations: gentle swaying, a bump or two, the air rushing through the blades, the sharp tang of jet fuel. I leaned over to see better, but when I focused all the way to the ground, my gut flip-flopped, my heart vaulted. I squeezed the seat cushion, my fingers digging into the vinyl. I hadn't yet recovered when trees gave way to a vertical drop of several thousand feet. Pressed hard against the seat, as though doing so would keep me from tumbling out, I swallowed to dislodge the lump in my throat so I could speak. No way would I let the pilot know how scared I was. It would ruin my new firefighter image.

"This beats any roller coaster ride," I said, forcing a grin.

He smiled back, reached above him to flip a switch. "Watch this." The engine noise stopped. Seconds passed. He flipped the switch again, and the engine noise returned. He gave me a rather wicked smile. Having no idea what had just happened, I smiled thinly.

His attention reverted back to our flight. "There's our first helispot."

He had to be kidding. This tiny, treeless patch was not remotely large enough to land on, but we were going to land there anyway. And we did, dirt and leaves whirling around us. Engine idling and blades still turning, the cockpit bounced up and down, as though anxious to be on its way.

"Don't forget," he yelled. "Crouch down when you get out, and until I'm gone."

I unbuckled my seat belt and climbed out. Blades whirred over my head; the forceful downdraft pressed on me like a vertical headwind. I hunched low and rushed to the edge of the clearing. Joe tossed out our gear and scurried to join me. Hunkered down, we watched the chopper lift off in another swirl of dust and fly away.

Now in comparative silence, I couldn't wait to ask Joe the burning question. "So what happened up there? When the engine got really quiet."

"Oh, that." He picked up a Pulaski. "He auto-rotated. Gliding without power. They learn it in case the engine dies."

Without power? Certainly he was joking. "Are you serious, he turned the engine *off*? As in *off—off*?"

"Yeah, those ex-Vietnam pilots are a bit crazy."

Crazy? The guy was insane.

Glenn told us to hustle, so we hustled. We cut overgrown brush, limbs—anything that could interfere with landings. Within an hour we finished our work. We used the wait-time for our next ride to eat lunch. Sitting on a tree stump, I peered into my sack. What was I thinking when I packed this? I didn't bring anywhere near enough food. *Oh well.* I bit off a chunk of cheese, stuffed a couple of saltines in my mouth, and washed it down with warm canteen water. Another bite of cheese, more crackers. I peeled the hardboiled egg and stuffed it whole into my mouth. All that was left was an apple, which I nibbled on until all that was left was the hard core and seeds. My mouth watered at Joe's double-decker sandwich, chips, oatmeal cookies, yogurt, apple, and thermos of milk. Joe must have sensed that I was still hungry, perhaps because it had taken me all of five minutes to eat everything.

"Want my yogurt?"

"I'm okay. Thanks, though," I said. *Strawberry.* I could taste it.

"Here, take it. I'll be fine."

I savored every smooth, fruity spoonful.

Joe closed up his lunchbox. "Um, would you . . . I mean . . . I'd like to take you out to dinner some time."

Just what I'd hoped to hear. "Sure!" And the door was now open to ask a *him* question. "I'm curious. Why does John call you Josephine?"

His cheeks tinged pink, and he shrugged. "Oh, I don't know. He's done that since I was a kid."

Tough, masculine, and that sweet innocence. I liked that. So different from Mark.

Here came the helicopter. Back onboard, it wasn't as scary this time. I even leaned a little further to see if maybe those tree tops were within reach.

That night I lay awake for a long time, reliving the day in movie-like sequences, jumping from frame to frame. At last asleep, I dreamed I had wings, soaring, dipping down to touch soft pine needles with my fingertips.


I GOT STUCK with station duty the day after all that excitement. Tom and Eric suffered the same fate, while everyone else flew to more helispots. Disappointed over missing all the fun, I grumbled to myself as I spent the morning cleaning out the fire cache and other mundane chores. After lunch, I frowned at the pile of tools in need of sharpening. Not my favorite task.

"Drop what you're doing," Eric said, as he dashed inside and snatched his fire pack off the shelf. "We've got a fire!"

# FIVE

I DROPPED WHAT I was doing.

Eric pressed hard on the gas pedal of the Model 20 tanker, stones ricocheting against wheel wells. From the front seat, I swiveled around to smile at Tom, who gave me a wide grin, his dark eyes sparkling.

"Guess getting stuck with station duty wasn't so bad after all," he said.

Once we reached Box Canyon, tight switchbacks and the two hundred gallons of water we carried slowed us down. A rough abandoned mining road got us close, but the fire lapped up a steep, rocky, grass-and-brush-covered hillside, with "inaccessible" written all over it. The tanker would be of no use here.

I buckled my canteen laden belt around my hips and secured a bandana around my neck. Water stayed attached to my body now, not inside my pack. Difficult terrain, combative plants, and higher-than-usual humidity would make for a tough, sweaty hike. I held my Pulaski at my side, stepping over rocks, maneuvering around prickly cactus and dagger-like agaves hidden by knee-high grass, searching for a route of least resistance. Of which there was none.

At the fire's edge, we spread out twenty feet apart to build line. My first swing, the Pulaski jerked to an abrupt halt on a rock, my wrists absorbing the shock. *Damn!* How in the world did plants find a foothold here with no soil? Worse yet, how could I stop the fire if I couldn't dig line?

A distant thunderstorm kicked up gusty winds, sending fire every which way. When the wind pulled a one-eighty, a cascading wave of fire barreled toward us like a high-speed train, flames roaring high above my head.

Eric's eyes widened. "Into the black! Now!"

I covered more ground in fewer seconds than I ever thought possible, somehow managing to avoid tripping over a rock, an agave, or my own feet, feeling the heat of the fast-moving grass fire. I stumbled, recovered, and ran into the black, where fire had already burned the vegetation, where I should be safe. But the all-encompassing smoke blinded and threatened to choke me. Breaths in shallow gasps, eyes smarting, I took a moment to tie my bandana over my nose and sucked cleaner air through the cloth. Eric coughed, and I recognized his tall silhouette through the wafting smoke. Relieved, I blinked tears from my eyes, rubbing them to improve my vision. But where was Tom? I called out his name, my voice cracking from the panic threatening to close my throat. I strained, listening for his response.

Not too soon I heard, "Here!" accompanied by the sound of boots thumping against rocks. Tom reached my side. "Wow. Was that ever a close call."

My relief was so profound, I wanted to hug him. Present danger over, we ventured out of our safety zone. My knees quivered from residual fear, my nerves tingly and jumpy. Our fire moved on, finding new fuel and a different course—we'd have to start over. Each swing of the Pulaski removed one rock or one plant closer to a fireline. Each swing hurt my wrists, scorching sun toasted my skin, and sweat burned my eyes. I held back a few frustrated tears. *This is so futile! We'll never catch this.* Eric tapped my shoulder and pointed to the sky. A small, fixed-wing aircraft vanished behind a hill.

"That's the lead plane scoping things out," he said, shielding his eyes from the glare. "Air tanker should be right behind it."

Here it came. Maybe slurry would do what we couldn't. The C-47 swept in low and slow, its belly doors dropping open, spreading a plume of pink across the fire's main path. Retardant smacked the ground hard, raising a cloud of ashes and splattering droplets for hundreds of yards. On our side of the fire, though, we faced more scraping and more digging out rocks to remove flammable grass.

Eric's head jerked skyward. "Here comes another drop!"

Heading straight for us, too. Somebody screwed up! A direct slurry hit could break bones. Or kill. We saw it coming and knew—there was no way could we outrun this.

Eric tossed his Pulaski aside. "Holy shit! Hit the dirt!"

I also pitched my Pulaski so it wouldn't impale me and dropped face down, wrapping my hands around my hardhat to keep it from getting ripped off. Paralyzed, heart thumping, I braced for impact. Turbines roared overhead. *This is it.* Splatters hit my back and legs, like a brief summer shower. At a moment when I should have been contemplating death, instead I thought the slurry smelled sweet, like the Pepto-Bismol it resembled.

Engine noises faded.

*Is it over?* I raised my head, then stood up. Tom too.

"Damn, that was close," Eric said, brushing himself off. His relief turned to anger. "Where the hell was the lead plane?"

No kidding. A warning would've been nice. We inspected our pink-speckled backsides. Tom chuckled. "Ha! Now everyone will know we fought the hottest part of the fire."

I'd heard it said that some firefighters intentionally placed themselves to get hit by slurry for bragging rights. Stupid craziness. Later, when dry slurry turned my collar stiff and scratchy, I covered the raw spot on the back of my neck with my bandana.

Eric's two-way radio spoke: Help had arrived from Sierra Vista and the Florida crew. I kept working, waiting to run into them, but our paths didn't cross. We three mopped up hotspots as best as we could, without water, or dirt, for that matter, both non-existent on that hell-in-disguise hill of rock.

After dark, with only the minimal glow of embers to guide us, I regretted leaving behind my fire pack and headlamp. None of us had thought we'd be out here this long. To make matters worse, as the fire died down, it got darker. Much darker. At midnight, without even a hint of moon or ambient light from a city, we made our way off the steep hillside. *Three Blind Mice.* Almost comical, if it hadn't been so painful. I stumbled over rocks, bumped into shindagger agaves that poked holes in my skin, and cursed the blackness. After at least an hour of this, we paused to take a breather. I rubbed my bruised, bleeding legs through my jeans. Eric collapsed onto a boulder and groaned.

"Damn. It's darker than the inside of a cow."

Tom chuckled. "That'd be pretty dark indeed."

I burst out laughing, and continued laughing until tears poured down my soot-blackened cheeks. Good analogy. I couldn't see either of them sitting right next to me. Then I had a sobering thought, *How in the world would we find the tanker?*

"I see it up ahead," Eric said later. What a relief. Thank God no one broke a leg. We threw our tools into the side boxes and drove back to the station. I leaned back and closed my eyes, exhausted but happy. I'd saved the world today. Or at least that one hillside.

# SIX

SPOILED AS THE only female on the crew, I liked being the center of attention. Then I found out another woman would join us for six weeks. Not only did I not want a roommate, but I did not want to share the attention from my crew. What if she worked harder than I did? Would she be competition in more ways than one?

Jodi arrived on Saturday afternoon. I forced a smile, evaluating the potential threat to my status at Florida. *A tomboy*, I thought, when she said she'd grown up on a ranch. I envisioned her doing cowboy things, like roping and branding cattle. Well, I could be both a woman and firefighter while keeping my femininity intact. Granted, I wore Levi's and work shirts on the job, but off the clock I loved my cutoffs and halter tops, or a sundress and Jean Naté body splash on an excursion to Tucson. When Jodi said she was engaged to be married, I inwardly celebrated. Still, selfishly, I worried: What if the guys liked her more than they liked me?

Jodi and I interacted little. Different squads, with different days off; we didn't see each other much. When her name came up in conversation among the guys, I listened carefully to their tone of voice. My ego wanted to know what they thought of her.

Late one night, Jodi and I sat on my bed in our pjs, discussing work and men. Curious, I asked her about the Forest Service job she'd held last summer.

She frowned. "It was *okay*. What really bugged me, though, is they put me on a tanker crew with another woman and a guy with health problems, then they refused to send us out on any fires."

This floored me. Why hire someone to fight fires if you weren't going to send them on any?

She assumed a crossed-legged position and faced me. "All we did was sit at high-fire-danger roadblocks the whole summer."

I couldn't relate at all. It simply made no sense.

BRIGHT AND EARLY, I sat up front in the six-pack crew-cab on the way to our job site, squished between Texas John and Robert, our third fire prevention technician, to work the gear shift between my knees. Three more of our crew sat in the back.

"I'm too big to sit in the middle," John had said, holding the door for me.

Good point.

A half-hour later, Texas John stared up at the mountains, and mused, "Dang it, we need some excitement around here. We should hike up there and put a lightning rod in a tree."

"John! That's awful." I couldn't believe he'd say such a thing. We weren't hired to *start* fires; we were hired to put them *out*.

"Well, heck. Awright then I won't," he said with a deep frown.

An elbow jabbed my side. I turned and glared at Texas John as he reached into his shirt pocket, comically raising his eyebrows up and down. He pretended to take out a book of matches, tear one off, turn the book over, strike it, then toss the imaginary lit match out the window. He snickered at first, then exploded into laughter. Soon we were all wiping tears from our eyes. Although his antics were funny, the reality is, some firefighters have been arrested for arson. My paycheck after the Kent Fire, with all the overtime and hazard pay, doubled my normal salary. I could see how this might tempt an unbalanced or greedy person to start a fire. I'd read about a firefighter who loved fire so much that he started one just to watch it burn. Texas John said all firefighters had a touch of pyromania. Really? Because I liked to fight fire, did that make me a pyromaniac? I didn't want to think so.

Madera Canyon Recreation Area was under our jurisdiction, and we cleaned it weekly. At the first picnic ground, Robert emptied the trash cans. Texas John and I raked cigarette butts and pop-top tabs. A bucket of soapy water took care of soda-sticky tables.

As a camping enthusiast, I used my share of stinky outhouses. I'd dash in and dash out as fast as possible. But I couldn't do that now. Sucking in a deep breath and holding it, I rushed in to check the toilet paper situation. It needed replacement, and I needed air. I dashed outside to breathe and get a package. With a reserve of air in my lungs, I ran inside, sprayed the seat with disinfectant, and wiped it down, ran back out to suck in another lungful. One more trip. Back inside, I found a pile of toilet paper on the floor. I picked it up with a rubber-gloved hand. *Shit*. Back to the truck to get a shovel. On the way I found a baby diaper stuck in a tree crotch. I cringed. What was wrong with people? Didn't they know what trash cans were for?

Texas John wanted to buy lunch at the Santa Rita Lodge. I treated myself to iced tea. Sitting on their patio, I enjoyed the lush oasis so different from the dry desert a few miles down the road. Gnarled, bright green sycamores lined the nearby creek, and the smell of water, damp earth, and leaf decay cleared the foul odor of the last toilet from my senses. Hummingbirds darted around me, sipping from hanging feeders.

"Oh, great," Texas John said, covering his plate with a hand. "Here comes a coati."

On the railing balanced an odd-looking creature: slinky like an otter, masked and striped like a raccoon. Boldly, it leaped onto our table, and snatched a French-fry right off John's plate. I laughed and pointed at the critter, thoroughly entertained.

Texas John shook his fist in the air. "Damn you. I'll skin you alive!"

It ran off, but not too far. How could someone not love wildlife encounters like this? But John had already told me that he killed coyotes for pelts, saying he sold them to be made into cheap coats. Just one more thing we disagreed on. I couldn't imagine killing any animal for its fur—or body parts for that matter. When I discovered my "lucky" rabbit's foot key chain was real, I couldn't get rid of it fast enough.

I BUMMED A ride after work with Pete, our crewmate from the east coast, to buy groceries and do laundry in Green Valley. Alone with him on the thirty-minute drive, being my sociable self, I tried to strike up a conversation. He sat stone-faced, seldom humoring me with a nod or sideways glance. On the drive back, I decided to test him by not talking to see if he would step up. Silence. Awkward. *He must not like me, but why?* Uncomfortable twists formed in my stomach.

Pete dropped me off. I stashed groceries and tucked clean clothes into the heavy wooden dresser, the only piece of real furniture in my room besides the bed. An apple box draped with a towel served as my nightstand. I tidied up a bit, sweeping dust bunnies and dirt off the bare wood floor. Ticking from my windup alarm clock echoed off the walls. *Only seven o'clock.* Laughter drifted from Pete and Mark's quarters, Florida's hotspot for nightly entertainment. They had the only television. I decided to walk over and visit with Mark.

Inside, a TV blared, leftover pizza sat on the table, and the air smelled of yeasty beer. Rum and coke in hand, I sat down on the couch between Mark and Tom. Mark swung his arm onto the couch behind me, discreetly fingering my hair. My neck tingled from his touch. Tom leaned against my shoulder, the contact intimate, warm. Flattered, I pretended not to notice the two men flirting with me at the same time.

Pete and Opie Taylor had already consumed enough alcohol to be loud and boisterous, drowning out the movie on the black-and-white set. Sitting there with four guys, I wondered how much my presence cramped their style. Maybe not much, since they certainly didn't curtail swearing. After a while, Opie Taylor's obnoxious behavior cramped mine. I finished my drink and stood to leave. Tom offered to walk me the short distance home. I smiled and said, "sure." We paused beneath a canopy of stars.

"Will you look at that," he said, gazing skyward.

A midnight-blue sky sparkled with pinpoints of light, the Milky Way as a sheer white brush stroke. The breeze carried a chill, raising goosebumps.

Tom faced me, his eyes full of affection. He placed his hands on my shoulders, sliding them gently down my arms, warming them. "You're a really fine woman, Linda. Everyone here thinks so."

I avoided acknowledging Tom's compliment because first off, I didn't believe everyone thought so. Second, his comment made me self-conscious. I felt the need to say something, so I protested, saying Pete couldn't stand me.

Tom shook his head. "That's not true."

That Tom found me attractive made my heart palpitate. At fifteen years my senior, his life experiences were way beyond mine, which made me both wary and curious. Could I believe what he said about me? Surely he'd met many women better than me. He leaned in for a kiss. I stopped him.

"I think it'd be better if we stayed friends," I said.

Dejected, he stood with a long face and lowered eyes. I figured he'd get over it. But I began to worry. We were such a close-knit group here. Was everyone back at Mark's speculating about what was going on between Tom and me? For sure Mark would be jealous. If I'd watched soap operas back then, I would've thought I was starring in one, but I wasn't sure I wanted to.

# SEVEN

BEFORE THE ALARM even thought about going off, I bounced out of bed, excited about the workday ahead. What would I do today? Maybe I'd be able to work with Mark. That would be great. Sometimes I thought he arranged for us to work together. It made me feel special. Working with Tom or Joe would be good, too. When Glenn sent me to work on a trail with Texas John and Opie Taylor, my heart sank. But trail work it would be. I heaved my fire pack off the shelf and carried it over to the truck. Always fire-ready, our packs followed us everywhere.

As I swung its thirty-pounds into the bed, Opie said, "Let me get that . . ." Before he finished the sentence—pack loaded. I turned to him and glared.

In a sing-song voice he said, "Guess I'm just used to those helpless Southern belles."

My mouth fell open. *Helpless? You think I'm helpless?* This made me furious. Too bad I could never think of great comeback lines.

Texas John parked at Madera's Nature Trail. Tourists avoiding the Santa Ritas' steep hikes frequented this trail with its gentle grade, winding through white oaks and pinyon pines, offering decent views of the rugged Mt. Wrightson and the flat desert of the Santa Cruz Valley below. I'd just started improving the tread by removing toe-trippers, when Texas John started yakking.

"Eee-yup, I was buddies with good ol' Marlin Perkins," he said in his thick southern drawl.

Skeptical, I gave him an I-don't-believe-you look. "Really. *The* Marlin Perkins." Famous host of TV's *Wild Kingdom*?

He crossed both arms on top of the shovel handle. "Oh yes, sweet thang, me and Marlin hunted lions on one of those, whadda-ya call 'em . . . safaris."

I shook my head and cleaned out a water bar so it would drain properly. I hated it when he called me sweet thing. I had serious doubts he really thought I was sweet. My activity disturbed an ant den, sending out its strong, pungent odor. I winced, checking reflexively to make sure the ants didn't swarm out to defend their territory.

"Did I tell you about that danged monkey?" he asked, still leaning on his shovel.

All clear with the ants. "No, John, you did not." I dragged a cut branch off the trail.

"Well, heck. It's a great story. You see there was this danged monkey who used sign language and mimicked people. So, I figured maybe that 'ol monkey would enjoy a good smoke." Texas John set his shovel aside and lit a cigarette.

"John, I don't think you're going to get me to believe this one." I scraped loose rock off the trail.

"Hey, Linda Lou, it's true. Just ask Glenn. I gave the monkey one, and I'll be danged if he didn't take a puff."

John calling me Linda "Lou" also irritated the daylights out of me. I happened to be quite fond of my middle name, Marie. However, John didn't see fit to call anyone by their real names, so I figured I'd have to get used to it.

That night I lay awake, contemplating my life at Florida. John and Opie were annoying, but I could handle them. At least I got along well with everyone else. What surprised me, though, is that although I'd been prepared for hard work, I never thought that working so darned hard would be so much fun.


ABOUT THE FOURTH of July, monsoon season arrived with its own unique fireworks. First, out popped dry lightning, setting fires here and there. It kept fire crews on their toes. A week or two later, torrential rains scoured the landscape, sometimes falling at a rate of several inches per hour. Nothing in the world smells as wonderful as a rain-washed desert. Much like sheets dried outdoors on a brisk, sunny day, spring water cupped in my hand before I sipped, an early morning hike in a forest of quaking aspens. Heaven should smell that good.

Mid-afternoon, lightning ignited several fires, with ours located in a roadless, remote canyon near the Mexican border. Remote plus roadless equaled a long, tough hike. Good thing Glenn arranged a helicopter ride.

Blades whirring to life, off we went. Confident and comfortable this time, I sat up front, electric with excitement for both the fire and flight. I even took advantage of the view through the floor as we passed over the smoky grass fire, heading for a hilltop landing spot. A figure stood ready to guide the pilot down. The chopper slowed, hovered, and landed gracefully in knee-high grass. An "all's good" nod from the pilot; I hopped out.

Our guide placed a hand on the back of my neck, reminding me to crouch down. His face lit up. "Linda! It's me, Tim!"

It took me a moment to recognize him. "Tim!" I knew him from the Santa Catalinas last summer. I'd often visited him and his Helitack crew. I felt so far removed now from *that* me, the office worker.

"I heard you made it to a fire crew," he said, beaming.

Word sure did get around. "Yup! No more timekeeping for me." Yeah, this felt good. I wanted to talk more, but we had no time.

With the fire contained earlier using a perimeter fireline by the Nogales suppression crew, we faced a long night of hard, dirty mop-up. Cooler temperatures, higher humidity, and calm winds helped, but the fire had scorched a hundred acres of rocky hills covered with sotols, a squatty, grass-like plant with sawtoothed leaves. After flames burned off the leaves, what remained resembled a giant pineapple. There were hundreds of them, many puffing smoke like tiny chimneys.

Headlamp lighting a small yellow circle in front of me, I weaved through the black and gray landscape until I found a sotol radiating red at its base. A hard push with my boot knocked it over, and I used my leg to prevent it from rolling down the hill. Scraping at the ground, I tried to muster enough dirt to smother the coals.

"HEY!"

I turned toward the voice in time to see a sotol-pineapple tumbling down the hill, starting little fires in unburned grass all the way to the bottom.

"I'll get it!" I scrambled down the ankle-twisting terrain. Supercharged with adrenaline, I smacked the flames out with my shovel. I stood over the sotol carcass, heart hammering. Where did that energy come from? I'd experienced that phenomenon often. When I needed it, it appeared.

Rolling, burning sotols had serious consequences, and by God we did not want to be on that rocky hillside any longer than necessary. A yell of, "Sotol!" sent everyone into action. Eric threw a Pulaski at one beginning its tumble downhill, imbedding the ax-head in the fleshy pulp and bringing it to a halt.

"Way to go, Eric!" a voice in the dark cried.

A guy from the Nogales crew tackled one as though playing touch football. "Oh no you don't . . . gotcha!"

What next? Lassos?

These antics struck me as hilarious. Once I reached a certain level of fatigue, everything struck me as hilarious. I laughed at that thought too. *Boy, I must be tired.*

Not far from me, two guys from the Nogales crew babbled to each other in Spanish. I recognized the word *mujer* as "woman," but not *guera*. They laughed and grinned at me. Obviously, they didn't realize I knew a little Spanish.

"You talking to me?" I asked, grinning myself.

Their eyes widened. *Oops.* One stuttered; both shook their heads adamantly. True: I didn't know that particular word, or if it was derogatory, but they didn't know that. A twinkle of delight rippled through me. *Let them wonder.*

We hiked out at three a.m., deadbeat, dirty, and footsore, and arrived as Mark and our relief crew pulled up to the staging area.

When he passed by me, he touched my hand and whispered, "So good to see you, Linda."

Sparks tingled through me, along with a wave of desire. The pull to stay was strong, but I had no say in the matter. My shift was over, and his had just begun.

Eric commandeered their truck for our return trip. I dozed in the passenger seat; three guys zonked out in the back. Eric startled me when he swerved to the side of the road.

His voice shook. "There. Look. An overturned car."

On the road's edge: a car tipped over on its side—its wheels still turning. All sleepiness evaporated. Eric picked up the radio mike and called for help. The two men didn't appear seriously hurt, so he gave them a hand to climb through the open driver's side window. One man suffered a cut on his forehead, blood dripping into his eyes. My first aid training kicked in.

"Eric. Shouldn't we help?" I asked.

He motioned me away from the men, his voice low. "We aren't supposed to. Too much liability. We could get sued."

After a shocked pause, I said, "Can't we at least give him a compress?"

"Well, okay. But that's all."

I walked to our truck, took out gauze pads from the first aid kit, and gave them to the injured man. Thanking me, he pressed them to his head.

"Let's go," Eric said.

I stared at him. "Aren't we going to wait for the ambulance?"

Eric's anxiety mounted. "They're on the way. Let's go."

This felt wrong. Could we get sued for helping? Not helping? I didn't know. Too tired to argue, I rode to Florida in silence. At five a.m., I went to bed, collapsed, and died.


MY FIRST DAY off, I took care of chores. Done by noon, I wandered down to the office to check my inbox, restless. Too bad I couldn't work seven days a week. I wanted to.

A little past five, crew-cabs pulled in, with everyone ready for a beer. I joined them. For the first time since I'd been with Mark, he seemed distant, preoccupied. This felt awful. Was he having second thoughts about us? I didn't want to break up with him, but wondered if I should do so before he broke up with me. Wouldn't that hurt less? Joe provided a timely diversion by asking me to lunch at the Summerhaven Inn in the Santa Catalina mountains the next weekend. Why not spend a whole day with him? I'd show Mark I didn't need him anyway. First I'd have to get through another whole week of dragging brush on Madera Canyon Road, though. That project just wouldn't go away.

When I entered the office, Texas John and Clark, with heads down and cigarettes in hand, wore serious expressions. This, in itself, was a big red flag. Serious anything for Texas John and Clark was an oxymoron. I never took John seriously, and Clark was known as the corny-joke king.

Texas John shook his head. "Woo-wee it smelled bad. At first I figured it was a dead cow. Never thought I'd find a body out there. Guy was bloated up like a whale, covered with maggots."

My stomach lurched. I got the picture. I turned around and left.

Once in the truck, Texas John started up again.

"Sheriff said it was probably a drug deal gone bad. Poor sucker. They shot him in the head and left him for coyotes."

Far too late to tell him to stop—the picture was permanently etched into my brain. No longer would I think of the experimental range as a place where cattle and deer roamed. Knowing executions took place here ruined my sense of security at Florida; or heck, the whole district. Texas John pointed out where he made the gruesome discovery. I wondered who else lay out there, hoping I wouldn't be the one to find them.

An invite to the lodge for drinks after work with the gang promised a needed distraction from a morbid day. When everyone gathered to leave, I asked Joe if we could go for a ride.

Parking where we could watch a distant storm, we leaned against his '56 primer-gray Chevy pickup. Lightning pulsed like the heartbeat of the universe, sending ragged bolts from cloud to cloud, firing down strikes on ridgelines of faraway mountains. Our conversation drifted to our first fire.

"You should've warned me not to put our packs there," Joe said, taking my hand, threading his fingers between mine.

I laughed, but quickly defended myself. "Oh no, no . . . I trusted you to know where it was safe to put them."

Wrapping his arm around my shoulder, he said, "I've never met a woman like you." He rubbed his thumb over my calluses, sending tingles up my arm. "Your hands are so small and delicate . . . I'm impressed by how hard you work."

His compliment felt strange, as though he was making a big deal out of nothing. Not that he'd offended me, but why would I do anything else *but* work hard?

"You don't have to prove anything, you know," he said.

Not too long ago, I didn't think so, either. But with Opie and Texas John's daily put-downs, sometimes I felt like I did.

Joe understood, and squeezed my hand. "Opie's an idiot. John is," he frowned, "well, John. You need to ignore them."

I wished I could. A chill made me shiver. Joe removed his Levi jacket and wrapped my shoulders against the mountain-cool air, then put his arm back. I waited for him to kiss me, but he didn't. Was he nervous? *I* made him nervous. Touching and sweet. Joe was both sexy and shy, a combination I liked.

That weekend, Joe and I drove to the Catalinas. Residual clouds from monsoon rains the night before swirled through the pines. The air was fragrant from soaked earth, and water droplets fell from needles when a breeze shook branches. It was downright cold for late July. We climbed the Mt. Bigelow lookout tower and visited Wilma, my friend from last summer; ate a leisurely lunch at the Inn. Clark had invited us to his house for a dinner party in Tucson, and we decided to take him up on it. On the drive, Joe said he worried about getting in the way of Mark and me.

"Don't," I said, after a brief pause.

In a secluded spot of Clark's backyard, we lay together on the lawn.

"I want to kiss you," he said. "But I don't know how."

More than eager to teach him, I did. And we practiced many times. He told me I was beautiful, and that he thought he loved me. *Beautiful?* No, I wasn't . . . but that he thought so? Yes, that felt wonderful. In my heart I wondered if I was falling in love with him too—but at the same time, I didn't believe I deserved his love. I asked him how he could love such a messed-up girl.

"Easy," he replied with conviction.


MARK AND JOE made a repair outside my quarters the next morning. Watching them, I felt like my emotions were split in half. They were exact opposites. Mark said thrilling and romantic things that made my insides melt, but could I trust what he said? Shy and reserved Joe said little, but his strong self-assurance was both masculine and sexy. He made me feel safe and secure. Who did I want to be with more? Did I have to choose? I felt like I was in the middle of a book, but hadn't read the beginning.

Mark hosted a birthday party for Opie Taylor on Sunday. I thought to pass, because obviously Opie would be there, but I liked being around everyone else. The heck with it, I'd go and have fun. Inside, loud music blared, and the laughter was alcohol fueled. Joe caught my eye when I joined the gang, and he smiled shyly at me. My heart did one of those flip-flop things.

In the center of the room stood Opie, teetering as he guzzled down a beer.

"Watch out," Mark said, laughing. "Two-beer Opie just passed his limit!"

Opie swaggered up to Joe with a drunken grin on his face. He poked a finger at Joe's chest. "I'll bet John calls you Josephine because you're, you know, one of *those.*"

Joe set down his beer, grabbed Opie, and tossed him over his shoulder. Leg muscles straining, everyone cheering him on, Joe carried a protesting Opie up the hill to the station's carp-filled irrigation tank, up the ladder, and tossed him in. Watching the spectacle in pure amazement, I thought, *Wow, did Joe really do that?* From what I knew about Joe it seemed out of character, but how delightful to see Opie get what he deserved.

The next morning, Opie Taylor stumbled in late for work. I kept my opinion to myself. *I hope you're so hungover you feel like crap.*

Clark pinched his nose. "P-U, you smell fishy."

There was a brief outburst of laughter, quickly brought under control when Glenn entered the room. Everyone respected Glenn, but I thought no one did more than me.

Glenn poured a cup of coffee and sat at his desk. "Range Management is building a deer fence. We'll need to harvest forty juniper posts."

Early on, I'd recognized that chainsaw operators commanded respect on the crew. Some kind of macho-guy thing. So, of course, I wanted to run one. Not to be macho, but to be a chainsaw expert. A sawyer. Even more, I wanted the respect that title carried. I had much to learn, though.

I clung to the armrest while we bounced over the rocky and rutted four-wheel-drive road to the remote Melendrez Pass, our post-cutting site. On the long drive, a sparkling glint drew my attention to the silver and turquoise necklace I wore. Four years ago, I'd purchased it on my family's first trip west. What a bunch of naïve tourists we were. We'd hiked, in sandals no less, to the bottom of Canyon de Chelly, a desolate, windswept, sandstone canyon with towering red monoliths: Mother Nature's high rises. We carried no water. In July. It's a wonder we didn't die of heatstroke or need an airlift out. In spite of my broken sandal strap, we made it back to the car. Once on the road, I coerced my dad to pull over at a Navajo roadside stand, where I selected this necklace from a blanket spread on the ground. Fourteen dollars exchanged hands, and it was mine. Years later, a friend told me the design represented earth and the universe. I decided that must have some kind of significance, so I never took it off. Truth be told: I also loved the way the silver contrasted against my dark tan.

All unloaded at the cutting site, sawyers and swampers were ready to go. Sawyers ran the chainsaw; swampers moved cut branches away so the sawyer didn't have to. I snagged the opportunity to work by Joe's side so I could learn, but also because I liked to be near him. While he cut, I swamped, deftly pulling branches out of his way. His strong, muscular body handled the chainsaw with ease. After break, he let me have a go.

I stuffed in earplugs, donned goggles, strapped on the special chaps to protect my legs, and pulled on leather gloves. More than ready to start, I paid close attention to Joe's instructions, and to his presence. He radiated self-confidence without one iota of arrogance, and the combination was hugely attractive.

"Let the weight of the saw do the cutting," he said. "Don't use the tip of the blade—it could kickback at you."

At first, the saw didn't feel too heavy. But it didn't take long for fourteen pounds to feel like forty. The saw's vibrations made my arms tingle and go numb. Chainsaw decibels rivaled strafing jets, even with earplugs. After two hours, Joe noticed I tired and offered to take over. With reluctance I agreed, understanding my fatigue made sawing more dangerous.

At the end of the day, we loaded the posts we'd cut. Tom and I squatted to lift the top, while Mark and Pete hoisted the butt end.

"Got it, Linda?" Tom asked.

*Of course I do.* "Umpf . . . yeah . . ." I staggered under the substantial weight, my knees wobbling as we carried it to our truck and slid it into the bed.

Seven posts taxed our truck's suspension, so we crept back to the station. I dozed, tired, but a satisfying kind of tired. I'd cut some trees and helped load them. I was quite proud of myself.

At the shop, I set our saw on the workbench and removed the cover plate. In a metal pan filled with old gasoline, I soaked and scrubbed each part caked with bar oil and sawdust. The chain always needed sharpening. If each tooth wasn't filed at a precise angle, the saw wouldn't cut worth a darn. Might as well beat the log in half with a stick.

Joe demonstrated how he sharpened the teeth. I gave it a shot and then asked for approval.

"Nope, not sharp enough."

Soon I'd discover that Joe had a knack for saw chain sharpening, one that most of us, including me, would never master.

After running the saw for hours, I anticipated sore muscles in the morning—but I woke up without pain. *Well, heck, I must be in great shape!* The day after, though, my right forearm hurt like a truck had run over it. Boy, did that ever deflate my ego.

EARLY ONE MORNING I woke burning with a high fever. No way could I make it to work. I stayed in bed, sweaty and miserable. Joe came by to check on me. "What can I do?"

"Make it go away," I said, letting out a moan.

Minutes later he placed a cool washcloth on my forehead. I fell asleep, and when I woke, there he sat, still by my side. *How sweet.*

"I bought you something," he said, reaching into his pocket.

*For me?* I sat up.

He presented me with a tiny velvet box.

I took in a sharp breath. *A diamond ring?* I'd no interest in getting married, or even having a serious relationship. Tentative, I lifted the lid to find a beautiful, delicate heart-shaped diamond pendant. Relieved, but feeling both guilty and afraid to accept such an extravagant gift, I thought not only did I not deserve this, but if I accepted it, did this mean we were a couple? Were these feelings for him "love?" For sure I found him sexually attractive. But it wasn't right to mislead him.

Gently, I returned the box. "It's lovely, but I can't accept this."

"Why not?" He sounded deeply wounded.

Chicken that I was, I didn't say what I was thinking. Instead, I said, "It must have cost a fortune."

The look on his face pierced my heart. Without wasting a second, I told him I loved it and let him fasten it around my neck.

# EIGHT

"YOU GOING TO the big bash tonight?" Jodi asked me in the morning.

Still feeling sick wasn't the only reason I hesitated. Two days prior, against my protests, Mark had confessed all to his wife. Guilt tortured, I wondered what to do. I thought I loved Mark, but he moved way too fast. My God, we barely knew each other. Only six weeks! If he left his wife, did this mean he expected us to marry? I didn't want to marry him either. If I went to the party, his wife might confront me. Just thinking about it made my stomach squirm. But stupid me, I went anyway, getting what I thought I deserved—icy stares from her that made me want to crawl under a rock and die.

I'd recovered enough by the next day to return to post cutting. This time, all of the saws refused to run. Stupid temperamental things. Joe removed the cover plate of a Homelite. I shadowed him for a while to learn whatever I could.

Jodi plopped down next to us. She fingered a blade of grass. "I'm bored. I want to chop down a tree."

Sounded good to me. The rest of the crew thought we'd lost our minds. They settled under pinyon-pines for a nap.

"Timber!" Jodi yelled as her tree hit the ground with a swoosh.

This was much harder than I thought it would be; a good swing chipped out a miniscule wedge. Another swing, another tiny chip. Paul Bunyan had one up on me. Last cut, and down it went. Like Jodi, I yelled, "Timber!" Okay, goofy, but satisfying.

Joe finally got the saws up and running, and soon we had many posts ready to load. *A good day*, I thought on the way back. *Cut five myself.*

By week three, it took longer to find the right trees; we'd cut all the ones close by. This project had long ago reached the tedious stage. Right after lunch, here came Tom and Texas John in their tanker. They parked, barreled out, and went about starting up the pumper motor and unrolling a length of hose.

Jodi and I exchanged puzzled expressions. *What the heck?*

Tom, grinning widely, opened the nozzle and soaked Pete from head to toe. Pete stood there for a moment, dumbfounded, water dripping from the end of his nose. Water fight declared!

At first, I stayed out of the fray, afraid I'd look silly—until Tom blasted me hard. While he turned to get Joe, I filled my hardhat with water, and snuck up behind him. "Hey, Tom?"

Tom turned, and I threw the water in his face. Shrieking, I ran from him as he chased me around the tanker, until he caught me around the waist. I squirmed and giggled until he let me go. Drenched, exhilarated, and cooled off, we sat down in the shade of oaks to dry.

Tom glanced at his watch. "Look at the time! We need to head back."

No sooner had we parked in front of the fire cache than Joe froze. His head snapped to look at me. "Where's the radio?"

My stomach tied into a massive knot. I'd carried the two-way radio on my belt, but removed it when the water fight began and set it on the bumper of the truck. I'd left it there.

"Too late now to go back and search," Joe said. "We'll have to wait until morning."

I'd be in so much trouble when Glenn found out. My stomach hurt just thinking about what he'd say.

All night long I lay awake. A lost radio. Glenn would be so disappointed in me. Thunder rumbled in the distance. *Great. Now it's probably getting wet.* Joe said I wouldn't be liable because he'd signed it out. Guilt ridden, I didn't want him to be liable either. Who knew how much those things cost. Would the government make us pay for it? Would we lose our jobs?

We left early in the morning.

"Don't want to drive over it," Joe said as we crept toward the cutting site. He hit the brakes. "There it is!"

What a relief it showed no damage. I think I aged five years that day.


WITH POST CUTTING completed, we returned to district maintenance. There was always something to do: Repair fence, paint or replace signs, and pick up trash. Tom, Eric, and I took leftover sign posts up to the bone yard, our outdoor storage area. Just as we finished, moody, charcoal-gray clouds gathered, blocking out the sun. Thunder rumbled. A stiff, rain-scented breeze delivered a few huge drops, raising tiny puffs of dust as they hit the ground. Then a deluge fell like an overturned bucket, sending us dashing for shelter underneath a small ramada. We were huddled close to stay dry, when something crawled across my boot. Shrieking, I grabbed Tom in a vain attempt to get my feet off the ground.

"What the . . . ?" Tom stared at the crazy woman latched onto his arm.

My voice quavered. "Did you see that?"

"See what? What are you talking about, Linda?"

"The centipede!" I squeaked out, hyperventilating. "I'm not kidding, it was at least a foot long!"

"Uh-uh, not me. Did you see it, Eric?"

"Are you sure you didn't imagine this, Linda?"

I did not imagine it. It looked like the creature in *The Tingler*, a terrifying movie I watched as a kid. Cold shivers traveled up and down my spine. Snakes? I hadn't seen one rattlesnake all summer. Scorpions? A boot stomp works great. Centipedes? My weakness: I turn into a screaming banshee.

# NINE

"THERE'S A WORKSHOP you have to attend," Glenn said to me after the crew left to start the day. That got my attention. *Just me?* He brought a mug of coffee to his desk and sat down. "It's for three days, paid." In his rough, calloused hands he held a letter, offering it with a gentle smile. "Sounds like a vacation to me."

I'd love a vacation. I read:

> *The Federal Women's Program will hold a three day workshop at the Stage Stop Motel in Patagonia, Arizona. All female employees will attend . . .*

Assertiveness training, conflict resolution, career advancement. What's assertiveness training? Never heard of it. Conflict resolution? Why did the Forest Service think there was conflict to resolve? What I didn't know was the Forest Service hadn't allowed women to work on fire crews until last year. This rocked their male-dominated world to its core, prompting the formation of this program. For me, this workshop was just a little getaway on the government's dime and nothing more.

Jodi had already left for college, so the next Monday Glenn dropped me off in Nogales to join Wanda, the district secretary, and Lourdes, her assistant, for the trip.

Wanda's petite stature belied her firecracker personality. "Chica!" she said, once we hit the road. "Whatever possessed you to want a man's job? Working around all those machismo men. Don't they get fresh with you?"

Her perception made me laugh. "Wanda, it's not at all what you think. I enjoy the work, and I'm friends with the guys. Well, most of them. I love my job."

"Well, I don't know how you do it. Seems to me they would get out of hand."

Lourdes was the most beautiful woman I'd ever met. Not beauty-queen beautiful, but what is that anyway? Although her lustrous black hair, light-cocoa skin, and chocolate eyes were all to be admired, her beauty came from within, manifesting as self-confidence and grace. If anyone needed to worry about guys getting fresh, it was Lourdes.

She leaned over from the back seat. "I'm so impressed by what you're doing. Men need women around to show them how to do things right the first time."

Wanda and I giggled deliciously. We were in for a great time.

We sailed along State Route 82 as it swept through grass-covered rolling hills. From the south, Mt. Wrightson's profile differed significantly from the one I viewed daily. Here, it had no vertical cliffs, with pines extending all the way to the top. Wanda had hit up a tortilla factory on the way, and we nibbled the warm flatbread, laughing and chatting about clothes, good Mexican food, and gossiping about the men on the district.

In tiny Patagonia, so small that if you blinked once you missed it, we pulled into the Stage Stop Motel, a rustic two-story building with, to my delight, a swimming pool. Good thing I'd thought to bring my swimsuit. After checking in, I took a seat in the conference room with thirty-six other women. The facilitator, Jan Qwill, casually sat on the table in front of the room, with legs crossed and shoes kicked off. With a welcoming smile, she asked us to introduce ourselves.

A pretty woman with fair skin and long dark hair smiled at me from the across the room. "I'm Donna, and I work on a tanker crew at Rustler Park, in the Chiricahuas."

When it came my turn, I introduced myself, proud to announce my position on the Santa Rita Suppression Crew at Florida Ranger Station. At the end, I found it surprising that only three other women were firefighters. Why so few?

Jan Qwill spoke passionately about women finding their place in the Forest Service, and she wanted to know if we'd encountered any obstacles.

"The guys are outwardly mean and degrading," Donna said. "If we get a fire call, they make me sit with the truck. One day they intentionally left me at the station. I hate it there."

How awful! During a break, I asked her, "Isn't there *anyone* backing you up?"

She shook her head with conviction. "Either they ignore what's going on, or make it clear I'm not wanted."

What could I say to make her feel better? "It's not like that everywhere. I love my job, and the guys don't give me a hard time . . . okay, there're a couple chauvinist pigs, but I get along great with the others."

Her eyes brightened. "You're so lucky."

At the end of the three-day workshop, Jan asked us to interview our male coworkers and document their opinions of women on fire crews. We'd regroup later to discuss our findings.

*Easy!* I'd return to report my crew supported me one-hundred percent. Well . . . minus two, but I had no doubt I'd be the envy of the group.

At Florida, I explained my assignment to Glenn.

"Well . . . okay," he said, pursing his lips. "Catch everyone before they go out first thing in the morning."

"I'll need to interview you too, you know."

Glenn's eyes met mine for a moment. He lowered his gaze, shook his head, and with one corner of his mouth lifting slightly, said, "I figured as much."

Per Glenn's request, everyone hung out in the office in the morning, while I stood, paper and pen in hand, ready to start. I pushed past my sudden nervousness and asked for a volunteer to go first.

Silence.

"Okay, I will." Glenn sat down and everyone else left.

Although skeptical of me the first day we met, checking my hands for calluses, my arms for strength, what did he think now? "You're doing just fine and you're a good hand."

By far the best compliment he could've given me. That's what I wanted to be. A good hand. Put me squarely in with the other hard-workers.

Both Robert and Joe said that as long as I could handle the work, I had just as much right to be there as any man. Robert's additional take on women crewmates differed in one significant way. "The guys work harder to impress her. She's working twice as hard to prove herself. More work gets done." He shrugged. "So what's the problem?"

Next Eric sat opposite me, avoiding eye contact. Forest Service cap in hand, he nervously turned it in circles as he spoke. "Heh, heh, you know the first time I heard women would join fire crews, I thought, 'Are you kidding me'?"

I waited for him to say I'd changed his mind.

"I still don't get it. Women don't belong on the fireline."

*What?* I'd been first on the line, initial attack, on both the Kent and Box Fire. I'd chased sotols all night with him on the Nogales blaze. It took a second for what he said to register, to feel the punch of his words. *I'm not wanted here.*

After Eric left, I stared at Mark, shocked, when he, of all people, said I had no business on a fire crew. Days earlier he'd said we were drifting apart, and he wasn't sure if he still loved me. In my mind, our relationship had ended that day. This was pure revenge. Damn him. He betrayed me.

When Texas John came into the room, he used getting a cup of coffee as an excuse to avoid facing me. "Women are too weak," he said.

*Coward.* I trembled in outrage. "Give me one example of when I didn't hold my own, John."

A vein popped out in John's neck, his face crimson. "What if I fell and broke my leg on a fire? You couldn't carry me out! I'd die!"

*Say something, anything. What about Skinny Wilson, the guy everyone calls a ninety-pound weakling?* I gritted my teeth. "John. No *one* person on our crew can carry out *anyone* who weighs over two hundred pounds. I mean, look at Skinny Wilson!"

He scoffed at my defense.

Near tears, fuming and shaking from the confrontation, next I had to face Opie Taylor. I braced myself—he was still mad I wouldn't have sex with him.

"What are you doing here?" he said with a sneer. "The only reason they hired you was to fill their "woman quota." You should quit—you make more work for everyone else."

Even though I expected this, the cruel words falling from his mouth stung like wasps. My throat closed, hurt. I sputtered some stupid, meaningless words, and he left, laughing at me.

While I struggled to compose myself, Tom sat down and eyed me curiously. I sucked in a deep breath before asking him the same question, certain he'd be on my side. But no, he didn't want me to go to fires either. He said he worried I'd get hurt. But I didn't want him to worry. Any of us could get hurt. I knew the risks. We all did.

After the interviews, I sat alone in disbelief. Only Glenn, Robert, and Joe approved of having me on the crew. Did the others feel threatened? Why? I did *not* take this job to prove I was as good as the men, I took it because I thought I'd enjoy the work. What hurt the most was that I thought these guys were my friends. All of the fun, sharing hard work . . . We were a team, or so I'd believed. I'd confused being liked with being accepted—not remotely the same thing. My wonderful world stood still.

On the road, I stared out the truck window and relived the whole event. What were the guys saying behind my back? That I was some weak, frail girl, who wanted to be a firefighter, but who was better off getting married and raising babies? Inside I was a tangle mess and invisible hands choked my throat. Should I quit? But then what would I do?

Ten minutes before five, everyone hung out by the shop, except me, poised to get the hell away from there. I hadn't said a word all day, impatient for the day to end so I could go home and cry.

Glenn called out to me. "Linda. I need you to load two Cubitainers into the back of my truck."

*What an odd request.* However, I picked up the square water containers, one in each hand, lugged them over to his truck, and hoisted each forty-two-pounder into the bed. I turned around to see everyone watching me.

In a gruff tone, Glenn said, "Let's not have any more doubts about who can handle the work around here."

A test. I guessed I passed. Embarrassing, but having Glenn stick up for me did help me feel better.

That night, I couldn't sleep. After many hours of ceiling watching, I gave up and flicked on my bedside lamp. I opened my journal and started writing:

*September 25th, Saturday*
*I really want to fight fires. I want to be able to withstand the pressures and the physical strength it takes—but am I willing to put up with this? I really thoroughly love being on fires—the glamour . . . it is so worth it to me. No one, including me, will ever know until I am presented a dangerous situation, what I will do. But dangerous situations can happen anytime, anywhere, on all types of jobs.*

Two weeks later, I attended Jan Qwill's follow-up workshop. Wanda, Lourdes, and I drove to Tucson, then east an hour on Interstate-10. There wasn't as much talking this time. I kept quiet, feeling thoughtful and not yet up to sharing. Exiting in Wilcox, we headed north and pulled into the Buckskin Guest Ranch mid-afternoon.

Tucked away in a remote area at the base of the rugged Galiuro Mountains, the guest ranch's adobe buildings were surrounded by scattered junipers and pinyon-pines. Peaceful, pastoral. I wistfully envisioned myself walking to the distant mountains and never coming back. At the front desk, I discovered I'd have my own room this time. After all I'd been through, I deserved it.

We gathered in a lobby filled with western décor. Saddle blankets and cowboy art decorated the walls; the life-size stuffed cow in a corner made me smile. *Only at a guest ranch.* It was good to see everyone again. I hugged Donna and whispered we needed to talk. All of us sat on overstuffed, brown leather chairs, or cross-legged atop giant pillows on the polished wood floor, to discuss our interview results. After a deep breath, I told everyone that only three of the guys approved of me on the crew, and those who I thought supported me, in fact, did not.

Jan asked me what I'd do. Venting must have helped. I said, "I'm not afraid of hard work. I love my job. I want to keep my job."

"Don't let them bully you into quitting," Jan said. "You know you can do the work because you've been *doing* the work."

After the meeting, Jan pressed a piece of paper with her phone number into my hand. Although I'd never see her again, our connection, and her advice, got me through more tough times yet to come. But now, back to Florida to face the men who didn't want me there.

# TEN

WHAT TO SAY, what to do? I hurt inside, like I'd swallowed poison not quite deadly enough to kill me. Glenn must have noticed, because he took me aside and said he had confidence in me. I nodded and tried not to choke up. But my tears fell after he left. Self-doubt lingered. What else had I misunderstood? Afraid to find out, I second-guessed every spoken word and action, questioned motives, skeptical of almost everyone. How much worse could things get?

A week after the workshop, I awoke early on Saturday morning to find Donna sitting by my front door. "Donna! You spent the night on my porch?"

"I wasn't sure you were home," she said. With a deep sigh, she added, "I quit my job."

My jaw dropped, and I inhaled a sharp breath. "You *what*? Why?"

"I just couldn't take it anymore. I wanted to stop and tell you how much I appreciate your support."

My heart ached for her. With Saturday a work day, I couldn't talk long. After she drove away, I stewed. One thing for sure, I wouldn't let the jerks here make *me* quit.

Later that week, Wanda paid Florida a surprise visit, at least for those of us who didn't know she was coming.

"We're having sensitivity training today," Glenn said, the lines in his face more pronounced. He took a seat behind his desk, removed his Stetson, and set it in front of him. Poor Wanda stood against a wall, doe-eyed and nervous, a notebook clutched to her chest, waiting for everyone to sit.

One quick scan around the room at the somber faces, and I thought, *Sensitivity training for a bunch of macho guys? Hilarious. Oh, yeah, this will go over just great.*

But training? No, this turned out to be nothing but a bitch session, which Opie Taylor and Texas John capitalized on to the fullest. However, their protests about women now sounded foolish, even childish. Afterwards, I laughed to myself. Why did I let those guys get to me? What a bunch of whiny babies.

*October 11ᵀʰ, Monday*
*295 90lb bags of cement went through my hands today!*

"We've got a Semi-truck arriving with a load of cement," Glenn said Monday morning. "Stick around and help unload."

I stood with five crewmates, staring inside the eighteen-wheeler, speechless. Eric decided forming a human chain would make the job easier. Tom passed one to my waiting arms, I turned and passed it to Skinny Wilson, and so on. Each time I took one, I swore it gained a pound. The heavy bags sagged in the middle, threatening to buckle and break open. For hours, we passed sack after sack, from person to person, stacking them in the hay barn.

After work, I ran a hot bath laced with Epsom salts, a trick my mom taught me to prevent soreness. I immersed myself into the soothing water and soaked for half an hour.

At morning coffee, several guys moaned about being sore.

"Really?" I said. "I'm not!"

Tom chuckled. "You got the lighter bags, that's why."

Eric joined in. "Yeah, Linda, the bags we gave you weighed nine pounds, not ninety."

I grinned at them, keeping my secret remedy secret.


MY FIRST FIRE season came to a close. Daytime temperatures hovered under eighty, and autumn rains fell. Sun rays slanted from the south, emphasizing the depth of the canyons, the steepness of cliffs, casting longer indigo shadows. This time of year always brought on a feeling of nostalgia for my childhood autumns. A touch of color appeared below Mt. Hopkins, Wrightson's sister peak.

"What kind of trees are those?" I turned to Joe, pointing to the patches of yellow contrasting the dark-green pines.

"Aspens," he replied.

"Really? I didn't know there were aspens up there." Now I felt homesick for the aspen grove I often visited in Prescott.

Funding for my position would run out on the twenty-first of October. Sad that my job would soon end, I arranged to return to Prescott for the winter.

At the end of my last day, Glenn made an announcement. "We need to throw Linda a party!"

"Hear! Hear!" Came the enthusiastic response. I smiled. These guys did like me, even if they thought I shouldn't fight fires. Although not yet five o'clock, everyone headed to the bunkhouse. Hard liquor of every kind imaginable worked its way around the room. Joe arrived late, about six, and we were already far ahead of him in drinking. And boy did he look handsome. I wanted to find a way to get him alone.

When laughter and recounts of the summer's adventures paused for a moment, Glenn motioned to me and patted his lap. "Come 'ere, Linda."

Everyone grinned at me. I decided what the heck and positioned myself on his knee. My face warmed when he put his arm around me. He then raised a bottle of Jack Daniels in the air. "Now that we know you can work as hard as we do, let's see if you can drink like us, too!"

A camera flashed, capturing me on Glenn's knee, the men with whom I worked side-by-side since May behind us, toasting the camera. I realized, in the end, I'd proved I was just as capable of the work as any of them. I belonged there as much as they did. I already knew I'd be back next summer. They could count on it.

# ELEVEN

PRESCOTT'S WINTER MORNING chill pinked my cheeks as I jogged down to the high school track to run two miles. It was always hard to get started, but once I hit my second wind, I could get beyond the pain of exertion. On Wednesdays, I stroked a mile in my swim fitness class at Yavapai College. Underneath the glass dome it always felt weird, and cold, to swim while watching drifting snowflakes outside above me.

My mom bought the Forest Service permit to cut firewood, and we were off. I revved up their chainsaw and cut logs into chunks, which us two tough women dragged back to our Suburban. Not sure what my dad thought of this, but that night a cheery fire warmed our living room.

Joe called often, which made me uncomfortable for two reasons: phone calls were hard for him; if I didn't talk, there were awkward silences, and I worried his feelings were stronger than mine. We never discussed the night of my goodbye party, when an intoxicated me brought Joe to my quarters, where we made love. What a careless, thoughtless thing I'd done. I'd stupidly disregarded how he might interpret that. I didn't want a serious relationship with him, or with anyone, and it was obvious I'd misled him. But because Joe lived so far away, I found it easy to avoid dealing with the complicated mess.

In mid-December, I applied for my second fire crew position, not for a minute doubting I wanted more. A week later, my older sister, Cindy, came for Christmas. My mom drove us to pick up some last minute gifts.

Cindy turned from the front seat to say to me, "When are you going to get a real-life job?"

A real-life job? I thought I had one.

"It doesn't take much intelligence to be a firefighter, you know. You should be looking for something else."

Tension permeated the car; almost palpable. *She thinks firefighters are stupid.* Including Glenn, Joe? Furious, but wanting to keep the peace—it was Christmas after all—I kept my mouth shut.

*December 31st, Friday*
*Snowed all day. Just beautiful. Another year coming to a close in a half hour. Very strange—how fast time goes by as one gets older. I don't think I'll be ready to have 1977 here; but there ain't too much I can do about it. Goodnight all.*

MID-MARCH, JOE surprised the heck out of me by calling from a motel in Prescott, wanting to see me. For an embarrassing moment, I couldn't speak. There was no avoiding the elephant in the room now; it had burst through the door and sat down on the couch. I decided I'd have to pay for that alcohol-clouded judgment. He'd come all that way, so I should see him, maybe try to explain . . .

But when Joe picked me up for an outing, my heart swelled with affection. It didn't hurt that he looked incredibly handsome and fit in his Levi jacket and jeans. We hugged, and I ran my fingers through his blond hair, noticing with pleasure he'd let it grow; just because I suggested he do so last summer.

Cold weather didn't deter us from hiking to my swimming hole at Wolf Creek. I started a snowball fight, stuffing ice crystals down his shirt, and soon we collapsed in breathless laughter. I said nothing about our *relationship*. Why spoil the wonderful, carefree day? When he dropped me off that night, I gave him a hug, and from the door, waved goodbye.

Then, in early April, Glenn called, the sound of his voice warming my heart.

"I've got a position for you at Florida on the fire crew. You interested?"

Of course I said yes. He'd even better news. "We're looking to hire early this year. We'll get back to you with a start date." After a distinct pause, he said, "I'm glad you're coming back."

Which was better? A job offer, or Glenn saying my return pleased him? Over the winter, I'd worried about how much he remembered, or even worse, didn't remember, about my goodbye party.


GLENN HAD AWAKENED me at one o'clock after the party broke up, tapping on my window and calling my name. What horrible timing: Joe was in bed with me.

"What should I do?" I whispered. Joe didn't reply. I staggered out of bed, steadying myself with a hand against the wall. I slipped on a robe and padded barefoot to the door. I invited Glenn in, and we sat on the couch, our shoulders touching. He reached out and ran his hand through my hair. Tingles ran down my spine.

"How come you look so different with your hair down?" His hands grasped mine. "I think the world of you, you know. I really like you."

Instant sobriety. My thoughts darted around in zigzags. This was Glenn? My supervisor; the man who had stood up for me last summer? The man I felt something for, but dismissed as admiration? For certain I'd never thought he had feelings for me. I wasn't appalled or disgusted. He was a fine person and I respected him. Now I worried that he might find out Joe was in my bedroom. I suggested we go outside.

There, he put his arms around me. "You're all a guy could ever want."

Enthralled by his declaration, I let him kiss me, his mouth tasting of whiskey and cigarettes. Glenn rambled for fifteen minutes, then left. Perfect timing. I dashed into the bathroom and vomited until I thought I'd die. Joe handed me a wet washcloth, and I pressed its coolness to my face. He helped me to bed, where I passed out. When I awoke, Joe had gone. Now late morning, waiting for my parents to pick me up, I nursed a headache the size of the Grand Canyon and a raw stomach, but not yet grasping all that had happened the night before.

But this current phone conversation with Glenn didn't give me any clue that he remembered telling me how he felt. Had he told me the truth? Or was it the alcohol talking? Our twenty year age difference didn't bother me, but did it bother him?

WHEN MY DAD heard of the job offer, he gave me "the" lecture: That I had no business working in a "man's job." That I needed to go get myself a "real" career. In our previous arguments, I'd acquiesced or sulked. In my father's world, no one had the right to contradict him, least of all his daughter. But this time, I stood my ground. This was my life and I wanted to fight fires. We argued for ten minutes, until I shut myself in my room to put an end to it. My mom knocked on my door, sat down next to me on the bed, and apologized for my dad's stubbornness.

"I'll worry," she said, her arm wrapped around me. "But I want you to do what makes you happy."

That night at the dinner table, I told my dad I wanted to buy a car.

He buttered a slice of bread. "Do you have enough money?"

"I've got twelve hundred dollars in the bank." My life's savings.

First thing in the morning, my dad called a local used car dealer. Two cars were available in my price range. The minute I saw the blue 1971 Toyota Corona station wagon, I wanted it. A friend insisted I name it, so I chose "Skyler."

The first thing I did was give my "baby" a wash and wax. I was buffing it out when I began to feel dizzy. Then my throat hurt. Within an hour I had a hundred-and-two degree fever. And wouldn't you know it, that's when the Nogales District called, telling me to report in three days. How could I manage that? I ached so much it hurt to lift my head off the pillow. When I could, I packed a little, slept a little, then packed a little more. Good thing earlier I'd completed the test for my "Red Card," the required proof of my fitness level. No way could I pass it when this sick.

On the morning of departure, still miserable, I placed a sheet of plywood in the back for the saggy mattresses at Florida, and everything else on top, clear up to the roof. Behind the seat I tucked in two cans of motor oil for my not-so-perfect car. I didn't care, though. It was all mine, and painted my favorite color. I slammed the hatchback and congratulated myself. Everything fit.

# TWELVE

## Summer of 1977: Florida Work Center, Santa Rita Mountains, Southern Arizona

I EXPERIENCED A pleasant coming-home feeling as I drove over the rattling cattle guard rails and entered the Florida complex in late afternoon. Feeling its magical spell once again, I realized that I'd missed this place. Raised high on a pole in front of the office, the American flag flapped gently in the breeze. I parked and stopped in to pick up a key. Eric sat at his desk.

"Hey, Linda! Welcome back."

"Good to be here," I croaked, coughing long and hard.

"Cripes, you sound awful," he said.

"Yeah . . . I'm still recovering from the flu."

Eric's face scrunched up in a grimace. "Well, that's no fun . . . Say, did you hear we're not a ranger station anymore? District decided since the ranger works in Nogales, not Florida, it misleads the public into thinking there's a ranger here. We're called the Florida Work Center now."

I rolled my eyes. Ridiculous. "Oh, good grief. The public thinks everyone who works for the Forest Service is a ranger, so what difference does it make?"

Eric broke into laughter. "Glenn thinks the new name makes Florida sound like a prison camp."

I smiled. "You mean it isn't?"

Eric grinned and handed over a key. "You've got the place next to Glenn."

Although smaller than last year's quarters, I didn't mind. I claimed the one bedroom. Jodi would stay in the private, enclosed porch. Like Jodi, many of the crew were attending college and wouldn't start until May. I felt privileged to arrive before most everyone else.

As soon as I unpacked, I called Joe from the office phone. He reminded me that he was still camping out on trail assignment. We had a comfortable conversation, and I figured he'd visit whenever he could.

Because they'd hired me early, I'd have to deal with winter still gripping the mountains. After a full day of hiring paperwork, I joined Pete to work the steep, rugged Florida Trail, with deep snow lingering on north facing slopes. Not yet recovered, hiking winded me, exacerbating a cough fierce enough to hack out a lung. To make things worse, no sun appeared on north slopes this time of year. My toes were frozen, my hands were numb. That afternoon it spit snow flurries. I tried imagining a blistering hot day, hoping it would help, but it didn't. I stopped to rest, but it was way too cold to sit for more than a few minutes. I'd have to keep moving, or I'd turn into Frosty the Snowman. It didn't help that just like last year, conversations with Pete came out forced and awkward. What a relief to finish the trail and put an end to cold feet and the cold shoulder.

I spent the next day working with Tom. Always good-natured, Tom was high on my "who I like to work with" list.

"Linda, I'm going to try my hand at wiring the new emergency lights for the tanker. Can't be that hard." Tom grinned through his long black mustache, brown eyes sparkling. "Maybe you can coach me along?"

"Me? Ha! You're too funny. I know nothing about wiring." But heck, if he could teach me, that'd be great.

Tom leaned inside the engine compartment, talking his way through the process. "Let's see . . . red to red, black to black. Logical, right?" He turned to me for confirmation.

I shrugged. "Sure, makes sense to me."

Startled by a puff of acrid smoke and flying sparks, we looked at each other and burst out laughing. After some head-scratching, Tom figured out his mistake. One more attempt, and the tanker's lights were up and running. Ecstatic, his success became my success. Tom said I shouldn't worry about making mistakes. That's how I'd learn new things.

On Joe's day off, I wondered why he hadn't come over or called. Earlier, he'd offered to change my car's oil, something that I usually did myself. But I thought, heck, that'd be nice, so I'd taken him up on it. I figured I must have misunderstood. Maybe he had other things to do. However, to make good on his offer, Joe showed up late that day. After he finished, he returned my car keys. I invited him in for iced tea.

"No thanks," he said, turning to leave.

Now I knew something was up. When I pried, he admitted that after leaving Prescott, he thought he'd made a mistake in coming to see me. He got the impression that I didn't want him there. In horror, I realized he must have picked up on my initial hesitation. Here I thought I'd hidden it so well. Before Joe came to Prescott, I'd regretted what happened. Not anymore. What did I feel now? Well, close to him, still attracted to him, but in love? I wasn't sure. I'd no idea where we stood, or where we were going, if anywhere. I just hoped we could at least still talk.

At work the next day, I helped with fire prep. I knew the drill. Like going through the decade-old boxes of C-rats to toss out the many bulging cans. Anything with tomato sauce went first: Botulism. Tools were sharpened, chainsaws were tuned. Shipments of supplies needed to be sorted and stored.

Glenn had been away my first week, but he greeted me now with his eyes and a rare, full smile radiating happiness. *To see me?* I searched his face for some kind of special acknowledgement, but it wasn't there. Until that moment, I hadn't realize I'd been waiting for affirmation. Deeply disappointed, my thoughts turned dark. For all I knew, he'd lied to me last October. *Heck, he probably did.*

Down to business, Glenn announced that everyone must attend a weeklong "pow-wow" at a Tucson hotel. I didn't give a hoot about the team-building meeting, but a week at the Santa Rita Hotel sounded nice. Away from the office, I also thought I'd have a chance to talk to Glenn alone. Call it what it was—an obsession—but I had to know if he really meant what he said that night. When the room cleared, I found the courage to ask Glenn if we could talk soon. He said okay. Again no sign if he knew what it was about, nor did he ask.

In the hotel lobby, Glenn took me aside, and asked what I wanted to talk about. Nervous, I checked to make sure no one could overhear. It was hard to begin, but I asked him if he remembered coming to my house after the party last year.

With eyes lowered, he removed his hat and ran his hand through thinning hair. "Mostly, but I was pretty drunk. A lot of what I said I don't remember." Just as Glenn was getting to what he *did* remember, we were interrupted.

Disappointed, and feeling I'd missed my only chance, I walked back to my room, where I plopped onto the bed. What was wrong with me? I had to let this thing with Glenn go. Someone knocked on my door. *Glenn?* No—it was Joe, wanting to talk, I assumed. But he had little to say, in fact, nothing to say. So we sat in silence. Why had he come? Last summer Joe had said he loved me. I didn't understand why he'd now taken a step back. I started to feel annoyed and angry. If he wanted me, then he'd have to fight for me. Other men were interested in me, and I, in them. And what about those confusing feelings I had for Glenn? If I ignored them, would they go away? I didn't believe so. Despite the stern lecture telling myself that Glenn was over twenty years older than me, as well as my supervisor, each time I saw him, my heart leapt, and my hands trembled. I couldn't deny that my existence seemed to revolve around his mere presence.


EASTER SUNDAY FELL on my regular workday. No one forewarned me about what to expect, maybe because they worried I'd call in sick. Easter in Madera Canyon delivered a different crowd not seen there any other time of the year. The peaceful canyon turned into Yellowstone National Park. On Memorial Day weekend. Times ten.

Fire Prevention Tech Robert and I cruised an overflowing picnic area. Where no tables were available, families had spread out blankets. Did people really think it was fun to be elbow-to-elbow in nature? I didn't get this. Robert placed warning citations on the double-parked vehicles lining the main road. Those people didn't know how lucky they were to get off with just a warning. Robert didn't believe in writing actual tickets. Poor, peaceful Madera Creek endured hordes of screaming kids, who trampled tender riparian plants. Robert calmly warned them to stay on existing paths. We carried large garbage sacks, filling them with dozens of soda and beer cans found floating in the water. Already I noticed forgotten Easter eggs tucked in tree crotches, under bushes, and in boulder crevices, but Robert said to leave them just in case kids hadn't found them yet. He hated to spoil the egg hunt, but admitted the forgotten ones would sure stink in a few days. This guy kept his cool the whole time. My head hurt when I got home that night like I'd tackled a shopping mall the day after Thanksgiving.

Monday, first in the office, I sat anticipating Glenn walking in the door. A truck pulled up, and I listened to his boots strike the wood floor. He glanced and nodded at me, hung his Stetson on the coat rack, and walked over to get coffee. Within moments, I started to shake, his presence charging me like an electric current. No man had ever affected me this way. No man had ever attracted me so strongly. I fantasized that we would sleep together, but worried that if it happened, he would lose respect for me, and I for him. Would it be better if we stayed away from each other? I dismissed that thought because I didn't like my answer. The arrival of crew members sent the day into motion.

Later, after work, I hung around the office, talking with the guys. There was no reason to rush home to an empty house. Glenn came in, smiled, nodded at me, and sat down at his desk. When the others departed, a wide-open opportunity for me to talk to Glenn presented itself. I could pick up where we'd left off at the hotel. But should I? What if he didn't share my feelings? Would I end up hurt and disillusioned? I decided to take the risk. I sat down in front of him to find out.

"I do have a special like for you," Glenn said, massaging his forehead as though stimulating his memory. "I don't remember exactly what I told you that night, and maybe it's best that I don't."

After an interminable minute, he offered no more.

Smiling, I said something lame to make him think this wasn't important. "Oh, that's okay." Okay? It was not only *not* okay, it hurt like hell. A "special like"? What was *that? Nowhere near love*, I thought. But why would he say something he didn't mean, even if he didn't remember saying it? *You must let this go.* But could I? Maybe I should focus more on Joe. But even he had me baffled. When he'd said he wanted to come see me, I'd replied, "Sure, come if you want." I didn't get why, if he wanted to see me, he didn't just show up. What did these guys want from me anyway?

OUR LAST CREWMEMBER arrived in late May, a direct order from Washington D.C. to fill the minority quota, or so the rumor said.

"Wait 'till you guys hear this," Eric said after delivering the new guy to his quarters. "So I get this phone call from the dispatcher's office saying our new hire is sitting at the Tucson airport waiting for a ride." He chuckled, shaking his head. "I walk into the Forest Service terminal, and here's this huge linebacker of a guy, black as the night is long. So I'm thinking, man, this is one big dude." He held his hand over his own six-foot-plus height. "We're driving back to Florida, and the poor guy asked a hundred times, 'What *towwnn* is this?' Farther we got from Tucson, the more scared he got."

Ed, a University of Georgia college student on a football scholarship, certainly fit the football player part. He was a big, brawny guy with a big laugh, so Mark nicknamed him, Big Ed. But why in heck would a football player from Georgia fly all the way to Arizona to be a firefighter? Tom asked him.

Ed's emphatic response was, "Oh, I didn't know this was a fire-*fighting* job."

*He what?*

Tom tipped his head sideways. "Really. So why are you here?"

Ed reared back, his eyes wide. "I thought I was gettin' me a cushy fire-*lookout* job."

He didn't know until he got here? Really? But a *cushy* lookout job? That's what I'd first thought when I filled in for Wilma, the Mt. Bigelow fire lookout, last summer in the Santa Catalina Mountains. Within five minutes she'd enlightened me on all of the responsibilities: locating smokes with the complicated Firefinder; knowing the difference between water dogs (vapors that appear when cold rain hits warm soil) and smoke; how not to report a campfire by mistake; talking on the two-way radio without sounding like an idiot. All had gone fine until a thunderstorm erupted. To avoid electrocution, I sat on a glass-footed stool. Lightning bursts turned the tiny room white with light, strikes hit the ground all around me, thunder claps boomed so loud they rattled the windows and shook the building. Hail beat against the glass panes until I thought sure they'd break. And those switchback steps, seventy-five feet worth, up and down at least twice a day, excluding bathroom breaks. Nope, being a fire lookout was not in any way, shape, or form cushy.

AS OF THIS summer, the Forest Service required all fire personnel to wear fire resistant Nomex pants and shirts, even when not firefighting. That was unwelcome news. I loved my comfy cotton workshirt and jeans. Nomex clothes didn't breathe worth a darn. Who needed that on a hundred-degree day?

"Why can't we carry them with us and change if we get a fire call?" Tom asked Eric.

Eric scowled. "Because Forest Service head-honchos think we sit around all day waiting for fires. I'm not crazy about this either, but we don't have a say."

That wasn't all we didn't have a say in. Eric said we'd also have to carry a fire shelter from now on. *More gear?* As if my pack wasn't heavy enough.

"Listen up about how this puppy works," Eric said, during the training session. "It's designed to protect you from becoming a crispy critter, but isn't failsafe. You'll have a better chance of surviving a burnover, though. I'm only going to show you once, because they're expensive, and they aren't reusable."

The fire shelter, tucked inside a compact orange canvas carry-case, shook out into what resembled an aluminum foil pup-tent. Eric lay face down and covered himself with the shelter. "I'm assuming you've already cleared the ground of flammables," he said from underneath. "To keep it from getting sucked off you when the fire passes over, put your elbows and feet into the corner pockets." He crawled out, stood up, and brushed himself off. "Remember, this is a last resort. Do *not* deploy it unless you have to."

I refused to accept I'd ever need to deploy—period. What fire official would ever let things get that bad? Certainly, they were on the ball, right?

Tom whispered in my ear, "We'd be a human baked potato."

Nervous, I laughed, but my skin crawled. I didn't want to bake in one of those things. Aside from the weight, the time it took to clear the ground, deploy, crawl under—I wasn't the only one who thought the time could be better spent making a last ditch effort to run like hell.

Texas John asked the question that was probably on everyone's mind but mine, because I refused to go there. "What would happen, Hoss, if a fire burned over me?"

Eric cleared his throat. "Well . . . it's not totally protective. You might get away with burns on elbows and feet in light fuels like grass . . . but a timber fire . . . well . . . I'm told severe burns are your least concern, because your lungs will blister from breathing the superheated air, and you'll suffocate from lack of oxygen."

Burned lungs? Blistered, peeling skin on feet and elbows? Suffocation? A death trap. Count me out. I'd rather take my chances and run like hell.

Texas John squared his shoulders and raised his eyebrows. "Well, hell's bells, why carry the durned things?"

"It's mandatory," Glenn said, his voice stern.

That ended the discussion and added one more thing to our gear.


ON MY DAYS off, other than grocery shopping and laundry, I stayed home. The last thing I wanted was to miss a fire call. After five, beer and bullshit often flowed at Pete and Mark's quarters. I ate a simple dinner, and then, wanting company, I walked over to visit. About an hour later, Tom and I moved outside to get away from the commotion so we could talk. Tom often said flattering things, which naturally I loved to hear.

"Everyone thinks you fit in here better than Jodi," he said.

I didn't respond—but how much I wanted to believe that. Although Jodi and I got along okay, I liked being the center of attention and wanted the guys to like me more than her—that darned ego thing.

Then Tom said, "Their only complaint . . ."

*Wait, they complain about me?*

" . . . is, they wished you drank more."

*They what?* That was too funny. I suppose the definition of "more" depended on whether they meant per hour or week.


JODI AND I shared a day off. Bored, we discussed our options.

"How about we catch some sun?" she asked. "I'm sick of my farmer's tan."

I didn't like my tan lines either. We decided the roof would make a suitable tanning bed. Jodi went to get a ladder while I gathered up towels, pillows, baby oil, a book, radio, and tall glasses of iced tea with lemon and Sweet-N-Low. It took us several trips up and down the ladder to get settled on our roof-top sunning spot. To maximize our new tan, we both took off our bikini tops, giggling about what we'd do if one of the guys came up the road. Could they see us?

At most, five minutes had passed, when Jodi said, "You know, it's hot up here."

"It is," I said, relieved she brought it up. "Too hot!"

We carried everything back down.

After quitting-time, I checked to see what the guys brought back from the mailbox. Thrilled when I saw the letter from my mom, I tore it open to find several pages in her lovely cursive handwriting: our cat's antics, the red-ripe tomatoes in the garden, and how she'd already picked sweet raspberries. Although I loved my independence, her letters tugged at me. I missed her. Would twinges of homesickness ever go away?

At work the next day, and enjoying the last of a cool morning, Jodi, Pete, Ed, and I waited on the office steps for the University of Arizona researchers we were asked to help. Like clockwork, at eight, cicadas began to buzz, signaling a hot day ahead. A white State of Arizona pickup swung up, and its driver waved us to follow. Dirt clouds billowed, suspended in the air, as the truck ahead of us sped off. Pete hung back so we wouldn't have to eat their dust.

Countless dirt roads zigzagged across the experimental range, an outdoor lab of sorts, for plant and animal studies. Cattle gave us curious glances as we whizzed by. Not much for them to eat here, so they ate everything and anything, evidenced by cactus thorns protruding from their mouths. *Someone must pull those out,* I thought, but I couldn't think of how.

An hour passed of turning onto roads with no names, and I worried about getting back by ourselves. I hated not knowing where we were, and Ed hated it even more. He hung out the window, craning his neck to find some sign of civilization. "What *towwnn* is this?"

Civilization to Ed: a grocery store, Circle K, McDonald's.

"There is no town, Ed!" I said with a laugh. His bug-eyed stare told me that wasn't the right answer.

At Study Plot #45, we pulled over to the side of the road. Walt and Annie unloaded white five-gallon buckets labeled with skull and cross-bones. *Poison? We're handling poison?* Could I pass on this?

Walt sat on his tailgate and explained how they wanted to exterminate both mesquite and catclaw acacia to make room for more grazing grasses. Kill trees so cattle could have more food? Sure, I hated to see them eating cactus, but poisoning trees, not to mention me? I didn't like either of those options. Now I wished Glenn had picked someone else for this project.

We waded through rustling, knee-high, tawny grass, stepping around the sharp spines of barrel and prickly pear cactus. Flies buzzed around my head; the sun blazed white-hot, searing exposed skin. Poor Ed clutched his chest, eyes wide, when I reminded him to watch out for diamondback rattlesnakes.

We stopped at a tree, its lacy leaves offering filtered shade.

"This is mesquite," Annie said. "Notice the leaf arrangement, and straight thorns."

She took another step, and stopped abruptly to unhook the curved thorn snagged in her jeans. "Catclaw acacia."

Much like the "Wait-a-minute" bushes I'd encountered on previous desert hikes, as in, "Wait a minute while I unhook myself."

By their furrowed brows and deep frowns, I figured Pete and Ed did *not* want to do this. Me either. Our reasons differed, though—they didn't want to deal with thorny plants, and I didn't want to handle poison. Thank goodness

I'd brought gloves. Jodi and I were to drop gigantic aspirin-like tablets at mesquites; Ed and Pete were to sprinkle granules around catclaw acacias.

We fanned out to cover more ground.

Ed called out in falsetto, "Here kitty, kitty, kitty . . . Where are you kitty? Oh, there you are. Baaad kitty. Hiding from ol' Ed. C'mon out from under there, kitty, Ed's got a treat for you . . . bwah-ha-ha."

*Silly boy.* Ed made me laugh until my eyes teared. Later I wondered if the plants died. Mesquites have to be the toughest tree on the planet. It didn't matter if they were burned, chopped down, or hit by lightning, they always grew back. I doubted you could successfully poison them either. I wanted to check to see if the stuff had worked, but I never could find the test plot again for the maze of roads.

# THIRTEEN

THE GOOD THING about this summer's crew: Opie Taylor didn't return. The bad thing about this summer's crew: Texas John and Pete did. At least I knew where I stood with John: I was the wrong sex in the wrong job. John I understood, and tried to ignore. Pete still mystified me.

I finished sharpening tools used on our last fire and stepped inside the fire cache to put them away. Pete stood at the work bench, repairing a chainsaw. I asked if I could help.

"Why? Do you think I can't handle this?" he asked, sounding irritated.

"Oh, no, of course not. I just thought I could give you a hand." Humiliating.

Why did I keep trying to be nice to this guy?

A few days later Skinny Wilson felt the need to tell me Pete didn't like working with me. That stung. Pete must have known his comment would get back to me and that stung more. Questions and self-doubt clouded my mind. Did he think I didn't work hard enough? Or that when I tried to be nice I was coming on to him? Nothing could have been further from the truth.

Glenn sent me with Pete in the morning to trim the huge oak trees lining the road to the campground in Madera. *Stuck alone all day with someone who doesn't like me? Just great.* I slid into the truck next to Pete, replaying the tape of what Skinny Wilson said on a continuous loop all the way to the job site.

Once there, anger fueled me like I'd overdosed on caffeine. I pushed hard, sawing limbs of the tall trees with a long-handled pruner, dragging trimmings to the trailer and flinging them inside. I crawled on top of the brush and stomped it down to compact the load. Pete ran the chainsaw, ignoring my furious pace. At lunch, I wolfed down my food, and went right back to work. Pete raised his eyebrows, but said not a word.

I stormed into my quarters at five-thirty, flinging the door shut with a satisfying slam. Exhausted, tearful, and feeling like no one believed I ever worked hard enough, I took a shower to wash off the sweat, dust, and bad mood. I changed into cut-offs and a filmy India gauze top to connect with my feminine side. Physically I felt better, but negative thoughts continued to spin around uselessly in my head. A few steps from my quarters, I sat down on the weathered bleachers of the former ballfield we used for P.T.s to calm my thoughts. Daylight faded, and a cool breeze drifted down the canyon, sweetly scented with oak and summer grasses.

A screen door slammed; footsteps headed my way: Pete, with two beers in hand. "Mind if I join ya?"

*Oh, great.* Resigned to his company, I accepted the offered beer. The bleachers creaked as he settled next to me and tipped his bottle up to take a swig. "Why'd you knock yourself out today?"

Surprised that he'd notice, or care—unlike me, I spoke my mind. "I'm sure having me around ruined your day." I immediately paid for my honesty with a major stomach twinge.

Amused, he offered a crooked smile. "What makes you think that?"

Was he serious? "You always give me a hard time! I must be doing something wrong."

"Who? Me? I give everyone a hard time." He grinned.

"I heard you don't like me." My chest tightened and my eyes watered, but blinked them back. I would *not* give him the satisfaction of reducing me to tears.

He glanced at me sideways, his mouth lifting in one corner. "You don't bother me."

What was that supposed to mean? That I wasn't important enough to be liked or disliked? I didn't respond. Crickets chirped, filling the silence between us. We finished our drinks and said goodnight. Unable to sleep, I ruminated about Pete's indifference. Pings of self-doubt again filled me. I wanted him to like me, but couldn't figure out how to make it happen.


BECAUSE OF A doctor's appointment, I missed going out with the crew, and Glenn asked me to ride along with him to check the station's water lines. Although I tried not to think about Glenn romantically, I couldn't control the thrill of his presence. At the Santa Rita Lodge, Glenn pulled into the empty parking lot. "I want to stop for a cup of coffee."

Inside, we perched on bar stools, waiting for someone to notice new customers. From the kitchen came the owner, who also served as our waitress. I recognized her from Monday cleanup days, when I ordered an iced tea and sat on the patio. With dark circles under her eyes, hair askew, and shoulders slumped—she always looked like she'd just crawled out of bed.

Moseying over to us, lit cigarette between her lips, she asked, "What'll you have?" She brushed stray hair from her eyes.

I ordered iced tea.

In his usual gruff demeanor, Glenn said, "I'd like a cup of coffee . . . *today's* coffee." He winked at me.

Her frown deepened as she snatched the coffee pot and poured the dark brew. She slammed the mug down in front of Glenn. Next she plopped down my glass of tea and retreated into the kitchen. We spent a silent, but comfortable, fifteen minutes, while Glenn drank his coffee and smoked another cigarette. I nursed my vile-tasting beverage, which had never spent any quality time with a real teabag. He tossed some change on the counter, and we left.

Back on the road, he gave me a wry smile. "Too damned cheap to brew a new pot."

For a moment, I thought to touch his arm when I laughed, but stopped myself. This was not the time or place, and besides, he didn't have feelings for me. At least, not that I could tell.

Most of the morning, we walked the water line originating from springs in the mountains. Springs always fascinated me: pure water, leaking out of the ground from rains and snowmelt, even after months of dry weather. I envisioned a labyrinth of tunnels, weaving and meandering underground, before finding a place to surface.

The sound of gurgling led us to a broken pipe. I returned to the truck and brought Glenn a hacksaw, two pipe wrenches, and a repair coupling. We sat on the ground while he patiently showed me how to install the part. He stood up and adjusted his cowboy hat.

"Good skill for you to learn," he said.

We found no more leaks to repair and returned to the station mid-afternoon. I assumed I'd be on my own until five, but Glenn wanted to show me how to splice rope. After a stern reminder to myself to not read into this, I sat with him on the steps of the fire cache, very close, almost touching. He smelled pleasantly of tobacco and leather.

"You start by untwining one end," he said, giving me a length of rope to unwind. "Now, overlap both ends and braid together." As he took my hands in his to demonstrate, his touch was electric. Our blue eyes met for a fleeting moment. He turned away.

This man was such an enigma. I wanted to know everything about him. Joe had mentioned that Glenn was a mule-skinner, someone who led pack-mule teams. Texas John told me about the metal plate in Glenn's head.

"He was riding Gardner Canyon Trail, oh, 'bout fourteen years ago. His horse spooked and fell, dumping him off. When the horse scrambled to get back up, it kicked Glenn in the head. Cracked his skull wide open. Ol' Jack was with him. He got out the radio to call for help, but accidentally dropped it. Batteries flew everywhere. Glenn was conscious at that point, 'cause he's told me he thought for sure he was dead if Jack couldn't get the radio to work. Jack managed to, and Glenn was air-lifted to Tucson. Tough old coot."

What if he'd died that day? I would've missed knowing him, learning from him. This tough, quiet man, full of backcountry knowledge and skills was essential to the operation of Florida. A *real* Forest Service employee. Why, he knew everything that *I* wanted to know: How to supervise a fire crew, fix a water line, build a fence, blaze a trail, ride a horse, pack mules up a mountainside . . . Would he teach me all of these things if I asked him to?

A few days later, Glenn surprised me by saying I'd ride with him to a meeting in Nogales. Why me? What would the crew think? But then I thought, *who cares?* Glenn lit a cigarette, turned on the Forest Service radio, and focused on the road.

After a few comments about work, he glanced over at me. "You know, I don't understand how the guys stay away from you."

For a heart-stopping moment, I couldn't think of anything to say. First off, the guys *didn't* stay away from me, but I didn't want him to know that. I forced a light-hearted laugh. But alarms went off in my head. Why would he say this? He must have feelings for me. Silence hung in the air for a few moments.

"Now, I want you to be okay with this. All will be fine," he said.

*Wait, what?* This was so off topic, he lost me.

"I'm going to assign you to the tanker crew with Tom and John."

My disappointment that he'd changed topics turned into an even bigger disappointment that he'd changed my assignment. Why? Did he think I couldn't handle the suppression crew? Did he worry I'd get hurt? I couldn't bring myself to ask.

"It'll be a good experience for you," he said, reaching in his pocket for a cigarette.

To heck with tanker experience. I wanted to stay on the suppression crew. We went to more fires than the tanker crew did.

As if reading my mind, Glenn said, "Don't worry, you'll still get to go to plenty of fires."

That didn't help. This felt like a demotion. I bit my lip and turned my face toward the window so he couldn't see the tears threatening to fall.

# FOURTEEN

*May 28<sup>TH</sup>, 1977*

*I had just finished writing what happened when I turned off the light and heard Glenn pull up at his house. And walk over here. And walk into this house looking for me.*

AT THE SOUND of my door opening, I leapt out of bed and dashed into the living room.

In the dim light, Glenn swayed slightly, the strong odor of whiskey surrounding him like an invisible cloud. "Linda, I need to talk to you."

My heart pounded so hard, I thought it would push right through my chest.

He stepped closer to me and fingered my hair where it lay upon my shoulder. "I think the world of you, you know."

Could he see me trembling in the dark? Or maybe he could feel me shake, because I sure could. He pulled me into his arms. "Linda, Linda . . . I really like you so much. I would love to make love to you, you know. I would. It would be wrong, but . . ."

All I could do was stammer, "I . . . I . . ."

Abruptly, he released me, and turned away. "God, Linda, this is wrong. I just can't do this."

Before I could react, he pulled me back into his arms. "Come over to my house. Please. I'll remember this moment, I promise. I won't forget."

A reality check. As much as I wanted him, I made a firm decision. No way would this happen unless I was willing to let it happen—and letting it happen while he was drunk did not work for me. I told him so. Angry, Glenn jumped into his truck and left. I went back to bed, but not to sleep. Despite my fear that he would hurt me emotionally, deeply, I couldn't think of a way to stop where we were going—to be honest, I didn't want to.

In the morning, on our day off, I walked next door to Glenn's house for answers—sober answers. Sitting at his kitchen table, I found the courage to ask him, "Why do you always have to be drunk to tell me how you feel?"

Glenn took my hand, pulled me over him, and kissed me, his fingers in my hair sending tingles down my neck. Drunk with desire, my knees weakened. I sat down on his lap, resting my head on his shoulder. How wonderful it was to have him hold me. My feelings were so strong, I had to say, "I love you."

He gently tucked my hair behind one ear. "You can't, you know, you just can't."

I didn't ask why. I didn't want to know. We talked briefly about the consequences of getting involved, with him being my supervisor and all. Probably more for his benefit than mine. I didn't care. Caught up in him, in the moment, we agreed to meet at a motel in Tucson.


LATE THAT AFTERNOON, I lay in Glenn's arms, a sheet draped across us. The industrial-strength drapes were drawn against the sun's rude glare, darkening the room. Did I dare ask him "what next?"

The romantic moment evaporated when he sat up straight. "Lord, I hope there isn't a fire. They'll wonder where we are. Let's go." After he put on his cowboy hat, he turned to me. "You aren't going to get squirrelly like women sometimes do after sex, are you?"

My mouth fell open for a moment, then shut. Somehow I managed to answer brightly, "Of course not."

I swung my purse onto my shoulder and followed him out the door. It hit me while descending the staircase, with my feet feeling unconnected to the earth. He didn't think getting involved was wrong because he was my supervisor—he thought it was wrong because I'd fallen in love with him and wanted a relationship with him, and he did not want one with me. How could I have been so blind? My soul shattered into thousands of glass shards, piercing my heart.

Together we walked in silence to the parking lot, where waves of heat undulated from the black asphalt, the air motionless, oppressive. Alone in my car, I lay my forehead on arms crossed over the steering wheel and sobbed.


TWO DAYS LATER, Glenn moved out of Florida to live on land he'd purchased at the base of the mountains. I knew this had nothing to do with me, but it still hurt. I didn't want to admit it, but maybe it was best to not have him living next door.

When I returned to work, I couldn't look at him. I didn't want Glenn to know what he'd done to me. He acted like nothing had happened between us.

*Focus, focus, focus. Think about your job and nothing else.*

# FIFTEEN

ON MONDAY, A routine cleanup day, I raked around a picnic table while Texas John shoveled out grills. Something wispy near Mt. Wrightson caught my eye. "John! Smoke!"

Texas John set down his bucket of ashes, tipped his hardhat up, and squinted where I pointed. "Well, I'll be hogtied, I think we got ourselves a fire." He grabbed the radio mike and called dispatch.

"Dispatcher, this is tanker two-two-zero."

"Go ahead two-two-zero."

"We got smoke up near Wrightson."

Static squawked. "Ten-four, two-two-zero. Report to Florida."

We raced back to the station, a surge of excitement erasing all my thoughts except the thrill of being first on the fire—initial attack.

Glenn waited for us with welcome news. The helicopter from the Catalinas was on the way. That saved us a five-mile hike, with an elevation gain of four thousand feet. Initial attack *and* a helicopter ride. What could be better?

Full of anticipatory tingles, I watched the helicopter approach, its blades chopping through the air. Taking advantage of reverse momentum to slow down, it made a wide half-circle, hovered for a moment, and settled in a whirl of dust. Helicopter rides rated near the top of my why-I-loved-my-job list. More fun than planes, they flew so close to tree tops I could wave at the squirrels. A Helitack crewman climbed out, placed a hand on his hardhat, crouched low, and scurried toward Glenn, downdraft flapping the legs of his Nomex pants. They shouted greetings and stood close to talk.

Standing in line, I waited for the crewman to jot down names and total weight with gear to calculate flight order. That done, he said, "First up: Barclay, Richardson, Linda—with Linda in front."

Same as before. Using last names for everyone but me. Amusing. I liked that a little chivalry sometimes snuck in.

Blades whirring overhead reminded me to duck low. I climbed into the front seat, the cockpit bouncing like an buoy. Joe said the privilege of sitting up front came from my weighing less, often matching a pilot's small stature. Friends said that if I believed that, I was *way* too naïve.

Engine high-pitched and whining, blades picking up speed, up we rose— while my darned stomach again took seconds to catch up. Soon we circled the Wrightson Fire, stirring smoke around like a giant blender. Our pilot made another pass through the shroud of smoke, flying blind. We hovered. And hovered.

"I can't land here," the pilot yelled. "It's too smoky."

I stared at him blankly. *Wow, I guess we're going back.*

"I'm going to hover as low as I can. You'll need to jump out."

*JUMP out? You want me to* jump *out?* Adrenaline kicked into overdrive; blood pulsed in my ears. I trembled as I stepped onto the skid, holding the door frame to steady myself. I leapt into the smoky abyss. Four feet later, I landed hard, stumbling a bit before gaining my footing. Crouched low, I scurried away from the spinning blades and squatted as close to the steep edge of the helispot as I dared, waiting for the others to join me. Seconds later, they knelt beside me, and with hands on hardhats, we watched the chopper fly away.

At the fire, we spread out ten feet apart and scratched a four-foot-wide line.

"Bump!" I said when I caught up to the next person on the line.

They bumped the next person, and so on. When lower limbs of a pine torched, my heart did an acrobatic flip as I remembered the training film about dangerous crown fires. Who wouldn't be afraid of a fire burning overhead? But winds were light; underbrush minimal. If anyone could call a fire an easy one, this was it.

By three a.m., we'd contained the eighteen-acre blaze. Wrapped in my Army jacket, I curled up on a bed of pine needles to nap, sandwiching my hands between knees for warmth, half-listening to a conversation.

"Man, are my dogs barking," Mark said, shucking his boots. "Did you hear what that Helitack guy said back there? 'We stop 'em, you mop 'em?'"

My eyes flew open. *What?*

"Yeah," someone replied. "Fly in, dig a little line, fly out. Lackeys. We do it all, thank-you-very-much."

Helitack crews thought they were above mop-up? Here, I'd envied their job.

In the morning I awoke to dew on my clothes, a golden sunrise, and the sound of hooves striking rocks and scuffling dirt.

*Do I hear horses?* I sat up. Glenn, on horseback, led pack mules carrying fresh food and water. Soon the aroma of coffee perking and hickory-smoked bacon sizzling in a skillet made me ravenous. Why did food eaten outside taste so much better? Maybe it was the fresh mountain air, or maybe it was because I hadn't eaten for hours—but this simple meal combined with the fragrance of sun-warmed pine . . . heaven.

Mop-up lasted for two long days until the fire was declared controlled. When the helicopter returned to give us a lift down, I was grateful, but felt guilty. After overhearing Mark's conversation, I wondered, *Is flying cheating?*


IN THE MOOD to do some shopping, I invited Jodi and Ed on a Tucson run. It'd give me a chance to ditch the Levi jeans attire—rare, but fun. I stepped into the yellow strappy sundress I'd made and placed the lovely straw-hat my best friend Gail had given me for my birthday on my head. I slipped on calf-sculpting Dr. Scholl's sandals and left my hair unbraided.

Cruising I-19 with windows wide open, a gust of wind blasted through the car, sending my hat sailing out a window. "Oh no!" I swerved off to the side of the road.

"I'll get it!" Ed said, jumping out.

My rearview mirror reflected Big Ed's huge bulk, dressed in a loud Hawaiian print shirt and baggy shorts, flip-flops flapping, chasing my hat down the interstate while it skipped along with the wind. What in the world were folks in passing cars thinking of *that?* With my hat now safely in the car, I thanked Ed profusely—one of those moments when I thoroughly enjoyed being treated like a woman. Who said I couldn't be both tough and feminine?

In big city Tucson, Ed was in his element—fast food joints galore; and Jodi and I hit up not a mall, but an Army surplus store to buy gear for our fire packs.

That night, Joe rode up to my quarters on his motorcycle. What a nice surprise! With my arms wrapped tight around his waist, we sped off into the desert. I pressed my body against his back and rested my cheek on his shoulder, the air rushing by, lost in the moment and the pleasant scent of his aftershave. His firm, muscular body felt good—very good. If we could have rode forever, with no destination, no stopping, it would have been . . . well . . . magical.


ALL OF US were ready to go out for the day, when in shuffled Big Ed a minute past eight, rubbing the sleep out of his eyes, boot laces dragging on the floor. He plopped into a chair, grunting and groaning with the exertion of bending over and tying the laces.

Mark folded his arms and laughed. "Are you dying over there, or what?"

"It's too damned early," Ed said.

Although I liked Big Ed, I didn't get this. I looked forward to every day and always arrived early.

Glenn shook his head and frowned. He had no patience for slackers. "The station's gasoline tank is leaking. We need to pump it dry and dig it up."

Sign post holes were bad enough, but a whole gas tank? I sighed.

With the ground as hard as concrete, we'd need heavy artillery. From the fire cache tool rack, I collected a digging bar. They weighed a ton, but I found them easier to use than a pick. Stabbing at the soil with the bar loosened a few inches. I stepped aside while Pete shoveled. Then more bar work. Then more shoveling. As the hole got deeper, I had to climb out and wait for dirt removal. I paced. Watching someone else work was about as interesting as watching rain form puddles.

Ed's turn was next for shovel duty. He stood in the expanding hole and wiped his brow with a bandana. "Lordy, Lordy, it's hotter than blue blazes." He removed his T-shirt and wrung out the sweat. "Don't know how y'all handle this."

I felt sorry for Ed. He did seem to suffer more than the rest of us. At break time, I walked up the hill to my quarters and made iced tea for everyone. Smiles of gratitude made it worth the trip. We sat in the shade, sipping, crunching ice cubes, speculating how much longer the backbreaking job would take. Definitely more than one day. Or two.

At eight-fifteen the next morning, I thought it odd Tom hadn't shown up for work yet—he was never late. By nine o'clock I couldn't shake an awful feeling of dread. Something was wrong. I said so, but everyone said I worried too much.

When Robert walked up to us at the gas tank, head down, brows drawn together, my heart turned cold. *No. Don't say it. I knew something was wrong.*

"Tom's been in an accident," he said.

*No, no, no . . . this can't be happening.*

"Clark and Pete found him next to his motorcycle in the middle of Box Canyon Road," Robert said. "He's in bad shape."

While the guys commiserated among themselves, I left, not wanting them to see me cry. On my bed, between sobs, I prayed to the powers that be, *Please don't let Tom die.* An hour later, wrung out, I forced myself back to digging. I had to do something, or I'd never stop crying.

When I arrived to work in the morning, I found everyone gathered in the office, solemn.

Perched on a table, head bowed, Pete said, "At first we thought he was already gone. Then he opened his eyes."

Clark's cigarette smoldered between his fingers, a long ash forming at the end. "We thought he'd die there. Took the ambulance forever to find us. I've never seen time move so slow."

Afraid I'd lose Tom, I poured all my despair into excavating that gas tank, refusing breaks or trading off.

More long days passed until I heard Tom would recover. But hearing it wasn't enough—I wanted to see him. Standing at his hospital room door, I winced at the unmistakable hospital smell of antiseptic and bleach. A heart monitor bleeped. Was that really Tom? A shattered leg in traction, a broken arm in a cast, his head wrapped in white gauze—he looked so . . . fragile. But his scratched and bruised face lit up when I approached his bed. I rested my hand oh-so-gently on his lower left arm, afraid my touch would hurt.

"Oh, Tom, I've been so worried about you." My voice cracked. My resolve not to cry failed. Tears began and soon flowed freely down my cheeks.

Tom's eyes moistened. "It's okay, Linda. I'm going to be just fine."

I both wanted and needed to believe him. I kissed him lightly above one eye, the only spot not red or purple. His eyelids threatened to close. "I'll come back to see you, Tom." I gave him a small smile. He feebly smiled back.

Weeks after Tom went home to recover, some of us stopped to check on his progress.

"You guys been to any fires?" he asked, his leg propped up on pillows.

"A few," Mark said.

"We sure miss you," I said. "When will you be coming back?"

Tom smiled, but with sad eyes. "Prognosis is not good." He sighed. "Looks like my firefighting days are over. I'm sure gonna miss them."

I understood why. I couldn't imagine not being able to fight fires.

"So did the sheriff ever figure out who hit you?" Mark asked.

Tom explained all he knew. "Rancher's kid didn't check for traffic when he pulled onto the main road. Broadsided me, panicked, and drove away." He didn't know if the kid had called for help.

Why did this have to happen to Tom? It was so unfair. Florida wouldn't be the same without him. I'd miss his laughter, gentle teasing. Yes, I sure would.


AT NINE A.M. on my day off, Glenn came to get me. "We've got another fire near Wrightson."

I didn't want a day off anyway. I changed clothes, sped over to the fire cache, and hopped into the loaded crew-cab. There'd be no helicopter this time, which was okay by me. Heaven forbid should we get spoiled.

Led by Mark, we pushed hard up to Baldy Saddle, loaded down with gear and tools for the long haul. Soon conversations ended: we were too winded to talk. This pushing so hard got a bit ridiculous. Sure, we were fit, but this was crazy. Of course we needed to get to the fire . . . but why wear ourselves out getting there? When some of us started to fall behind, Mark stopped for a quick breather; so short, we didn't even sit down. Repeated several times, each break was just long enough to catch our breath. Last stop, a woman in her sixties rounded a bend.

She smiled at the panting, sweaty firefighters, and said, "Hello."

"Ma'am, you need to turn around," Mark said. "There's a fire up ahead."

Alarmed, she quickly left. Pushing top speed, and a hiker at an even pace had overtaken us. A hiker forty years older than we were. How ironic was that?

More pushing hard until we arrived at flames meandering through pine needles and lazy smoke drifting between trees. That's when I felt a new burst of adrenaline kick in. Eric assigned one squad to start there and waved for me and another crewman to follow him across treacherous scree. Without warning, the rocks gave way, pitching me sideways into the slope. *Whoops!* I stuck out an arm to break my fall, but it twisted backward as I hit the ground. Pain screamed through my shoulder. In agony, I held the arm against my ribs, rolling from side to side, my breath coming in short, quick snatches. Meanwhile, emotionless voices discussed my fate, akin to talking about what they ate for dinner last night.

"Guess we need to call a helicopter to fly her out."

"Yeah, probably should call a helicopter."

Mortified, I thought, *Fly me out for a strained muscle? No! Even worse, the whole forest would overhear that I got hurt.* That would be humiliating. Blind with pain, I rolled one more time, desperate to make it stop. Something I did helped. Maneuvering to my knees, I then stood. I couldn't let them send me down. They'd label me a wimp, or blame me for getting hurt, or throw the "See, women don't belong here" line at me.

I sucked in a shaky breath. "I want to stay."

Eric and Mike turned to look at each other, and then at me, their faces blank.

"Are you sure?" Mike asked.

"Yes."

Jaw set tight, I followed them, determined to continue.

Minutes later, a plane engine droned overhead, the C-47 swooping in low. No drop. It circled around and came back again. At a safe distance, I watched the belly doors open, spilling the dark pink retardant across the head of the fire. Flames knocked down, I dug in to scratch line. I kept my elbow close to my side, which allowed me to use the injured arm. "Rock!" a voice yelled from above. *Where? Yikes!* I scurried to avoid the dislodged stone tumbling end-over-end down the slope and watched it narrowly miss my leg.

Daytime slipped sideways into evening. Ed mopped his face with a red bandana. "Doggone it, I wish that moon would turn it up a notch. Man, I'm having a Big Mac attack. When's feeding time at this zoo?"

Ed thought there should be a McDonald's within fifteen minutes of his whereabouts on the entire planet. I had to laugh. "You are something else, Ed. Do you ever think of anything besides food?"

"Is there anything else to think about?"

Mark's voice echoed in the darkness. "Hey, Ed, smile so's we can see ya!"

Ed roared. He knew exactly what Mark meant. I laughed, too, my fatigue adding to the humorous vision of a bright, floating Cheshire-cat smile.

Later that night we contained the fire, and took a break. Army jacket zipped up tight, I vied for a spot next to a burning stump to keep warm. I found a position that rested my arm, and napped for a couple hours, turning over when the side opposite the fire got cold. Then the stump burned out. I shivered. It was freezing at nine thousand feet. Joe slept nearby, but he'd foiled my attempt to move closer, saying we shouldn't show affection at work. His rebuff stung. What difference did it make? *Besides*, I thought, annoyed, *sharing warmth makes sense.*

No cooked breakfast greeted us this morning. A cold C-rat filled my empty stomach, but left me craving pancakes with maple syrup, bacon, and *steaming* black coffee. Ten minutes later (that's all it takes to scarf down a C-rat), I joined Joe for mop-up. I threw a shovelful of dirt onto glowing coals and turned when Joe whistled.

"Look at that," he said.

All that remained of the beheaded Douglas fir was a tall, ragged, three-foot-diameter stump. This was not a lightning strike. This poor tree got a full-brunt slurry hit. Good thing I never felt the urge to purposely place myself under a drop in order to claim bragging rights. Back at my hotspot, I chopped apart the smoldering log to aid in cooling. Time for a heat check. I removed a glove and held my hand over the charcoal. Still warm. Back to dumping soil on the coals, chopping and scattering pieces.

Another twelve hours slipped away; daylight to dusk, dusk to dark. Nightfall helped a great deal with mop-up. Hotspots virtually screamed, "*Over here!*"

"Found one," I said to Joe.

He finished his heat check. "Okay, be right there."

Joe shoveled out and scattered hot coals; I chopped at the charred stump, breaking it into pieces.

"How's the shoulder?" he asked.

"Just a strained muscle. It's not too bad." Which was a big fat lie—it hurt like hell. But I appreciated that he'd asked. So far, he was the only one who had.

On break, I curled into a fetal position to nap, shivering in my damp clothes. When I awoke, daylight had crept into the sky, turning it turquoise and gold. No chirping birds welcomed the sun this morning. Smoke, fire, planes, and humans had frightened them off to safer places. Once the sun cleared the horizon, the cloud-free sky deepened to cobalt blue, and temperatures soared. Hard to believe an hour ago I couldn't get warm.

Glenn declared the fire controlled, but with the helicopter busy elsewhere, we'd have to hike out. Well, so be it. Five miles that would feel like ten. At least my shoulder pain had reduced to a dull ache. Down, down, down we zigzagged on seemingly endless switchbacks, past huge granite outcrops painted with multi-colored lichen: orange, chartreuse, sea-foam green. This trail was a rough one, and I tried to step on flat rocks to avoid the painful poke on the bottoms of my feet. I focused on the rhythm of my steps, the thump of my boots striking dirt, and then on rewards at the end . . . real food, a shower, and bed—maybe in reverse order.

Those stairs to my quarters *must* have grown taller the past few days. I fell onto the couch—did that ever feel good. What would feel even better required me to move. *Yeah, I should shower.* I sat up, tugged off my boots and sweat-soaked socks, and fingered my poor little aching toes. Two were red and blistered. The bottoms of my feet were also red and burned like I'd been walking barefoot on hot asphalt. If I stank, I couldn't tell. Everything reeked of smoke. Amazing how I never noticed that until I got home. My pants and shirt were so stiff with multiple layers of dried sweat, they could've walked to the laundry basket on their own. I stood under the blast of warm water, savoring the removal of several day's accumulation of filth. Being that dirty always gave me a whole new appreciation of being clean.

Refreshed, I enjoyed that wonderful feeling of mission accomplished. Even my shoulder felt better. Now for dinner and an early bedtime—all of which wouldn't happen because someone pounded on the front door.

# SIXTEEN

"FIRE CALL TO the Kaibab National Forest," Eric said. "You're going with John and Rico."

Tired? Not anymore. I stuffed clothes into my duffle bag. What would it be like going off-district with Texas John in charge? He yakked more than he worked. Rico, the tanker foreman in Nogales, had taken Tom's place, and I'd no clue what to expect from him. But, it's a fire, and I'm raring to go. And different from any fire I'd battled so far—not only off-district in an unfamiliar part of Northern Arizona, but also to what the Forest Service calls a "Project Fire." From what I'd gathered, this meant "a really big one."

Before leaving, I slapped together a cheese sandwich to eat along the way. A couple hours later, Texas John exited at a rest stop lit up like a used car lot. People milled around, stretching, walking dogs. Children squealed and chased each other, releasing pent-up energy. Returning from the bathroom, I found John talking to a tanker crew from the Catalinas who were headed to the same fire. Instant comrades. I stood back while John bragged about our busy season. He always managed to monopolize a conversation, so I didn't get a chance to talk to one of the guys I knew. Too bad I couldn't ditch my crew and ride with the Catalina guys.

I dozed during the long drive, waking on occasion to read signs indicating how much farther we had to go. John swung into fire camp near midnight. Generators hummed, charging floodlights strung between trees to keep darkness away. People scurried between tents; a truck driver unloaded his rig of supplies. Cardboard signs hung on trees, designating sleeping areas for the many crews. Branches, serving as clotheslines, sported socks and underwear. Prone figures sprawled under canopies, engaged in the kind of deep sleep that comes from total exhaustion.

We ate a late dinner at one of the many picnic tables inside a circus-sized tent. My stomach a bundle of nerves, I had no appetite and ate little. From a trash can filled with ice, I helped myself to a can of orange juice for later.

Mealtime over, off we went to patrol a bulldozed fireline for hotspots. At the first one, Rico unrolled hose, and Texas John started up the pump. I took a Pulaski and headed over to chop at the smoldering log.

John grabbed the handle of my tool. "I'll get this."

*What the hell?* "Let go," I said, tightening my grip. "I'm getting this."

After a brief tug of war, I won, but that didn't end the battle. John was on a mission to keep me from working. If this included getting me to sulk in the truck, well, that would never happen. Rico stayed out of the conflict, so I was mad at him too. Some time passed. Certain the shift was about over, I pulled out my pocket watch. *Only one o'clock?* Unbelievable. I had to stop checking.

Sixteen hours after we'd begun, I spread out my sleeping bag on ground and collapsed. Texas John disappeared to do who-knows-what. He returned too soon.

"Woo-wee," he said, standing over me.

I squeezed my eyes tight. *Go away.*

"Just imagine that." Cellophane crinkled.

I sat up and sighed. "What?" Would he ever leave me alone?

"I just heard a guy got hauled off to the hospital because an ant crawled in his ear." He lit his cigarette. "'Bout drove him crazy."

*In his ear?* Alarmed, and now wide-awake, I flipped my sleeping bag over, sweeping pine needles aside to look for ants. None, but I never did get any sleep. Every little tickle jolted me upright to brush off imaginary insects. *Thanks, John.*

After another long night mopping-up, we returned to camp. I plopped down on my back. Sleep deprivation often led to more sleep deprivation. I draped an arm over my eyes to block out the sun.

"Hey, lookie over there," Texas John said. "That's the all-women Indian crew. Supposed to be really somethin'. Call themselves the Apache 8." He snickered and made a Groucho Marx face. "Woo-wee, wouldn't I like to be on that crew."

*Ugh.* "You're sick, John."

What he said registered. *All women?* I sat up. Some carried shovels and Pulaskis; several balanced chainsaws on their shoulders, all with long black hair contrasted against yellow fire shirts. They seemed so strong and confident. I flopped back down. *Do they have it better than me?* I wondered. *Am I as good as they are?*

Snatches of sleep were interrupted by helicopters, truck engines, and generators. Four hours later, I was getting ready to start another shift, when Rico rushed up. "We're leaving! Flagstaff's got a big one on Mt. Elden, and they need us right away."

There went our plan to sneak in a visit to the north rim of the Grand Canyon. I doubted we could've pulled that off anyway.

Off we sped, heading south on a three-hour drive to a city in crisis. Drowsy, my head lolled to the right. I woke with a start, my head resting on John's shoulder. *That* had to stop. An elbow poked my side.

"Lookie there," Texas John said.

The tall, mushroom-shaped cloud of smoke on the horizon filled my stomach with dread. *Oh. My. God. Is that Flagstaff burning?*

# SEVENTEEN

RICO TWISTED THE dial to a Flagstaff radio station.

"The Radio Fire has consumed over four thousand acres of heavy timber and is growing. If you are in an evacuation area, get out now!"

Evacuations. What were we getting into? Far more danger than I wanted to take on with these two guys. How much I wished Joe or Glenn were here.

On the horizon, orange flames formed a necklace around Mt. Elden's ridges, writhing like solar flares. The sky glowed an iridescent orange, as though it, too, was on fire. Captivating. Breathtaking. A chill shimmied up my backbone. Frightening.

Texas John left to check in at the fire command center. Rico watched fire camp activity. I worried myself sick. I'd never been to a fire that threatened homes before. Would they make us put out house fires? I'd no idea how to do that. Making my fears worse, the faces all around me were grave, their concerns extending well beyond saving trees.

John returned with our assignment.

"They've got everyone evacuated," he said, rummaging for a cigarette from his pocket. "They want us on patrol for spot fires."

Texas John took the wheel. Rico offered to sit in the middle, which I appreciated. Down the twenty-foot-wide line we crept. Fire on our left, homes on our right. I rolled up my window to keep smoke from filling the cab, but it still worked its way inside. Our headlights bounced back off the swirling smoke, making it impossible to see where we were going, so John turned them off. Radiant firelight made our surroundings appear surreal and otherworldly.

"I'd be heartsick if that was my house," I said, as we crept by a two-story structure.

"We aren't supposed to put out house fires," Rico said.

*Oh, thank goodness.*

Firelight cast strange shadows onto the walls of the home—sinuous figures that danced and waved. As smoke drifted through the backyard, the silhouettes of a swing-set and a bicycle floated in and out of sight. Smoke engulfed our tanker like fog rolling in from the ocean.

Texas John hit the brakes. "I can't see a durned thing."

For five long minutes, we sat, engine idling. Texas John lit a cigarette. Great. Just what I needed. More smoke. A breeze cleared our view, and we continued. A puff of wind, created by the super-heated air, rustled through the trees, spurring flames. Instinctively I cowered away from the window when a tree flared brilliant orange. Despite the fiery display, the line held. We advanced slowly, never reaching a speed worthy of second gear. I watched in and among the homes for spot fires to our right; Rico watched the fire on the left; John focused on the bulldozed fireline ahead.

An hour past midnight, a Forest Service truck approached from the opposite direction. Texas John parked and jumped out to talk to the driver. Rico napped. I decided to get out and stretch. I leaned against the truck to watch fire do its thing—turn matter into carbon. Moments later came a change in the wind, and a change in the fire's behavior. Alarmed, I realized the line might not hold. If it didn't, no way did we have enough water onboard, or enough time, to stop the flames from overtaking us. I yelled at John. He glanced at me, but kept talking. I yelled again, pointing to the approaching flames.

"What? Oops. Guess we oughta get going," he said, sporting a sheepish grin.

"Jesus, John, what were you waiting for?" I said as we hustled back into the vehicle. The other driver did the same, and sped off.

Rico sat up straight, startled by slamming doors. "Hey, what's going on?"

I pounded the dash with my fist. "Go John! Go!"

"I'm going!"

Rico paled. "Shit! Go, go, go!"

With flames licking at the side of the truck, John pressed down on the gas pedal, hitting rocks and ruts hard. I clung to the dash, tossed against the door, against Rico. By the time we reached safety, I trembled, and blood pulsed in my ears. Oddly, though, my first thought was, *I wonder if the paint blistered?* Even odder, my second thought was, *Who'd explain to Glenn how that happened and why?*

"Whassa matter, Linda Lou? Fire a little too close for ya'll?" Texas John said, chuckling.

Acid dripped from my voice. "It seems to me you'd know that fire and gas tanks don't mix."

John smirked. Rico said nothing.

We circled around into the neighborhood and checked to see if the line had held. It had.

"Well, since we're out here, might as well fill up the gas tank," John said.

I glared at him. *Yeah, so you can blow us up royally next time.*

Texas John pulled into an all-night service station, started the self-service pump, and went inside for coffee. I plugged two quarters into a vending machine. *No Snickers?* Darn. I chose a PayDay instead. Took me thirty seconds to devour it. Tasted pretty darned good. I bought another and ate it just as fast. Not quite as good. My body hummed from the sugar overload. I leaned against the tanker, needing the support, and debated on buying a third one. I talked myself out of it. What I really needed was sleep, not more sugar. A car pulled up beside our tanker. Out stepped a man, his forehead deeply lined in concern. He opened the passenger side door, offering his hand to a very distraught woman. They walked over to me.

"Excuse us," the man said, his arm tight around the woman, who seemed to need his support. "We saw your Forest Service truck, and my wife insisted we stop."

Puzzled, I smiled and waited for him to explain.

"We were evacuated last night," he said. "We just wanted to thank you for protecting our home." His wife sniffled, dabbed her red eyes with a sodden tissue, nodding.

All of my fatigue, crankiness, and anger disappeared. Their gratitude made my day. Heck, it made my whole summer.

Mid-morning, with another shift over, I walked to a long table with basins of water, soap, and towels. I scrubbed my face, lower arms, and hands in the cold water, and dried off. In line at the mess tent, I let them fill my plate with whatever and ate mindlessly. Back to a clean basin to brush my teeth. Now for sleep. But my mind would not shut off. Visions of fire, smoke, homes in danger—all kept me awake. By noon, it hit ninety degrees. A bead of sweat trickled down my forehead; I wiped it away, only to feel another one form. Insects buzzed around my face. Five minutes felt like sixty. At last, time to go back to work. Better than lying there waiting for sleep that didn't want to come.

Our final night out, we patrolled, creeping along in first gear. I kept nodding off, lulled by the slow going, fatigue, and darkness. Our motion stopped. *Did we run out of gas?* I turned to Texas John. He'd fallen asleep, head lolled down.

I shook his shoulder. "John! Wake up!" His eyes flickered open.

"Huh? What?"

"You fell asleep. Why don't you let me drive for a while?"

"I wasn't asleep," he said, straightening his shoulders. "Just resting my eyes."

*Liar.* He didn't want me to drive. Or Rico either, for that matter.

Late in the morning, fire officials released us. Rico said the Florida and Nogales crews were battling a huge fire in the Huachuca Mountains, east of the Santa Ritas. I worried all the way back about my precious mountains. What if we had a fire? Who'd put it out?

Late evening, we arrived at the empty Florida complex. No lights shone in the windows, no government trucks were parked in their spots—a blanket of silence covered the entire station. Had time frozen while I'd been away? For eight solid days, I'd been traveling to, fighting, or returning from, fires. Those eight days felt like three weeks. And fire season had just begun.

FIRST THING, I replenished my fire pack, exchanged dull tools for sharp, and cleaned out the tanker. When I reached behind the seat to pick up trash, pain ripped through the shoulder I'd hurt before, rendering me incoherent. Gasping for breath, I held my arm to my side and waited for the agony to subside. *Damn, strained it again.* By now I considered all aches and pains the price I paid to do my job. I'd just have to be more careful.

EXTREME FIRE DANGER required extreme measures. The entire Coronado National Forest was closed to the public in mid-June. Glenn assigned me to the roadblock on Madera Canyon Road and asked Mark to loan me a uniform shirt so I'd look official. My bathroom mirror reflected an image I liked. Forest Service green might become my new favorite color.

Skinny Wilson and I manned the roadblock—a barricade placed in the travel lane. We sat on the side of the road, baking in the truck's cab, watching heat rise from the asphalt in visible waves. Kind of like sitting next to a blast furnace. Not many cars came up here in the summer, making for a long, long day. Skinny Wilson's smug comments made it seem even longer. If I mentioned the intricacies of tuning a saw—oh, heck, he'd perfected that years ago. Bring up the art of tool sharpening, he'd perfected that years ago, too. Because Skinny was only eighteen, I figured he must've learned this stuff in kindergarten.

At last, a car approached. I didn't mind talking to John Q. Public and strolled out to greet the driver. Skinny stayed in the cab engrossed in a *Playboy* magazine. A middle-aged couple, dressed in matching khaki shirts, with binoculars hanging around their necks, returned my "hello" with a smile. Their disappointment over the road closure turned into sympathy for our hot job, and they offered us cold drinks from their cooler. Those were the nice folks. Another car approached. This time, four overweight men, beers in hand, eyed me skeptically as I explained the situation.

The driver's round face reddened. "Hell, I pay for these facilities with my tax dollars. In fact, I pay your salary." Guffaws came from the passengers.

"I'm sorry sir," I said. "If you'd like, I can give you the phone number for the district ranger."

"I ain't calling no stinkin' district ranger," the man said. He made a U-turn, and, thank goodness, drove away.

The following week, Mark took Skinny Wilson's place. Last summer, Mark's company would've been great, this summer, not so great—in fact, awful. Not sure how we got on the topic, but Mark brought up the subject of women on fire crews, saying they belonged in the office, not on the line. Arguing would have made things worse, so I spent the day giving him the silent treatment, which he reciprocated. That he'd loved me last summer, but hated me now, was something I blamed on myself. If only I'd made a decision about us sooner, maybe things wouldn't be this way.

The rotten day with Mark put me in a rotten mood once home. Joe rode past my house on his motorcycle.

I waved him down, yelling, "Take me!"

I straddled the seat, wrapped my arms around him, and let him whisk me away. Parked in the desert to watch the sunset, Joe took my hand, laced his fingers between mine, and said I was beautiful. That he repeated this often didn't make me believe it one iota, but the pleasure that he thought so lingered for hours. There wasn't any place else I wanted to be other than with him, right there, right then.


THE OFFICE SCREEN door squeaked when I opened it in the morning and banged when it shut behind me. I peeked into my inbox. *A letter from Mom!* Inside, she'd stuffed newspaper clippings about out-of-control blazes reaching from California to Alaska, designating the summer of '77 the worst in recent history. Why didn't we get to go anywhere? So far, nothing but false alarms; and in one instance, three days in a row. Each time, we scrambled to the trucks and raced out of the complex, only to turn right around. Boy was that disappointing.

It wasn't the same as going to a fire, but when we started a spring improvement project at Kent Springs, I figured that at least it would distract me from all the fires we were missing. We bounced up the access road with far less urgency than last summer's haul-ass trip *en route* to the Kent Fire. Understandably, I'd missed the beauty of this idyllic forest setting on the crazy ride with Scott that May morning. Tall, gnarled sycamores with white and green mottled bark lined a musical creek in the deep, shadowy canyon. Water tumbled between and spilled over boulders; spiky, golden columbines nodded on the edges; limpid pools beckoned me to plunge in—maybe I would this weekend.

Lacy, bright-green bracken grew in abundance where we would build the wildlife watering trough. A V-shaped trench filled with concrete would funnel water into a concrete spring-box. White-tailed deer, black bears, squirrels, and coatis would soon appreciate a drink here.

Texas John and I unloaded sacks of cement. We'd add gravel and water to make concrete. Plenty of water here.

"Head down the trail a ways," Mark said. "There's a rockslide with gravel just the right size."

Rock is extremely heavy, even when it comes in small pieces—not that I didn't know that, but I'd never backpacked rock before. I held an old fire pack open while Texas John shoveled, and shoveled, and shoveled.

"Geez, John, you've got it overflowing!" Even if I could lift it, I'd lose the top third carrying it. He took some gravel out, grumbling about weak girls. Then he filled his pack half-full. *That figures.* With a bit of a wobble I carried the pack to the spring. Many trips later, a suitable pile had formed.

Mark crawled out of the trench, and in a voice thick with sarcasm, said, "Are we having fun yet?"

Maybe he wasn't, but I sure was.

"Your turn," he said to me, avoiding eye contact.

*Fine, don't look at me,* I thought. But this treatment hurt. Despite all that happened between us, I didn't hate Mark. I sincerely regretted the awful mess we got into, but just because everything fell apart, didn't mean he had to be such a jerk.

I slid into the trench, fully immersed in the earthy scent of rich, black humus. My boots sank deep into the mud. *Rats. I hope they don't leak.* I forced the shovel into the muck with my foot, then strained to lift the load. The heavy clay resisted, then a sucking sound accompanied the successful scoop. I tried to fling the mud off the shovel, but it wouldn't budge. Beating the shovel on a rock accomplished nothing. Mark handed me a second shovel to scrape the mud off the first one. Meanwhile, Texas John bailed out the trench as water seeped in from the spring. At four o'clock, we called it a day.

After a week of digging and bailing, we mixed concrete. As I sloshed the mixture forward and back in the wheelbarrow with a hoe, my thoughts wandered. Last night Joe had slept over. While I curled up next to him, he whispered that he loved me more than anything. On one level, I thought I loved Joe more than I'd ever loved anyone else, but would I never love anyone else but him? I wondered if that was possible. I'd loved before, but it didn't last. Would this?

Now for the hard part: hauling the concrete uphill to the trench. The terrain made using a wheelbarrow impossible, so we filled five-gallon buckets instead. I started out with one, but all the weight on one side threw me off balance. Two were heavier, but easier to carry—although after many trips, I wondered if my arms had lengthened a couple inches. Late afternoon, I watched Mark smooth the surface with a trowel.

"We should add a date, like the CCCs did," I said, proud of our work.

"You are not writing in my fresh concrete!" Mark gathered tools and stomped back to the truck.

*Spoilsport.* I should've done it anyway.


TWO WEEKS CRAWLED by like drunken snails, and still no fire calls. What a letdown. The action earlier this summer had spoiled me. I wanted more excitement. I wanted to go to another fire. Instead, I got culverts. Roadway culverts were something I'd never known existed, but Glenn changed that forever.

Flash floods from sudden rains washed sand and debris into the corrugated metal pipes along Box Canyon Road. If "someone" didn't clean them once in a while, water backs up and washes the road out. Glenn's "someone" would be Texas John, Skinny Wilson, and me: A long day ahead with two annoying companions. Yeah, I really wanted to go on another fire.

After arriving at the first culvert, I slid down the steep embankment to reach the opening. I crouched low, extended my shovel into the three-foot diameter pipe, dragged out a load of sand, pitched it downhill, and then went back in for more.

Texas John lit a cigarette and waved out the match. "Ya know, Linda Lou, you could crawl inside and push that sand out."

I flung the load off my shovel. "Fat chance, John, be my guest."

He chuckled. "I'm too big."

Again, what could I say?

"Watch out for snakes," he said as I leaned into the pipe.

I turned to glare at him. "Thanks."

A car with out-of-state plates pulled over to the side of the road next to our parked truck. The man, dressed in a shirt and tie, walked up to us with an "I'm lost" expression on his face. With a sly smile and a wink in my direction, Texas John asked how he could be of assistance.

The driver said, "I tried to take a short cut, and must've made a wrong turn. Where am I?"

Texas John didn't skip a beat. "Well, Hoss, you're in Texas."

The man's mouth formed a perfect "O" as it registered that somehow he'd driven through the entire state of New Mexico without knowing it. John continued stringing him along for at least five minutes; after which, I couldn't stand it one second longer.

"John's just joking with you. You're still in Arizona." I sent the relieved man on his way with directions to the interstate.

With hands on hips, John said, "Why'd you have to go and spoil my fun?"

"Because enough is enough! You were being mean." I let out a huge sigh. Only thirteen more miles of culverts to go . . .


I INVITED JOE on a long weekend in Prescott. Not only did I want to spend quality time with him away from work, but I wanted my parents to meet him. Quite unnerving, though, when I introduced a very shy Joe to my folks: a polite handshake with my dad, a smile and hello to my mom. When I walked in the kitchen to see Joe and my mom chatting away, I was so relieved. I should've known she'd work her magic on him.

Early Saturday, Joe and I explored the local swap meet, finding a few treasures. That night he took me to dinner at a swanky restaurant, where we lingered over good wine and conversation. Sunday, we hiked to Wolf Creek, making love to the sounds of rushing water. Late afternoon we headed back to Florida, with me in disbelief our three days together were already over. I almost didn't want to return to work.


WHAT A LONG Monday. In addition to having the post-vacation blues, rumors flew that funding was running out, and we'd be laid-off soon. I lowered and folded the American flag around 5:15, a ritual I enjoyed. Neat bundle in hand, I entered the office to stow it away. Hearing Glenn on the phone, I stopped. He acknowledged my presence with a nod and motioned for me to sit. I poised on the edge of his desk. He finished the call and placed the receiver in the cradle. My inquisitive eyes met his steady gaze. From that connection I knew: we had another fire.

"You're going to Northern Arizona," he said.

He reached out, and gently squeezed my hand. My heart squeezed. Confused, and frankly a bit scared, I waited to see what he'd do next—which was to let my hand go and pick up the receiver to make another call. The warmth of his touch lingered.

After he finished, I dialed my mom to let her know I'd be off-district again. She answered the phone upset and crying.

"We lost Tabitha," she said, sobbing.

In horror, I listened as she explained that our kitty had been hit by a car and had to be put down. *Tabitha, dead!* I hated that I couldn't console her very long, or let her console me. Right now, I had to get to a fire.

With raw grief, I stared into the dark outside the truck window in a trance. Tabitha had come west with us, spending the five days driving cross-country on my lap. Although she was the family cat, she'd favored me. When I realized that just last Saturday she'd slept on my bed, tears poured down my face, and I stifled sobs so no one could hear me cry.

Preoccupied with my loss, somehow I blotted out the entire experience on the Hualapai Reservation. Weeks later, I'd hear Mark tell all of the screw-ups on this fire: how we'd wandered around for hours in the dark, looking for the tools left for us to pick up and not finding them; how rhythmic drumbeats had kept us awake when we tried to sleep; how the crew boss had insisted that east was north, even after the sun came up in his "north." I have no memory of these events.

What do I remember? I remember being in incredible emotional turmoil: Tabitha was gone, leaving a gaping hole in my heart; I loved both Joe, and, unfortunately, Glenn; Mark and I were at odds with each other, but he did notice that something was wrong with me. He didn't pry—which was fine. I doubted I would've felt comfortable bawling on his shoulder. And I also remember those eerie, obscure, crashing sounds echoing in the night air deep within the dark forest. Downright spooky.

"What *is* that?" I asked Mark, my nerves tingling.

He glanced over at me. "Trees falling."

*Oh.*

Later that night, I heard a creak and faint snap—close—very close. I burst into a dead run, heading for who-knows-where. Heart pounding, out of breath and hopefully out of the way of a falling tree, I waited. Nothing happened, but I remained on super-high-alert the rest of our shift.

TYPICAL OF THE way most major fires end, Mother Nature waved her magic wand and delivered rain. I have no memory of the drive back to Florida.

Up the stairs I trudged to find Jodi in our kitchen, stirring something on the stove. She turned to me. "Welcome home!"

It was good to see her. I peeked into the pot. "Whatcha fixing?" Anything not canned would be great.

"SpaghettiOs!" she said with glee.

Last summer Jodi had admitted she couldn't cook, so no surprise here.

I opened the fridge to investigate options. After a sandwich, time for a shower.

I rubbed my scalp with my fingertips to begin untangling hair kinked and matted from week-old sweat. Determined to remove all the soot with only one shower, I spent extra time scrubbing. Momentarily refreshed, I sat on the couch to share my fire adventure and see what Jodi had been up to. She got two sentences out before someone knocked on the door. We stared at each other with raised eyebrows. *Another one?*

# EIGHTEEN

ERIC STRODE INTO the living room, removed his cap, and turned to me with a sheepish smile. "Are you up for another fire?"

I guessed he thought I'd reply, "Are you nuts?" But I'd already forgotten I'd just returned from one a few hours ago. I gave him my best "I'm not tired" smile, and sat up straight. "Sure, where to?"

"Northern California. The Klamath. Pack fast, plane's waiting."

Jodi watched as I stuffed clothes into my duffel bag, disappointed she couldn't go with college starting next week. Who knew how long I'd be gone. We hugged goodbye.

Glenn rounded up a crew of eight, and for the first time since I'd worked there, said he would join us. "They're so desperate for bodies, next thing you know they'll be hiring people off the street." Eventually, they did.

Soon, I stood next to Joe and the rest of my crew in the Forest Service's terminal at Tucson International Airport. Blinding white, florescent lights charged up my body's dead batteries. Other crews milled around, with not another woman in sight, but I'd gotten used to that. Although a bundle of nervous energy, I figured I *must* be tired. If I'd learned anything about being a firefighter, it was to sleep whenever possible. I curled up on the floor, using my pack for a pillow, but the cold concrete made my shoulder and hip ache, ruining my nap attempts. We waited, and waited some more. Hurry up and wait—typical government way. At last, nineteen men and one woman boarded the chartered plane. From my window seat, I watched Tucson's lights fade as we headed to the northwest.

THE THUMP OF lowering landing gear woke me from a fitful doze, and I strained to see signs of where we were out the window, but it was pitch-black dark. Too bad I didn't have a map. I have great memories of family vacations, when I watched my dad pore over our travel route, puffing on his pipe filled with fragrant cherry tobacco, marking sightseeing destinations. I'd learned to love maps from those trips.

It was pre-dawn in Medford when I stumbled onto a different plane headed to Eureka. Once seated, I scrunched up to take advantage of yet another catnap opportunity. At daybreak, I woke, stretched, and gazed out the tiny window at endless acres of forest. Idaho? Montana? Then I noticed large, treeless concentric circles dotting the landscape. The work of a gigantic cookie cutter? Alien landing sites? I asked Joe.

He leaned over me to see. "Clear cutting. It's a logging practice."

"Well, that's ugly."

"I hear it's easier than selectively harvesting individual trees."

His explanation didn't change my opinion.

In Eureka they herded us like cattle onto a waiting school bus. A few jokesters in the group "mooed." I snagged a window seat and leaned my forehead against the cool glass in fatigue. I watched another day end, then drifted off.

A cloudless dawn revealed a forest I couldn't see for all the trees. Hunger pangs reminded me I hadn't eaten since I left Florida, not even peanuts on the plane. When were they going to feed us? Our bus pulled into a parking lot amidst a group of rustic buildings. This Forest Service work center rivaled Florida: quaint, and possibly historic. A delightful thought occurred to me that I could apply there if I wanted to.

An employee led us to a mess hall, where I stood in line to place my breakfast order: scrambled eggs, toast, and bacon. I filled a mug with coffee, which I'd just started to appreciate. That hot breakfast Glenn and Texas John made in June, on top of the mountain . . . was it really this summer, or last? It now seemed so long ago.

On the bus, I realized that this was how I envisioned the life of a hotshot when I'd first met them—traveling in scenic western forests to fight fires. The dense, fragrant woodlands of leafy hardwoods here reminded me of my former Upper New York State home. I bet there were many lakes out there, too. The swift Salmon River, tumbling beside the winding road, churned with white-water rapids. An orange sun glowed through a distinctive brown haze, and sweet wood smoke drifted in through the window. We were getting close.

Green canvas tents, school buses, Forest Service vehicles, and rows of porta potties with their sickeningly-sweet scent, spread out across acres of open meadow, forming the fire camp. Noisy generators hummed; off-duty firefighters, support personnel, and venders milled around. We sat with our gear while Glenn disappeared to obtain our orders. The Forest Service, after all, is a government agency, full of red tape and formality. They considered firefighting a war—in fact, they'd been engaged in fire wars for over a century.

Glenn briefed us on the Hog-Fong Fire. "No containment yet of the nearly fifty-thousand-acre blaze. Embers have been starting spot fires miles ahead of the main fire. Hard to get a line around it."

*Miles ahead of the main fire?* I'd no idea that was possible.

Hours passed before I climbed, at last, into the back of an Army open-bed transport truck and took a seat next to Joe. I was grateful to have both him and Glenn on this trip. Our convoy sped down a dusty logging road, which coated us with red, powdery soil rolling off the dual rear tires—suffocating. I tied a bandana over my nose. I wanted to see where we were going, but I had to squeeze my eyes shut to keep out the dust. It was oddly disorienting riding backward with my eyes closed, but at least I didn't get carsick.

At day's end, we reached the outlying spike camp. Stiff from the uncomfortable ride, I climbed out of the truck and instinctively brushed off dirt. Futile, of course. I didn't bother to look at my face, figuring it matched everyone else's.

Tools in hands, headlamps shining light along the way, we marched single file up and down endless, undulating hills. While these hills weren't as steep as in the Santa Ritas, my leg muscles were feeling the uphill portions enough to appreciate the downhill stretches. After two hours, I started real work—chopping limbs and digging out brush to create a six-foot-wide line. All trimmings went outside of our clearing, away from the approaching fire, the one we hadn't yet seen. No adrenaline—this was just plain hard work. Tools chinked against rocks, saw engines buzzed, spewing blue exhaust and wood chips, disrupting this peaceful forest. Did the trees know their fate? Did they know we were there to help?

After twelve hours, we marched the two hours to spike camp for food and rest. By the time I'd stood in line to eat, stood in line for a disposable sleeping bag, and stood in line to wash up—only six hours remained, and I planned on making the most of them.

Disposable sleeping bags? Who knew you could make sleeping bags out of paper. Multiple layers of tissue, topped with a waterproof surface, provided warmth, but offered little padding against the hard ground. My damp clothes would make for a cold night, so I wiggled all the way inside the bag, and removed my socks, pants, both shirts and my bra. How to do that without exposing any skin? I decided I didn't care. The guys never tried to take a peek at me undressing anyway—at least as far as I knew. Fire clothes wadded into a pillow, I curled up on my side, willing my body to relax.

If I slept, I didn't remember doing so. Glenn made the rounds with our wake-up call—a nudge with his boot. I dressed inside my paper bag, more challenging than it was to take my clothes off, and changed only socks and underwear—the essentials.

Next, I stood in line for my sack lunch (dinner, breakfast, whatever meal it was). After tossing the bologna, which I detested, I ate the bland white-bread-cheese sandwich and washed it down with apple juice. I tucked the orange and Snickers bar into my Army jacket pocket and strapped on my fire shelter and canteens.

"We're going to help with a backfire today," Glenn announced.

Backfires burn out vegetation in front of an advancing blaze to starve it of fuel—fighting fire with fire. I'd learned about it in training, but never had the opportunity to see it in action. At least it would be more exciting than building line for a fire that we hadn't actually seen yet. Swept up by a storm of anticipation, I stood with my crew, ready to take it on.

Again in single file we marched through the powdery soil, stirring up our own dust clouds. Soon, I stood with my crew, awestruck, before a dramatic scene of men and machines, working like a colony of ants, to clear a thousand-foot-wide fireline: man versus nature.

Mark's jaw dropped. "Holy moly! Look at that!"

Two massive D-9 Caterpillar bulldozers created billows of red dust as they ripped towering fir trees from the ground. Deafening clanks and squeaks from equipment drowned out our voices. Diesel exhaust fouled the essence of freshly turned soil. Sawyers added to the cacophony, running chainsaws at full throttle, as they, too, downed the tall trees. Unable to match the efficiency of the dozers, I overheard the sawyers were asked to leave. In less than an hour, a swath of evergreens was turned into immense stacks of slash at the inner edge of the fire break, ready for ignition. I'd never seen anything so destructive happen so fast. Next, several men went about setting those piles ablaze.

Drip torches worked better than lighter fluid, with slash igniting as though it had been soaked in gasoline. In an out-of-body experience, I watched myself watch a wall of flame grow as tall as a twenty-story building. I turned away, raising a gloved hand to protect my cheek from the intense heat. Fear formed in the pit of my stomach as flames leapt into canopies, searching for more fuel, turning majestic pines into giant torches. Smoke boiled and rolled hundreds of feet above the forest canopy. The sky turned red. With the wind at our backs working like a bellows, the inferno uttered an unearthly, guttural roar, engulfing entire trees in seconds. Alarm grew exponentially in my chest with each passing second. *How much worse is this going to get?* My instincts told me to run, but my feet remained firmly planted. Ash collected on my clothes and drifted to the ground around my boots like gray snow, never to melt. My thoughts turned to the fire shelter I carried around my waist. Bile rose into my throat. *I sure hope the men in charge know what they're doing. If they screw up, we're all dead.*

Glenn cupped his hands around his mouth and yelled for us to follow him.

Reluctant to walk away from the spectacular fire show even though the magnitude of what I just saw frightened me, I had to force myself to move. Although alarming, the fire was also captivating.

Glenn pointed at me and eight of the men. "You go with Arnie. The rest, follow me."

I stood with my squad while Arnie gave directions. "We're working in pairs, a couple hundred feet apart. You need to stay awake and alert, and watch for spot fires."

Texas John, with arms folded across his barrel chest, narrowed his eyes at Arnie. "Hey, Hoss, so what're you gonna do all night?"

"Me? I'm gonna walk up and down the line to make sure no one is sleeping on the job."

"Well, awright, then," Texas John said, apparently satisfied Arnie wouldn't be slacking off. What arrogant nerve. John wasn't exactly Mr. Hard Worker.

Arnie left Greg and me at a large rock outcrop, which served as a fairly safe place to watch—rocks are, after all, noncombustible. I'd no idea what time it was—time had no meaning on a fireline. You worked until it was time to stop working, and often beyond that.

I sat facing the backfire to watch for a wind change, which could make the fire jump the line. Greg had our backs, watching for a spot fire, which could entrap us. We turned off our headlamps to conserve batteries. Sparks floated and danced like forest fairies, snuffing out as they cooled; a phantom tree, consumed by flames, crashed to earth, echoing inside the deep, dark woods. *When a tree falls in the forest, and no one's around to hear it, does it make a sound?*

Greg's voice drifted from above me. "How's it going?"

A human voice, amidst all of the forest and fire sounds, at that moment sounded strange, incongruous. "Fine," I said after a pause.

"Wasn't that backfire something?" Greg asked.

More than something. "All I could think about was what a joke our fire shelters are. And hoping that nobody screws up and gets us killed."

We both agreed; even knowing it probably meant a death sentence, if it came right down to it, we'd run like hell before we'd ever deploy.

Our vigil continued: watching and listening for any sounds or sights signaling a problem with the fire. It was hard to stay awake—I rubbed my eyes, hoping it would help. Snapping twigs and thumping against rocks startled them wide open. *Bear?*

"Hey guys." Arnie shut off his headlamp so he wouldn't blind us. He sat down on the ground near me. "Things are quiet. They're predicting light winds tonight."

We talked for a few minutes, and Arnie stood up to go check on the others, assuring us he'd be back later. His footsteps faded as he made his way down the fireline.

I listened to the fire dwindle to a gentle crackling, nodded off, then jerked awake. I stood up and stretched. My movement stirred Greg.

"Wow, I'm beat," he said in the middle of a yawn.

My yawn echoed his. Awake for more than twenty four hours, I was beyond tired. My body felt foreign and unwieldy, like it belonged to someone else. We conversed a little to keep ourselves awake. Greg had just joined our crew this summer. What a way to start out.

"So far," he said, " I love it."

I could relate.

Arnie returned at two o'clock. "This section's looking good, so we'll be relocating. I'll gather up the squad, then come back for you."

"Don't you want us to come with you now?" I asked.

"Nah, stay put."

Although it didn't make sense to me, I didn't question him.

At my post, exhaustion won. I drifted off and awakened with a start. *Damn. How long did I sleep?* "Hey, Greg, what time you got?"

"I've got . . ." He flipped on his headlamp. "I've got four-thirty."

"That's what I've got! Where the heck is Arnie?" Panic rose in my throat. What now?

Greg slid down from his perch, sending loose rocks tumbling. "So what do you think we should do?"

I couldn't see the point of sitting there any longer. "Let's try to find them."

Following the cleared line, I mulled over our dilemma. *Maybe they found a spot fire. Or got lost? Geez, if they got lost, where does that leave Greg and me?*

Two figures approached us from the other direction.

"Have you seen Arnie?" I asked Texas John and a Nogales crewman.

"Not since he told us to wait," John said. "They must be further up the line."

Positive they were ahead, the four of us trudged onward. Not convinced John knew where we were going, I worried we were hiking the wrong way. Then I heard voices, and multiple headlamps shone through the trees like tiny search lights. Another crew.

"We can't seem to find our people," Texas John told the crew boss.

*What? He's making it sound like we got lost!*

"Haven't seen anyone but you," the man said. "But you can't stick around here. We're getting ready to backfire. They're probably looking for you, maybe they're farther down the line, or, you could go back to camp. That way," he pointed behind us, "you'll walk right into it."

Insanity! Why did Arnie walk off and leave four people behind? Worse yet, why didn't anyone else notice we were missing? Because we didn't have a radio, it made more sense to return to camp. My headlamp lit only the ground in front of me as I stared at my feet following the path. Beyond the beam it was pitch-black, ominous, and silent. The conversation tumbled around my tired brain cells. The crew boss had said they were getting ready to backfire. *Backfire! They could've burned us up!* I had no desire to die, even in the line of duty, but to die because of someone's incompetence? I clenched my fists, livid.

Anger gave me plenty of energy for the hike to camp. Early morning light filtered its way through the smoky haze, making it appear as though we were camped by the ocean, with the fog rolling in. It should have smelled smoky, too, but I'd been breathing it for so long, that I didn't notice anymore. Texas John tiptoed through the many sleeping crews, looking for ours.

Returning, he said simply, "They're here."

"What do you mean . . . our crew? Here?"

Texas John stared at the ground. "Yeah, they've been here a couple hours."

I lost it. "Unbelievable! So where are they?"

He gestured.

On the way to confront anyone and everyone, I ran into Mark first. He turned to glare at me. "So where the hell have *you* guys been?"

My voice shook. "*We* waited for over two hours for Arnie to come back for us, like he said he would. But we never saw him again!"

"Well, I don't know what happened, but Glenn's pretty PO'd at you guys."

I stormed over to Glenn, but before I could say a word, his steel-blue eyes flashed in anger at me. "Don't you *ever* get separated from the crew again."

Tears welled up; my throat clamped shut. To have him mad at me hurt more than I could cope with right then. Too exhausted to defend myself, I stomped off, dropped to the ground, and curled up in a ball. *Don't you dare cry.* I closed my eyes and commanded myself to go to sleep. Something hit the ground, close, and my eyes popped open. In a heap next to me lay a sleeping bag, and Mark was walking away. Too tired to analyze why he'd done something nice for me, I crawled inside the bag, reliving the confrontation under closed eyelids. I never mentioned the incident again. Neither did anyone else.

# NINETEEN

EVERY DAY, I went through the motions of working with my brain turned off—a fire-fighting zombie: hike two hours in, build line, chop limbs, scrape ground, hike two hours out, eat, try to get some sleep—until I didn't know what day it was, nor how long I'd been out there.

On day "whatever," I awoke to a raw throat that hurt so much to swallow, my eyes watered. *Damn. What a lousy time to get sick.*

"Better go get checked," Glenn said. "We sure don't need you going out tonight if you're sick."

I pulled on my boots and dragged myself over to the first aid tent. I waited my turn, watching two medics treat nasty blisters and poison oak. *Poison oak? Thank goodness I didn't find that.*

"Let's take a look," the youthful white-shirted man said to me. He reached for a tongue depressor and a flashlight, and peered down my throat. The light clicked off. "Smoke inhalation. I've seen dozens of cases today." He handed me a package of lozenges. "Sorry, but it'll get worse before it gets better."

*Great.* I swallowed hard, flinching.

"So what's the diagnosis?" Glenn asked when I returned.

"I'm not sick," I said, unable to speak above a whisper.

"Stay here and rest anyway."

I sulked, worried what the guys would say about me staying behind. Would they call me a wimp? How would I ever live this down?

When everyone returned, I overheard stories about getting stung by ground-nesting bees. Not that I wished I'd gotten stung, but I didn't like missing out on anything.

The next shift, I returned to the fireline, glad to be back, despite my sore throat. At break time, I huddled around a burning stump with Joe and Pete on this stone-cold night. Deep in the bottom of my pack, I found a few packets of instant coffee, which I shared. We perched our canteen cups on rocks near the flames, waiting for the water to boil. Unwrapping my *Snickers* bar, saved from lunch, caught Pete's attention.

"Trade ya," he said, offering me a box of raisins.

I glared at him, and laughed. "Ha! Not for ten boxes of raisins."

We sipped coffee, staring into the meager fire. Pete tossed in a few branches to keep it stoked. I dreamed of a real bed, real food, and most of all, real sleep.

*Linda Strader*

Shortly before dawn, something about the air smelled different. *Rain?* A few sprinkles tapped lightly on my hardhat. After seeing nothing but smoke-hazed skies for days, this gray sky filled me with hope. Maybe we'd get a handle on this fire. Sprinkles soon turned to a steady downpour. I unpacked my poncho and slipped it over my head. It kept my upper body dry, but not lower extremities. I sought shelter under tree canopies, sitting to arrange my poncho like a tent over my feet. Motionless, I hung my head, staring at drops falling from the edge of the hood, waiting for direction.

At last we could return to spike camp, but we faced a long, slog of a hike in the pouring rain. The temperatures dropped into the forties, making my breath visible as white, vaporous puffs. With faces streaked with soot and lined with fatigue, everyone shouldered their gear. After several miles, the lack of sleep caught up with me; my legs were incredibly heavy, like I'd tied thirty-pound weights to my ankles. To keep going, I repeated my mantra: *You can do this—and you will. You can do this—and you will.* Mark didn't want to take any breaks, and at one point screamed at us to hurry up. That did it. Emotional overload and fatigue did me in. I just couldn't keep up with Mark's death-hike pace. I plopped down on a log.

Joe stopped and turned. "What's wrong?"

I choked back a sob, my voice catching. "I can't go on."

He sat down next to me. "Sure you can. To hell with Mark."

"I don't understand why he's hiking so fast," I said, composing myself. "Aren't we supposed to stick together?"

"Yeah, John's way behind us, so Mark *should* slow down."

We decided to wait for Texas John. Fifteen minutes later he appeared, huffing and puffing, his face beet-red. "Hoo-boy, this is tough going."

Alarmed, I worried he'd drop dead in front of us.

"You okay?" Joe asked.

"Gimme a minute," Texas John said, panting. He took off his pack and dropped it on the ground. Then fished in his pocket for a cigarette.

*You've got to be kidding me. Smoke? When you can't breathe?*

"I've got one of them muscle cramps in the back of m'legs." He took a deep drag. "It's drinking milk. Dang it, milk is causing cramps."

*Where did all this milk come from?* I wondered.

After John's face lost its redness, we pushed onward. Again, he dropped behind us. Joe and I finally caught up with Mark.

"Geez, you guys are slow," Mark said.

Furious, I clenched my jaw. Joe put his hand on my arm, a reminder not to say something I'd regret later.

We continued our trek. Rain continued to fall. Wet and chilled to the bone, I trudged through a dismal black and gray landscape, which smelled of wet charcoal, soggy ground, and decay. Rivulets of gray ash trickled across the path, while the newly disturbed red soil turned to sticky muck. Rainwater trickled off my poncho and down my pant legs; my boots seeped water, which squished between my toes. Two more hours passed. Through the trees I saw the green canvas tents of spike camp—not fancy accommodations by any means, but at least they'd be dry inside. My three tent-mates gave me privacy so I could take off my wet clothes before getting into my sleeping bag. Snuggled inside the cocoon of warmth, I gave them the all clear. Steady rain pattered on the tent roof as I drifted off into my first sound sleep in many days.

Water, water everywhere. I woke up. *Great. I have to pee.* Maybe the rain would stop. I waited. It didn't. Finally, I *had* to get up, rain or no rain.

Joe heard me stir, and said sleepily, "Where're you going? It's pouring."

"Yeah, I know, but I can't wait one second longer."

"Ooh . . ." He rolled over and went back to sleep.

An overfull bladder made it painful to pull on my cold, damp clothes. Without taking the time to even lace up my boots, I made a mad dash to the porta potties. Halfway back to the tent, I overheard the camp boss tell Glenn that we would leave soon. I delivered the news to Joe, who sat up, mumbled something unintelligible, and flopped back down. I shucked my boots and wet clothes, and crawled back inside my bag to wait.

At last, the rain stopped. Off to base camp in the Army trucks, only this time without the dust bath. In the old sawmill building where we would standby, at least a hundred firefighters filled the windowless space, their voices echoing off the aluminum walls. Some slept, others sat in circles, playing cards or talking. There were still no other women that I could see, but I'd gotten used to, and liked being the only one.

Glenn said we'd get a couple days of R and R. Before releasing us, though, officials wanted to make sure we weren't needed on another fire. At first, my inner voice screamed, "No! I want to go home!" Dedicated to my job, though, I'd go wherever they sent me.

Compared to spike camp, base camp resembled a five-star motel. Together, Joe and I picked up air mattresses so we wouldn't have to sleep on the cold concrete floor. Bed made up, I searched for the promised hot shower.

Semi-trucks had been converted into individual shower stalls, erasing my mental image of four canvas walls with a hose hanging from a pole, like at Girl Scout camp. I savored luxurious hot water, scrubbing with the fragrant soap bar at black soot and shampooing twice. I dried off with a giant paper towel and dressed in clean, smokeless clothes. *Boy, I'm hungry!* Even heated C-rats would be good after so many cheese sandwiches, but the roast chicken, fresh steamed vegetables, and piping hot rice that filled my plate more than satisfied my craving for real food. I'd dropped off my tray when I noticed a steel drum filled with dry ice. *Hmmm . . . what's in here? Ice cream bars!* I devoured the treat in record time, and stuffed full, talked myself out of seconds.

Sated, Joe and I went exploring. We window-shopped firefighter style, wandering through concessionaire tents selling socks, underwear, tobacco, and toiletries. I didn't need anything, but I did grab two pairs of the kind of Nomex pants Joe and I both preferred, made like Levi's, right down to the watch pocket.

Curious, we roamed the old sawmill operation, poking around the abandoned equipment. Joe fascinated me with all his knowledge of how machinery worked. Finally alone behind old logging equipment, we decided that no one could see us. Getting lost in kissing made up for not touching each other in ages.

"You're so beautiful," he said, searching my eyes and clasping my hands.

*No,* I thought, *I'm not.* However, I never tired of hearing him say so. I loved him, but what about the love I felt for Glenn? Why is it that someone can tear your heart out, stomp on it, and you can still love them?

There was little to occupy my free time, but it didn't matter. I couldn't seem to get enough sleep. After nap number four, I wanted to use the payphone to call home, but the line was still too long. Meetings with fire officials kept Glenn busy. Greg, engaged with a crew from the northwest, laughed at their stories of stinging bees, bad food, and getting rain-soaked. A captive audience listened to Texas John tell his tall stories. Somber discussions about the reliability of our fire shelters came up, too. A loud voice over the PA system echoed in the cavernous room, halting conversations.

"This just out," the man said. "Elvis Presley died suddenly today at the age of forty-two."

At first, there was only silence in the room, and then murmurs as everyone absorbed the news. If I hadn't known better, I'd have thought Texas John had tears in his eyes. In no time, however, he'd captured a new audience, perhaps telling them how he'd met "The King." Who knows, maybe he had.

On the second day in camp, Glenn returned from briefing. "They don't need us here, but they won't release us." He ran his hand through his hair, probably missing his cowboy hat, which he'd left at Florida. "We're going to standby in Medford."

Oregon? I'd always wanted to see Oregon. Maybe we'd get sent to a fire in Idaho, another place I'd been wanting to go.

In Medford, a bus delivered us to the Air Force base, where we'd stay in barracks. R and R meant a bit more here than at fire camp. The real bed, off the floor, with a real pillow, called to me when I sat on the edge. *Nice.* I curled up and slept.

Early evening, we all went to see the first *Star Wars* movie. Joe and I munched on hot buttered popcorn while the movie transported us to another galaxy. Disoriented when we left the theater, I felt a weird disconnect with reality. What had I missed outside this world of fire?

Joe and I explored the base to pass time. Every chance possible, we kissed, never able to get enough of each other. It'd been ages since we made love. Where could we go without getting caught? Where there's a will, there's a way, and we found it.

Less concerned with getting us home in a timely fashion than they'd been with getting us here, fire officials made us wait two long days. With so many fire crews needing a lift home, it was hard to find a chartered plane we'd all fit in, so Glenn chose four of us to fly via commercial airliner out of Yreka. We grinned at each other. Unlike the charter, we'd get a meal onboard. A bus delivered us to Yreka, where we had an hour to kill before our flight.

As a desert dweller now, large bodies of water brought out my child-like glee. "I *have* to see the ocean," I told Joe with a wide grin. "We're *so* close!"

It'd been years since I walked on a beach. I longed to look for shells, to feel the sand under my feet. Too bad sheer cliffs kept us from access. By Joe's side at an overlook, I made do with experiencing the ocean from afar. Strong sea breezes fluttered my hair, cooled my skin, and brought the taste of seaweed. Gentle waves shushed; sandpipers scampered and pecked at the sand. Overhead, gulls screeched, soaring and diving. The brief experience was restorative, and exactly what I needed. Joe pulled out his pocket watch. "We better get back."


LIKE A LOYAL friend, Florida had waited for my return. Tomorrow would be my last day here. I reported to work in the morning, turning in my gear, key and driver's license. Glenn allowed me to clean up the house and pack on government time.

On departure day, I simultaneously wanted to go home and not go home. I missed my mom so much my heart ached, but I sensed that Florida wanted me to stay. Joe did too.

After stashing the last box into Skyler, I turned toward the government truck pulling in behind me. Glenn. My breath hitched. *Get a grip.* I cared for him more than I knew was right. He stood before me, his thumbs hooked through the belt loops of his Levi's, his cowboy boots shuffling in the dirt. He gazed at me from under the brim of his ever-present Stetson. That always got to me.

In his slow, deep voice, he said, "I want you to know that I think you did a real good job in Northern California on a tough assignment."

My heart somersaulted. From a man who said little, that simple sentence touched deep into my soul. He was proud of me. Not sure what to say or do, all I managed was, "Thanks." But I also stood there waiting for him to give me some kind of sign . . . that what had happened in that motel meant more to him than sex. But it was not there. I desperately wanted to hug him, but feared he would not hug me back, or worse, back off. Driving away, I checked my rearview mirror to see if he watched me leave. He did.

IN PRESCOTT, I rushed to enroll in forestry-related classes at Yavapai College, which I hoped would advance my new career. Despite the aching in my legs from hiking up and down all those hills on the Klamath, I had a lightness in my step. There were so many challenges last summer: brutal long hours, backbreaking work, intense heat, danger, smoke inhalation, bad food, and no sleep for days on end. Why did I put up with it? Because this job made me feel important; it gave me a purpose in life. Plus, if I could handle those grueling conditions, I could do anything; and what I wanted, more than anything, was a permanent Forest Service position.

# TWENTY

MY FIRST COLLEGE experience. Would classes be too hard? Hungry to learn, I pored over the homework, reading and studying. When I picked up my mid-term grades, I twirled in a circle, ecstatic: I'd aced everything!

Joe called almost every day. I missed him so much, and he said he missed me too, promising to come up when he completed the last of trail work.

Every Saturday, I visited the bustling Prescott swap meet: trucks with antiques in the back, tables laden with curios and oddities, blankets displaying someone's future treasure—there was so much to see. I waded through the crowd and picked up a cat figurine from a tailgate. My mom would love it. A voice from behind me made me turn.

"Linda, fancy seeing you here."

Roy—my former love from two years ago—the vagabond who broke my heart more times than I could count. Despite breaking my heart, he'd left a place-marker there, and now he was back. How could I say "no" when he asked to see me later? We could be friends, there was nothing wrong with that. Around seven he picked me up to go for a drive.

"I'm seeing someone," I said when I scooted onto the seat. "We're serious."

Roy steered toward the Granite Dells, a place we'd visited often: climbing the gigantic boulders, tossing a stick for his black lab, Yankee, picking cattails for my mom. Tonight, a star-studded sky and a touch of fall in the air brought back memories of the last time we were together.

"I've given up on my girlfriend. I could never marry a girl like her." He smiled that Bob Dylan smile at me. "You're still so pretty. Remember all the good times we had? Maybe what was between us is still there. But I don't want to interfere with what you've got going on with Joe."

Damn him. He always did this. Every time I moved on, he came back, wanting to pick up where we'd left off. Did he know he could get to me? He must.

"I'm going to Alaska. Need to get my head together. But I do want to be with you. No matter what happens, I won't forget you. You're such a deep and sensitive person." He took a lock of my hair and let it slip through his fingers. "I still care a great deal about you."

Every nerve in my body tingled. Every hurtful thing he'd said in the past was forgotten. No matter how long we were apart, this always happened. I didn't say much, didn't answer his questions . . . I just couldn't.

At home, I lay in bed, replaying his words in my head. Not too long ago, I would've been thrilled to hear Roy say these things, but now, I doubted his sincerity. I'd heard this all before. But I knew I would always love him. Now what? Should I believe him this time?

To be fair and honest, when Joe called, I told him about Roy—that I still felt something for him. Although Joe admitted that this news hurt, he told me to do whatever felt right. It broke my heart to break his. I churned inside with so many conflicted feelings. How would I know what was right?

Joe continued to call when home from trail work. I also continued to hear from Roy. There was more talk of leaving, but not to Alaska. He now spoke of Northern California, or maybe Idaho. If he bought land in Idaho, would I come live with him? I didn't respond.

One morning in October I awoke and decided to cut class. I needed to see Joe. Now. I tossed some clothes into a suitcase, gassed up Skyler, and drove. Miles clicked by on the odometer: fifty, one hundred, two hundred. The radio played "99 Miles From LA" during the final stretch—I counted the telephone poles. *Please be there . . .*

Swinging into Joe's driveway, I brimmed with anticipation, my heart beating fast. His mother, who I'd let in on my surprise visit, opened the door and whispered that Joe had just returned from trail work. I found him in his bedroom, reading a letter I'd sent him. Even with a week's worth of stubble and his clothes smudged in bar oil and trail dirt, he was incredibly handsome. Sensing movement, he glanced up; his eyes widened, and I dropped into his lap, embracing him as tightly as my arms could manage. Moaning, he ran his fingers through my hair and kissed me deeply. I responded in kind, my heart racing, my passion growing. My love for Joe felt real, and unlike with Roy, grounded. It made no sense to let go of what we had.

# TWENTY-ONE

## Summer of 1978: Florida Work Center,
## Santa Rita Mountains, Southern Arizona

IN EARLY APRIL, the much anticipated job offer came from Gary, Jodi's brother, who'd taken Eric's place. I'd live in the same quarters I'd occupied my first summer. Jodi had married and moved to northeastern Arizona. Scott had also moved on. My new roommate would fill Scott's fire prevention technician position. I didn't like the idea of a new roommate, or, honestly, of having a roommate at all. What if we didn't get along?

Gary delivered some great news, reducing my roommate worries. "Guess last summer was too much for John. He didn't reapply."

"Really?" Okay, not nice to gloat, but I couldn't help myself. I'd handled last year's summer of fire; Texas John had not.

"We've got several newcomers. And you know Joe's waiting on that job offer."

Last month, I'd helped Joe fill out an application for a career-conditional appointment with the Forest Service in Northern Arizona. If he got it, he was one step closer to a permanent government job. I wanted him to get it, but dreaded the thought of him leaving.

Early April in Prescott usually delivered unsettled weather. True to the calendar, snow flurries swirled around me Saturday morning as I left. Four hours later, I arrived at Florida, a steady drizzle falling on this cold, gray day.

As I eased into the narrow driveway next to my quarters, Glenn approached my car, the collar of his wool-lined denim jacket turned up to ward off the chill, Stetson firmly in place to shed the rain. To have him here, on a Saturday, waiting for me? I had to control the urge to leap out of Skyler and took a moment to regroup before opening the door. I stood before him while he placed a key in my hand, telling me that everything should be in working order.

"You might want to turn the heat on," he said with a wry smile.

His eyes held mine for what I swore lasted one second longer than necessary. Or maybe I wished that. It hurts when you care about someone who doesn't care about you, but it happens all the time—not that knowing frequency helps much. The smart thing to do would've been to write him off, but unfortunately, the heart doesn't comprehend "smart." What also didn't help was that I'd given Glenn a piece of my heart last year, and he still had it.

I kept my voice casual. "I will. It's cold!"

A long pause. "Okay, then." He headed toward the office.

I carried my luggage into my former bedroom and hooked up my brand-new stereo. What to play? Linda Ronstadt's "Heart Like a Wheel" drifted through the rooms, my tears falling as the lyrics hit home.

Sunday I returned from grocery shopping to find the house full of boxes, houseplants, and a dog. Out of the second bedroom strolled my roommate, as far from the outdoorsy type as I could imagine: Farrah Fawcett hair, eye makeup, and, as I'd soon learn, wearing contact lenses, which were forbidden for fire personnel.

*Oh, brother.* "So, is this your first Forest Service job?" I asked.

"Yes! I had to vacate my apartment, so I hope you don't mind, but I brought everything."

I could tell.

"Um, well, I'm not sure we have room for all of this," I said, cringing when she set a fern on my new turntable.

"Sure we do. I'll make room." She unloaded and placed her albums beside mine in my wooden crate.

Alarmed, I said, "Hey, not there, they'll get mixed up!"

"Phoo," she said with a dismissive wave of her hand. "I'll remember which ones are mine."

*Miss Prissy*, I deemed her, swooped in and took over the place. I'd hoped for interesting and fun times here this summer. Only day two and already I had a bad feeling. Then I decided I shouldn't be so quick to judge my roommate. Maybe we'd become friends.

Besides my roommate, I had several new people to get used to. Gary seemed outgoing and friendly like his sister Jodi, but how would he be as a supervisor? Paul made me wonder why an English major wanted a firefighting job. He had no muscle definition, and soft, uncalloused hands. Probably never held a tool in his life. Did he have any clue what this was about? Brian, the guy with a muscle-builder's physique, spouted irritating bravado.

"Aw, heck, this is nothing," Brian said during training. "I've fought structure fires for years. Wildland fires will be a piece of cake. After all, you don't have a building about to fall on your head."

"Granted," I said, respecting his line of work. "Except that you don't have to worry about firestorms, crown fires, blow-ups, steep terrain, slurry drops, falling trees, lightning strikes, rattlesnakes, or sixteen-hour shifts for days on end . . . do you?" *Wait until his first fire. I'll ask him if he still thinks this is a 'piece of cake.'*

When Joe came over later, I suggested we go somewhere, anywhere. I needed to get away. A few miles below the station, we built a campfire, munched crackers and cheese, and sipped red wine. Time alone with him was just what I needed. The sky shone white with stars; a meteor streaked toward the horizon. I made a wish. *Let this be a good summer.* If it hadn't been so cold, we would've spent the night.

WAY TOO MUCH station duty and training took place over the first few weeks. Drove me crazy with boredom. Then I learned we'd take part in a "prescribed burn," a fairly new practice to reduce wildfire danger. The Forest Service used to call them "controlled burns." A few years ago, a control burn almost torched the Palisades Ranger Station. So much for being under control. I wondered how many similar incidents had prompted the name change. About the same time, Fire Control Officers became Fire Management Officers, too. At any rate, prescribed burning promised some excitement. At least there'd be fire involved.

Earlier in the spring, the crew had thinned dense stands of pinyon-pine in Gardner Canyon, located on the east side of the mountain, and stacked trimmings in piles. Now we'd set those piles ablaze. We started work at three in the afternoon, prepared for an all-nighter.

Ranches inside the national forest boundary kept cattle in check with multiple fences. I rode shotgun, so gate duty fell on me. Clark pulled up to the first Texas gate. I dreaded these stupid gates, made of barbed wire strung to juniper branches. To loosen the tension so I could unhook the closure loop, I wrapped my arm around the gate post, and squeezed. It didn't budge.

"Hey, Linda, need help?" Clark hollered from the idling truck.

"No, I've got it." *Damn thing, get off there!* I fought with it some more, squeezing even tighter. Every single time I did this, I swore it took ten times longer than it should. I could only imagine what the guys were saying while I struggled.

At last I got it open, and our vehicles drove through. Closing took more finagling, but without eyes on me this time.

Jostling over four-wheel-drive roads for an hour, my internal organs felt a bit rearranged when we finally reached the burn site. Sometimes I wondered if it would be easier to hike than drive.

Mark filled a drip torch. "I'll light a few piles and see how they burn." Then he laughed. "We sure don't want to call dispatch to report we set the whole mountain on fire."

When he lit my pile, I stepped back from the intense heat as it whooshed into a bright burst of orange—popping, snapping, and sending up tendrils of flame and smoke. I worked the perimeter, redistributing branches to make sure everything burned clean, keeping a close eye on where floating sparks landed. Soon the flames subsided, and the pile was reduced to a smoldering heap. Joe's pile still had some major flames going on. I walked over. "Need any help?"

"Yeah, got any marshmallows?"

I laughed. It was hard to be near Joe, especially in the dark, and not be able to touch him. How did people manage to have a relationship with someone they worked with and not run into complications like this? A branch tumbled from the stack. I picked it up and tossed it back in.

"Want to come for dinner tomorrow?" I asked.

"Sure, I can do that."

In the distance, someone sang "When smoke gets in your eyes . . ." A sliver of moon rose. Our bonfires simmered down. Mark lit some more.

What a long night. Weary, I opened my front door to find clothes draped on the couch, an overturned shoe in the middle of the floor, and dirty dishes in the sink. Jodi and I'd always kept a neat house. This would drive me nuts. The bathroom door swung open.

"Out all night?" Miss Prissy asked, padding out in her short terry robe.

I swallowed the confrontational words on the tip of my tongue. "Yeah, I'm kinda tired."

"So what did you do?"

"Burned slash piles," I said, opening the fridge. Uninspired by its contents, I debated on cereal. "Easier than a real fire."

"Oh, yeah? Can't be that hard. I happen to know a firefighter, and he said they never did anything but sit around and wait for fires, and when they got one, they squirted some water on it and went home."

I froze with my hand holding the fridge door. She thought my job was easy? Did she and Brian know each other? Let me get her on a fireline. Or digging some ditches. Or building some fence. Or, dammit, hiking five miles to work trail, and *then* get a fire call and hike ten more miles.

She left for work, and I went to take a shower. I picked a soggy towel off the floor and moved her beauty products aside so I could brush my teeth. *God help me, I want my own place.*


I'D GONE GROCERY shopping and reached behind the car seat for my purse. Excruciating pain tore through my shoulder once again. This was happening way too often. With reluctance, because I hated admitting any pain was debilitating, I decided I'd have to see a doctor. First, though, I asked Eric to file a belated accident report. No way would I be paying for this myself.

The doctor asked a few questions, lifted my arm up and down, took x-rays. "You dislocated your shoulder, overstretching the tendon. I could operate, but you could end up with a frozen shoulder."

*Dislocated?* No wonder it'd hurt so much. But wait . . . *Surgery? Frozen shoulder?* I choked. "Isn't there some kind of exercise I could do?"

He shook his head.

I would not let this injury affect me. I'd work through this. I wouldn't have an operation that could possibly make me worse.

"FLORIDA ISN'T COMPLYING with new government building color standards," Glenn said Monday morning. "Supposedly, they're too reflective. I don't get this. They've been the same for decades, and I never thought they stood out."

Change the color? Why? I loved the pale yellow.

Clark squashed his first cigarette butt in the overflowing Smokey the Bear ashtray. "Don't tell me we're painting them redwood, or I'll puke." The Forest Service stained everything made of wood the same shade.

Glenn tossed paint chips on his desk. *Brown and beige?* I couldn't imagine anything uglier. An awful roommate, Florida's charm swirling down the drain . . . what if Joe ended up leaving for a new job? This summer headed downhill like a sled on ice.

On our first painting day, I volunteered to do the trim. Clark often teased that there never was enough time to do it right, but always enough time to do it over. Not in my world. Glenn had drilled a solid work ethic into me from day one. Make time to do it right. I scraped loose paint, swept cobwebs and washed off dirt. When the newbies slopped paint over flakes and dirt, I inwardly fumed.

That evening, I vented my frustrations to Joe. "The paint won't stick! This is bullshit!"

"Cows do too."

It took me a second, and I smiled.

"Don't sweat it," he said. "Do your job like you always do and ignore the idiots."

That was hard for me. I didn't get their attitudes.

Curled in the crook of Joe's shoulder, before falling asleep I thought about how I needed him as my ally and friend as much as I needed his love. To think he might leave opened a hole in my heart.

OUT OF HABIT, I arrived at the office thirty minutes before anyone else. In past summers, I loved our pre-work meeting. I'd perch on a table, hardhat in hand, swinging my legs in anticipation of a fun day. We shared stories, laughed, and joked. This summer, there was little of that, but I had to get away from my roommate so I wouldn't kill, I mean, strangle her.

Clark arrived soon after me and made coffee. Others meandered in a few minutes before eight. Miss Prissy, at eight-thirty. She was always late. Why didn't anyone get on her case? She got away with things here that no one else could have. I'd witnessed her femme fatale performances:

"Could one of you strong handsome men lift this box for me?" and, "I'm afraid if I fill the gas can I'll spill some on my uniform, would one of you sweeties help me out?"

Lord help *me*. Worse yet, the guys fell for it. For two summers, I'd fought hard to earn their respect, to be recognized as a hardworking crewmember. Would she undo all of that?

Glenn's truck pulled in, the door slammed, his footsteps sounding hollow as they struck the wood floor. He headed straight for the coffee urn.

"You didn't reuse yesterday's coffee grounds, did you, Clark?" he said, winking at me.

Clark snorted. "Heck no, that was John's lazy trick."

Though not a regular coffee drinker, I still couldn't imagine reusing coffee grounds.

Coffee and lit cigarette in hand, Glenn sat down behind his desk. He assigned a variety of tasks to everyone, and then turned to me. "You're in charge of Paul today."

I frowned. I didn't much like Paul. I didn't much like that next building up for painting was my place. I wished we could have painted it last—or not at all.

Paul and I set up in the shade of my backyard. Upside down buckets served as stools. I prepped the door, scraping and sanding. Paul took forever to even get the paint can open. Pausing, assessing, studying . . . What was he waiting for?

By nine o'clock, I'd discovered Paul's fixation with time. Which would've been fine if he wore a watch, but he didn't. Every fifteen minutes he asked, "So what time is it now?"

By mid-morning, his clock watching had already driven me crazy. I snapped. "It's not break time, lunch time, or quitting time! When it is, I'll let you know."

He reared back, startled, and raised his brows. I muttered under my breath.

Right after our ten o'clock break, Paul disappeared. *Where the heck is he going?* Fifteen minutes later he returned, only to leave again shortly thereafter. At noon, I reminded him to wash his brush before leaving. Paul rose from his seat and glared at me, his mouth gaped open. What was his problem? If he didn't like me being in charge, tough.

At one o'clock, I settled in to paint. No sign of Paul until one-fifteen. Just thirty minutes later, he set down his brush and walked away. I'd had enough. After not finding him anywhere in sight, I banged on the door of his quarters. "Paul? You in there?"

He opened the door wearing a ridiculous, stupid grin.

"What the heck are you doing?" I said through clenched teeth.

Paul folded his arms across his chest, his lips forming a ludicrous smirk. "I'm counting my fire shirts."

Now *my* mouth gaped open. *You're doing what?* "Get back to work, Paul."

His grin vanished. As I walked away, I shuddered. I *really* didn't want to know what he was doing in there. I mentally ticked off Paul's annoying behaviors: no work ethic, showed up late, did as little as possible, and gave himself permission to take a break whenever he felt like it. What irked me the most was I thought Paul resented me. First chance I got, I told Gary.

"You're being too sensitive," he said, snickering. "He's just teasing."

Was I? I didn't think so. Well, if Gary had no intention of sticking up for me, then I'd have to stick up for myself.

# TWENTY-TWO

JOE CAME OVER to my quarters after work to tell me he got the job. *No!* My eyes welled up. I choked back a sob.

His brow furrowed, and he took my hands. "If you don't want me to take it, I won't."

I protested. "No, you must take it! This is your career."

We talked much of the night. He didn't understand how I could both want him to go and need him to stay. After he fell asleep, I lay awake. How often would we see each other? When? Even harder for me, I envied, and wanted, the opportunity he would soon have: a permanent Forest Service job. Would I ever get that chance?

Two weeks later, we spent our last night together at his place. The alarm clock bleeped at four a.m., but it didn't wake me up. I hadn't slept at all. I helped him load his truck, and we got into our respective vehicles. At my turnoff, he pulled over. I did too. He pointed a finger at his chest, drew a heart in the air, and pointed at me. *I love you.* I nodded and repeated the motions back to him. Tears poured down my face as I steered toward the station. Aside from Tom's accident, this was my worst day at Florida. How would I manage without him?

Up early on my day off, I decided to do some housecleaning. Glenn knocked on my open front door. I invited him in, wondering what he wanted.

Voice firm, if not demanding, he said, "Something's going on with you. What's wrong?"

Did he ask this because he cared about me, or because he thought my emotions got in the way of work? Easier to lie. "Nothing, I'm fine."

"Well, okay then. Just checking. You can talk to me, you know." He left.

I stood in the middle of my living room, stunned. What just happened here? The last thing I needed was for him play with my emotions on top of Joe leaving. The more I tried to understand Glenn, the more I realized I never would.

THROW A BUNCH of emotions into a blender, punch high, pour into a glass, and let them settle. What would float to the top today? I'd lost my motivation, but still showed up for work early. Would my "I'm fine" mask succeed? I didn't want Glenn asking me more questions, afraid I would read something into them that wasn't there. Somehow I managed to get through another day. No word from Joe all week. Why didn't he write?

Painting the buildings wasn't near enough to keep my mind occupied. It left way too much time to think. *I miss Joe. I hate it here,* I thought, dipping my brush into the paint can.

Gary dashed from around the corner of the house, startling me. "Let's go! We've got a fire!"

Moments later, crew-cabs loaded, we sped off to the Chiricahua Mountains, a forested range east of the Santa Ritas, where we'd join the efforts of several other crews on a slow-moving blaze in high timber.

"I'm going to put you in charge of a squad," Gary said.

About time. With this being Paul's and Brian's first fire, I checked on them often.

"Down to bare mineral soil," I reminded Brian. He grunted and scraped more.

There was no sight of Paul for quite a while. I found him way behind the rest of us, pawing at the ground with a McCleod, a firefighter's version of a rake. I told him to pick up the pace, this was a fire, not trail maintenance. He laughed at me. Later, I caught him carrying a tool on his shoulder—a safety violation. When I spoke a few sharp words about the correct way to carry a tool, he gave me an angry glare. It was tough being a supervisor, I got that, but did I have to put up with this crap?

That night after we were released, I rode back wondering how I could've handled Paul better without Gary accusing me of being too sensitive. Should I have reported Paul on the spot? That would've made things worse. I wished I could ask Joe what he would've done.

Days later, four of us arrived back at the station just past five, with a truck full of fencing supplies. Late didn't bother me, I figured it balanced the days when we knocked off a little early. As soon as Gary parked, Brian and Paul jumped out, heading for their quarters.

"Hey!" Gary said. "Where the hell do you think you're going? You need to help unload."

"It's after five. We're off the clock," Paul shouted over his shoulder.

Gary voiced what I already knew to be true. "Those two guys have to be the most worthless ones we've got."

*Well, halleluiah!* That incident, on top of everything else Paul did, must surely be grounds for dismissal. But nothing happened, not even a reprimand. What did you have to do to get fired from this outfit? Frustrated, I became silent and brooding. I didn't realize anyone noticed until Mark commented that I didn't laugh anymore. Why would I? Idiots for coworkers, no camaraderie, only a few fires, Joe gone and an unbearable roommate . . . I dreaded the rest of the summer.


I CAME HOME from grocery shopping to find a party going on next door, so I popped over to join them. Glenn was there, which was unusual for him this summer, since he didn't live at Florida anymore. I joined the group in the living room.

Mark paced, flailing his arms. " . . . and she said was going to file an EEO discrimination complaint!"

I gathered that Mark meant my roommate, the only other "she" here.

"Against who?" I asked.

Eric turned toward me. "Against Glenn."

*Glenn? Why that little . . .* What audacity to accuse the last person on the planet that would ever discriminate against anyone, anywhere, at any time. I attempted to gauge Glenn's reaction, but he just stared into his whiskey. I wanted to tell him that I would never do such a thing, and that I thought the woman was a lunatic.

Heated discussion over, the guys shifted to another topic. Glenn stood up and took me aside. Cupping my elbow with his hand, he said, "Can we talk?"

Minutes ago, I wanted this. Now, wary, but also wanting to hear what he had to say, I followed him outside for privacy.

Glenn stood intimately close to me, his head lowered, and then looked into my eyes from under the brim of his Stetson. "You know, I think the world of you."

My inner voice screamed, *No, no, no, he will only hurt you again!* but the part that still loved him wanted him to kiss me, and I let him. However, the words I wanted to hear more than anything, that he loved me, weren't spoken. Even though it wrenched my heart to do so, I pushed him away. Angry, he left. I stood there for a few minutes, reeling, near tears. How do you extract someone from your heart once they are firmly embedded there?

About three a.m., I staggered home from *two* too many drinks. Flat on my back, I tried to sleep; but when I closed my eyes, the room spun. With eyes open the room spun. Somehow I made it to work the next morning despite a hangover so brutal, it hurt to blink. Good thing we had station duty; I could handle sweeping out the fire cache, but not much more. At eleven, I gave myself a pep talk. *Only five more hours to go.* That's when Gary burst into the shop saying: "We've got a fire!"

My headache vanished.

It returned an hour later.

# TWENTY-THREE

SMOKE-CLOUDS ROLLED and churned from steep, rocky slopes beneath the vertical cliffs forming Pusche Ridge, an area in the Santa Catalina Mountains known for its inaccessible terrain.

Gary turned on the local radio station. "Today's forecast calls for a temperature of one-oh-eight, so stay cool Tucson, and stay indoors."

*Like that would happen.* Tightening the knot in my stomach—not a single shade tree in sight. *They aren't really going to make us go up there—are they?* I'd always made a concerted effort not to be a complainer about firefighting hardships; after all, I'd chosen and loved my job. But with that scorching forecast and those barren slopes, the fire posed less danger to me than did possible heat exhaustion, or worse, heat stroke. Too bad Brian had missed this fire. I would've loved to see him tackle this "piece of cake."

Fire camp, tucked into a grove of scrawny palo verdes, offered scant shade—that's the desert for you. Gary returned with our orders: "We've got the night shift."

Working at night would be great, except we'd start now. I swung my fire pack onto my back, tied my canteens and fire shelter around my hips. Up we marched on a scree covered, ladder-steep slope. Noon-high blistering sun penetrated both of my shirts, searing my skin. I paused for a sip of water. What few plants grew here hugged the ground, except the notorious and well-armed shindagger agave. Midday glare washed out colors, leaving a palette of tan and muted greens in those areas not already blackened by fire. Bone-dry air sucked out any scents other than baked earth and wafting smoke.

Gary stopped. "Crew coming through, step aside."

Men plodded by, faces drawn and withered from working in the blazing sun. One of the guys stopped in front of me. "Can you spare a canteen?"

Give him my water? The guy must be sun-crazed. "Uh, well, I'm just starting a shift," I said.

"Okay, never mind." He moved on.

As I walked away, I felt a twinge of guilt. *Should I have? Wait, no, he's almost back to camp. I need my water.*

Stumbling over the rough terrain, we reached the slow-moving fire, which burned through succulent agave leaves, making a sound much like popcorn. At least agaves didn't ignite like grass. No big threat here.

Hours later, my muscles and patience taxed, I couldn't tell if we'd made much progress. Sweat evaporated before I felt a single drop. I stopped to take a sip of my precious water. *Not too much . . . make it last.* I wanted to drink more, but fought the urge. I could be out here sixteen hours. I replaced the cap and screwed it tight—heaven forbid should any leak out. My head pounded; a combination of dehydration and a hangover. *Dumb shit. No more drinking on weeknights.*

Gary suggested a break. Sitting in full, unrelenting sun, on ground hotter than the air offered no relief, though. We gave up after only five minutes.

"Am I the only one who thinks building line here is futile?" I asked, back to chopping at plants wedged between rocks.

Gary mopped his brow with a bandana. "Yeah, but this is bighorn sheep habitat. They're worried about loss of food."

Okay, so we were saving habitat. Not much glamour, though. Without threats to life and property, we wouldn't be making headlines for our efforts. That's the news media for you.

What a difference it made when the blistering sun ducked below the horizon. Although still in the nineties, relative to daytime heat, this cooler air made me feel downright perky. All night we chopped and scraped. Bugs danced around my headlamp, both distracting and annoying. My feet hurt from walking on sharp rocks, and I stumbled more often, from that and fatigue. Gradually, the midnight blue sky lightened to soft turquoise. Our shift ended.

In gold morning light, we slid down the rocky hillside to camp before the sun threatened a repeat performance. Only a meager cup of water sloshed in one canteen. I let go of my guilt for not sharing with that guy yesterday.

Burned out from the heat, hard work, and water rationing, I dumped my pack under one of those palo verdes and went in search of a cold drink. I filled a paper cup with DayGlo-green Gatorade from an industrial size Igloo cooler. Guzzling it all at once coated my dry throat with the sweet, icy-cold beverage. With eyes closed, I relished the flavor, texture, and dust removal. *Damn that was good.* I refilled my canteens with cool water. Under the scrawny tree, I spread out my paper sleeping bag and collapsed flat on my back, every drop of moisture sucked out of me—a desiccated carcass.

Gary handed me a box. "C-rat?"

I passed. I sat up, opened my pack, and nibbled some trail mix—but I wasn't hungry. What I really wanted was a gallon of Gatorade, but I didn't want to be a pig and drink it all.

Laying spread-eagled on my sleeping bag, I prayed for a breeze. But there wasn't even a whisper. I stripped down to underwear, but kept on my work shirt. Out of the corner of my eye, I noticed a firefighter gawk at my bare legs. Unbelievable. How could anyone think of sex while sweaty, dirty, and beyond exhaustion? I shut my eyes. Flies pestered me, their annoying little feet tickling. Loud snoring and an occasional grunt came from the others. How could they sleep? All I did was doze off a few times.

We were back up the hill one more time that night, but found no hotspots. Unlike many fires, where rain helped more than anything else to snuff them out, this one starved itself out as it connected with those enormous rock outcroppings.

"Why didn't they drop slurry?" I asked Gary as we slid and skidded down the hillside.

"They didn't want to scare the sheep."

I hadn't thought of how terrifying a low-flying plane would be to wildlife. I pondered the fate of the sheep residents, wherever they were hiding. They have amazing agility to navigate terrain no other animal dared to tread; *Including humans,* I thought wearily. My aching feet were nowhere near as tough as sheeps' hooves.

When we pulled into the station, I felt a renewed appreciation for Florida's cool, woodland setting. And although the Santa Rita Mountains had steep slopes, at least there were trees.


A WEEK LATER, Glenn pulled up alongside us at the fire cache as we unloaded at the end of the day. He stepped out, paused, stared at the ground, and shook his head. "Well, it's official. District's out of money. We can't keep you guys on any longer."

My heart plummeted. Laid-off in July? I hadn't made anywhere near enough money yet. What would I do the rest of the summer?

"Catalinas have an opening on the hotshots and several on the trail crew," Glenn said. "Let me know if you want a transfer and we'll fill out the paperwork." He drove away.

*Hotshots? Hey, maybe this would work out just great.*

"I want the hotshot crew," I said, parking in front of Glenn's desk.

He took a drag on his cigarette. "I don't see why not; you've got the most fire experience of all the seasonals here."

That made sense. Maybe he could pull some strings for me, too. He'd do that for me, wouldn't he? Ecstatic I'd be on the hotshots, I also rejoiced in no more Paul, Brian, or Miss Prissy. Yes, I still loved Florida. But I had to get away from here, *and,* I thought sadly, *from Glenn.*

"I'm going to the Catalinas," I said to Miss Prissy, placing my hardhat on the dining table.

"Me too," she chirped from the kitchen.

"You are?" *Damn.*

She sashayed out the front door. "I'm off to Pete's."

I sighed. Why couldn't I get away from her? But she'd never make the hotshots, so I'd be good. In the kitchen, I noticed she'd already started packing. *Wait a minute.* In the boxes were many familiar items—familiar, because they were mine! Furious, I stomped over to Pete's to confront her.

"Hey! Your boxes are filled with my stuff!"

"Oh really? I couldn't remember what was mine."

"So you took everything, just in case it was?"

She flipped her bangs. "Whatever."

*Arghh!* I stormed home to retrieve my belongings.

In the morning, Glenn came to my quarters as I finished packing.

"They offered you trail crew," he said.

Crushed, I asked why.

"Hate to say this, you know . . . but . . . they said no women allowed. Greg got the job."

*What?* I fumed. I had more experience than Greg. That job belonged to me. But, trail crew beat getting laid off, so I took it. Furious, though, I couldn't stop thinking, *They didn't give me the job because I'm a girl.*

# TWENTY-FOUR

PUSHING THROUGH TUCSON, with its stop, go, stop, go heavy traffic, reminded me of one big reason I loved my job—living and working in nature. When I left the madness behind and began climbing up the Catalina Highway, I turned off the AC and opened my window to enjoy cool, pine-scented air. Dramatic granite cliffs lined the road, with tall ponderosas perched high above. At the Windy Point overlook, entertaining rock formations called "hoodoos," balanced as though a sneeze would knock them over. A faint outline of the Baboquivari Mountains on the western horizon rose above the Tucson haze. Every twist and turn in the road brought back memories of working at Palisades Ranger Station in 1975 as a fire crew timekeeper. *Look at me now,* I thought with pride.

I parked Skyler in front of the Helitack base at Sollers Point. I'd always admired this homey two-story redwood house, with its hand-laid rock walls and white shuttered windows. A steep, green-shingled roof shed occasional heavy winter snows. Another flood of memories, and a particularly happy one: the walk on the short-cut trail winding through the forest to have dinner with the Helitack crew.

Lofty pines stood as sentinels, their needles sunlit and shimmering, rustling in the breeze like wheat in a field. No sign of life outside, so I knocked on the door. It swung open to reveal a small, slender woman, with eyes so vividly green that I found it hard not to stare. She introduced herself as Bev, formerly of the Helitack crew. Although her frame was petite, her arms were strong. She'd already gained my respect, and would soon gain my friendship.

"Make yourself at home," she said. "I'll be staying in Tucson on weekends, so pick any room you want. You're the first one here."

Hardwood floors and pine paneling lent warmth to the living room. A long blue couch and two padded armchairs faced the giant stone fireplace. In the galley kitchen, I recognized the huge stove for large-scale meal preparations. I ran my hand over the smooth, shellacked surface of the pine dining table, where I'd enjoyed taco night with Al, Tim, and the guys back then. They'd always welcomed me, made me feel a part of their "family."

I picked a bedroom on the first floor and unloaded my car. After I unpacked, Bev and I chatted about our respective jobs. I told her I'd really wanted the hotshot job, but Glenn had said they wouldn't take women.

Her eyes widened. "You should go talk to McKelsey's assistant, Frank, about that."

Bev's shock at my news got me thinking: maybe Glenn had misunderstood. My confidence renewed, I decided to straighten it all out with Frank.

Palisades Ranger Station had changed little over the past three years. I approached the pert, college-aged woman behind the counter and asked if I could see Frank. Head held high, she walked purposefully to the back, stopped in a doorway, and spoke softly to someone inside.

Returning, she said, "Frank will see you."

Once inside the dark-paneled room, a man in uniform waved me over to the chair in front of his desk. Burgundy leather squeaked when I sat, and the brass tacks on the armrest felt cool under my fingers. A wiry man with a meticulous goatee stared at me with chilling gray eyes that matched his thinning hair.

"So, what can I do you for?" he asked, leaning back in his chair, lacing his fingers behind his head and propping his black leather boots on his desk with a thump.

Disturbed by his unwavering gaze, my bravery faltered. *What's the best way to say this?* "Umm, well, I'm confused why I didn't make the hotshots. I have three years fire experience."

Frank lowered his feet and leaned forward, forming a teepee with his fingers, frigid eyes locked on mine. "I don't want women on my hotshot crew."

The walls closed in on me. "But . . . I . . . I'm qualified," I said, surprising myself with the audacity to talk back to someone older than me, much less someone older *and* a man.

"Qualifications have nothing to do with it. Women don't belong on hotshot crews."

His matter-of-fact tone staggered me. Perspiration formed on my upper lip, my face flushed, but still I managed to say, "That's not fair."

He shrugged.

Angry, embarrassed, and insulted . . . like an idiot, I just sat there. I couldn't seem to make myself leave.

He took the opportunity to fill in the silence. "So, do you want the trail position or not?"

I kept the job because I needed the work. On the return to Sollers, humiliated, my face burned and a few tears fell. *Okay, so I'm on a trail crew. Bev said we'd work until September. That's longer than the hotshots will work, so that's a good thing. But this is discrimination—isn't it?*

Bev's green eyes narrowed when I told her what had happened. "You should file an EEO complaint."

What would happen to me if I did file a complaint with the Equal Employment Opportunity Commission? I considered calling Jan Qwill from the Federal Women's Program for advice and support. Wasn't that what the organization was for? But no, I could handle this; however I needed to hear from Joe. I checked my inbox. Still no word. I wrote another letter, telling him what happened, asking him to write soon.

The following morning I took a chair into the living room for our staff meeting. Miss Prissy hadn't showed up, yet. Good.

"Tim's our supervisor, but he won't be going out with us," Bev said. "He wants us to finish as many trails as possible before funds run out."

The front door opened and slammed. Miss Prissy swept into the room, flipping her bangs from her eyes with a toss of her head. "Sorry, running a little late."

Bev squared her shoulders and blinked hard. "Yeah. Right. Be on time tomorrow."

But the next day, Miss Prissy banged in late again, offering Bev a phony smile. "Traffic."

Bev again firmly told her, "You *must* be on time."

*Yes!* Finally, someone put the twit in her place.

Our discussion about finding potable water sources while on trail for five days continued.

"We'll get water from springs," Bev said. "It can't be trusted, though. It takes so long for water to boil and sterilize at high elevations, make sure you bring iodine tablets."

Up jumped Miss Prissy, who then flounced off into the kitchen.

Bev mouthed at me, "What the heck?"

I smiled and shrugged. Five minutes later, Prissy returned with a bowl of cereal, sat down, and scooped it into her mouth, oblivious to the stares directed at her from everyone in the room.

Bev, like me, could not believe this. "You need to eat breakfast *before* you come to work."

Vindication. Miss Prissy would not get away with anything here like she had at Florida. I wondered how she'd fair camping out all week. I never found out, though. She transferred to another district within a week, and good riddance. Soon after she left, I thumbed through my albums to play one in particular. It was not there. Panicked, I flipped through them. At least five were missing. Furious, at first I wanted to write and demand she return them, *now*, but that might backfire. Instead, I toned down my anger, and wrote her to please return what she'd taken by mistake.

I spent Friday night alone in the big house. Well, not quite alone; field mice lived there too. I curled up with every square-inch of skin covered by blanket, petrified the scurrying rodents would jump onto the bed. I'd just drifted off when I felt something run across me. I bounded out of bed, shrieked, and danced around like hot coals covered the floor. That did it—I needed to set more traps.

In the morning, I headed down the mountain to buy camping supplies. At a sporting goods store, a friendly sales clerk helped me find the perfect backpack—the first sticker shock. A down sleeping bag was the second sticker shock. Synthetic would have to do. An Insolite pad came highly recommended, so I placed it on the counter, too. Third sticker shock. From a display, I picked up a bottle of biodegradable soap. *Safe for the environment*, I thought. *That's important.* I added it to the ticket. The sum total? A substantial cash outlay. But, I justified it by thinking I'd use it all, even after the job ended.

Grocery shopping, I scanned the aisles for backpack-friendly, non-perishable food. I skipped canned goods, which were too heavy. Feeling the budget pinch, I resorted to instant soup, saltines, peanut butter, Pop Tarts, Tang, tea, and trail mix. At the checkout, I splurged on a big fat paperback: M.M. Kaye's *The Far Pavilions*.

After a late dinner, I hopped onto my bed and turned on the TV. The office phone rang. *Hey, maybe a fire!* I dashed to answer it, finding McKelsey on the line—not calling about a fire, or even work. Instead, he invited me up to his place, saying he'd like to talk. I hesitated . . . why would he want to talk to me? *He's Tim's boss, so technically he's mine, too. I should go.*

Underneath the starriest of skies, I parked next to the spacious log cabin behind the Palisades office. *So this is one of the perks of being a Forest Service official.* He opened the door before I knocked.

"C'mon in. What can I get you? Beer, wine . . . scotch?" He held up his half-full glass.

Drinks surprised me. "Umm, wine, please."

"Make yourself comfortable," he said, heading for the kitchen.

I sat on a rustic leather sofa. Outdoorsy paintings of deer or fishermen hung on the walls, but dim lighting made it hard to see much detail. A candle burned next to a half-empty bottle of scotch on the coffee table. The air was hazed from his cigarette smoldering in a clay ashtray.

McKelsey returned and sat down next to me. I accepted the glass of dark red wine, and took a sip. He picked up his cigarette and took a drag.

Smoke wafted from his mouth as he spoke. "I remember you well from back in '75. You were so cute and sweet. No wonder so many of the hotshots asked you out."

At the time, only nineteen years old, living among over twenty, sexy firefighters, with no other unattached women around—sure, many asked me out. A big deal for the shy girl I was back then. But why was he bringing this up again? I smiled, uneasy, as his eyes tried to latch onto mine. At that point, I suspected what he was up to, and I wanted *out*. I set my glass down and stood. He rose, took my arm, and tugged me toward an open door, beyond which I could clearly see his bed.

"C'mon . . . whaddaya say?"

Alarmed, I made for the front door. "No! Let me go."

He blocked my hasty exit with an outstretched arm across the doorway, a seductive smile crossing his face. "You don't know what you're missing."

Now *that* disgusted me. "Oh, yes I do. Let me go."

"Are you sure?" He moved aside.

"Yes." I dashed out and sped home.

In bed, I kept replaying what happened. How stupid of me to have gone to his place. He could have raped me. Would he fire me for turning him down? What a long, sleepless night.

# TWENTY-FIVE

EARLY MORNING AT the trailhead had a bit of chill, but that wouldn't last long. I strapped on my new pack, stuffed full, and secured six, one-quart canteens to its frame. Even though the weight wobbled my knees a bit, I reminded myself: *There's nothing worse than thirst.* Good thing we'd be hiking downhill. After emerging from the shady forest, we followed steep switchbacks for two miles. I stopped for a water break, taking in the panoramic views of city, desert, and blue-hazed mountains, including the Santa Ritas. They tugged at my heart. Did anyone there miss me?

Bev found a perfect camping spot: shady, flat, and protected from wind, with few rocks and plenty of firewood. Although most outdoor lovers share a code of ethics not to steal (so I was assured), we hid our backpacks, just in case. Sans pack, I floated down the trail for the next few miles to our work start-point. Even with mild temperatures, the Arizona sun blazed high in a cloudless sky. I tied my bandana around my forehead to keep sweat from stinging my eyes. No chainsaws were allowed in wilderness areas, so I swung a Pulaski at the rubbery, resilient, manzanita stems growing into the tread.

Allowing time to hike back, we quit at four, and trudged uphill to camp. Our backpacks were right where we'd left them, and I went about setting up for the night. Easy to do. No need for a tent in this glorious weather.

"I'm going to clean up," Bev said. "Coming?"

With a towel and biodegradable soap in hand, I joined her to bathe in a nearby creek. It was fun having a woman to share this with. We stripped down at the water's edge, giggling and talking. Before opening the soap, I read the label for the first time: Warning: Not safe for use in rivers and lakes. *Well, isn't that just great.*

I lowered one foot into the crystal clear water and shrieked. "It's freezing! I want to be clean, but . . ."

"Just go for it!" Bev plunged in, screeching while splashing water over herself.

"The water's fine, so come on in." I'd heard that lie before. After the initial shock, teeth chattering, I bathed, probably breaking the world record. It was worth it though—every bone-chilling second. Exhilarated and refreshed, I also felt virtuous for not polluting the water with biodegradable, but not environmentally safe, camping soap.

The guys had built a fire to cook dinner while we bathed. Into a large pot went potatoes, assorted vegetables, and beans. "Stone Soup," without the stone, of course. While it simmered, I rested my back against a tree to listen to rustling leaves, the low voices of my crew and birds twittering as they roosted for the night.

There wasn't much talking while devouring our hard-earned feast. Mr. Sun slid below tree tops, and the dry mountain air cooled quickly. Sitting fireside, we spooked ourselves for a while with ghost stories, leaving enough daylight for me to start my book. I snuggled into my sleeping bag where my eyelids soon became heavy, the book dropping from my hands as I went comatose.

THE SHORT TRAILS took about a week to complete, and the ten-mile trail, several weeks. Every Friday I checked for letters. Today, there was one from my mom, and finally, one from Joe:

> Dear Linda Marie,
>     I'll be in down there on the sixteenth, and can't wait to see you.
> Love you, Joe.

*The sixteenth? When is that?* I scrambled for a calendar. *Tomorrow!* Anticipation kept me awake all night. Our time together went way too fast.

THANK GOODNESS TRAIL work kept me from seeing McKelsey much. The term "sexual harassment" wasn't even in my vocabulary. All I knew was that when I had seen him, his leering made me nervous and self-conscious. I wished he would quit staring at me.

After another week out on trail, I lugged my gear into the house. *Here I come, hot shower.*

The office phone jangled, and Bev answered it.

"Okay, I can have four ready in fifteen minutes." She hung up. "You guys up for a couple snag fires? Hotshots are out of state, so we're it for fire suppression."

*Heck yes!* Fire packs loaded, we sped down the Catalina Highway and turned onto a narrow dirt road. We bounced on that for a while, reaching a stretch requiring four-wheel-drive, something we didn't have. Thunder grumbled in the distance, the air scented with rain.

"Maybe the fires will get rained out, but we can't be sure," Bev said, handing me a two-way radio after attaching one to her belt.

An hour later, we split up into teams. Dave and I found our snag with fire dancing from cavities inside the dead tree. An ideal solution would have been to cut it down, but we didn't have a saw. Instead, we dug a line around the potential fall zone. Lightning flashed; a thunder explosion made us jump. An instant later, torrential rain sent us scrambling for cover. Squatting under a ponderosa, we formed a tent over our heads with our ponchos as the forest disappeared in a white veil.

"Well?" Dave yelled over the din. "Now what?"

"Let's wait and see if it stops," I hollered back.

It would not be prudent to jump the gun, leave, and have the fire take off later. Huddled under our makeshift shelter, we waited, listening. More rumbles and more flashes. I sat, impatient, hoping the rain would quit soon— already my pant legs were wet, and I felt a damp chill creeping under my poncho. An unearthly silence replaced the thunder bursts, but the rain kept pummeling down. The forest seemed to hold its breath, as though waiting for something to happen. Me too. Then a blinding, all-encompassing flash, combined with an explosive clap, shook the earth beneath us. Dave and I bolted upright as though jerked like puppets. If my heart could have left my chest, I swore it just did.

"Jesus!" Dave yelled, his voice muffled by the pounding deluge. "Lightning strike!"

"Too damn close for me! This fire isn't going anywhere." I radioed Bev. "We're outta here!"

"Us too!" came her staticky reply.

Dave and I hustled down the trail until the ground turned into slippery, slimy goo, sticking to our boots, slowing us down. I figured it'd be easier once on the trail, but instead, the well-worn path ran with water several inches deep. Slogging for what seemed like ages, we rendezvoused with the others. Because I could see my breath, I guessed the temperature had dropped into the thirties. Feet sloshing inside my boots, my clothes soaking wet, shivering uncontrollably: I dreaded the long haul to our truck. Bright headlights ahead pierced the inky darkness, blinding me. *What nutcase would be out in a storm like this?*

The truck stopped and the window rolled down. Tim said, "I thought you guys would appreciate a lift."

A chance to get out of the cold and rain? I could've kissed him. Once at Sollers, Bev and Felipe left for Tucson. After changing into dry clothes, I put the kettle on and poured two mugs of tea. I carried them out to the living room to find Dave tending the fireplace.

"I decided we needed a fire." He tossed in a log and reached for the steaming mug. "Thanks."

I sat cross-legged on the rug in front of the hearth, wrapping both hands around the cup. "Oh, this is nice."

Dave gazed into the warm, friendly glow. "Amazing, isn't it? How differently we think of fire in a fireplace as opposed to one raging out of control?"

My mind drifted to a childhood memory: I'm five years old. A wintery Saturday night, my dad lights a fire in our fireplace. We pop popcorn and watch Perry Mason. I lay with my older sister on the rug in front of the hearth, head in hands, staring into the flames, reciting: "Ladybug, ladybug, fly away home. Your house is on fire, and your children are all gone." Why were nursery rhymes so morbid?

Dave lay with his head propped on one arm—firelight reflected in his dark eyes. We watched orange flame tendrils and talked at length, beyond firefighting, beyond trail work. I regretted we hadn't talked more. My thoughts strayed. Handsome guy . . . dark hair and complexion, and that sexy wisp of a mustache. Before this moment, I'd never thought much about him. Now I wondered what he thought about me. Would I let him kiss me if he tried to?

"Well, I'm beat," he said, interrupting my fantasy.

We said goodnight. Despite all the excitement, I didn't have any trouble falling into a deep, dreamless sleep, waking only once to the sound of mice acrobatics.

Bright and early, Tim sent us to check on the snag fires. Dave and I found our tree still standing, covered with black charcoal, but with no signs of fire. Curious about the proximity of last night's lightning strike, we decided to investigate.

"Which way do you think?" I asked.

"Over here," he replied, walking north.

Too close to where we'd sat huddled from the storm, I stopped and stared. A huge tree trunk stood splintered and ragged, as though a bomb had exploded from inside. Large spears of wood were scattered everywhere, with some stuck upright into the ground like wooden lightning bolts, frozen mid-strike.

Dave's face turned solemn. "We could've been impaled."

Goosebumps prickled on the back of my neck. "Or fried."


ON A NEW trail the next week, after a day of hard work, I discovered our camping spot had many stones hidden in the pine needles. Even pebbles felt humungous during the night, especially when positioned under my hip bone. After much fussing to get the ground just right, I lay on my back, gazing up at stars and the smiling moon cradling Venus. A canyon wren whistled its cadence. Boughs rustled . . . I drifted off.

I awoke at daybreak, with a lingering ghost of a dream, or was it real? All night, I sensed invisible hands pushing me to roll over. Now, puzzled, my first inclination was to blame one of the guys. After a few minutes, my fuzzy brain-fog lifted. It had been the gusty wind not a person. I laughed out loud, grateful I'd not made any accusations.

Tired, and lonely for Joe, I walked into my bedroom on Friday afternoon to find him sitting on my bed. Ecstatic, I tackled him before he could say a word. At times like this, I loved him so much. It was hard to see him leave on Sunday, but we'd be together soon.

Mild days on splendid wilderness trails; chilly nights with friends by the campfire; daytime skies a stunning blue, and nighttime skies angelically starry. Hard work aside, what could possibly be better? Although I didn't regret taking the trail job, I decided to file an EEO complaint against Frank. It was plain and simple: he discriminated against me. At the supervisor's office in downtown Tucson, I met with the personnel clerk.

"This process is completely safe from repercussions and considered confidential information," she said reassuringly.

At the moment, I didn't understand the implications of the information *not* being confidential or safe from repercussions, but felt a strong conviction to fill out the forms anyway.

Layoffs came in late September. When I watched everyone leave one by one, a hole expanded in my chest. I'd sure miss everyone. To counter the sad parting, though, I was excited that Joe had asked me to stay with him over the winter. Did we have enough in common to live together? Aside from our love and mutual physical attraction, we shared the passion of our Forest Service jobs and hard work, pine-scented air, the desert, hiking, wilderness camping; and the biggie—not being stuck in an office all day. It made sense to me to find out.

That night, packing to leave, it dawned on me Miss Prissy had never responded about my albums. The urge to track her down and throttle her was strong; but instead, I opted against jail time, chalking it up to one of life's lessons about rotten roommates.

First, I spent a week with my mom. Next, I joined Joe in his nineteen-foot travel-trailer at the Springerville KOA, in northeastern Arizona.

THE WHITE MOUNTAINS: what a great place to be in autumn! During peak fall color, no less. Joe and I toured his district, and when we drove through a logging site, I convinced him to rescue a blue spruce seedling for my mom to plant in her backyard.

In Joe's tiny trailer, I made myself at home. Settled in, I searched for a temporary job, which proved futile. Boredom set in fast. To make living there tougher, Prescott's winters had nothing on Springerville. By mid-November, the bitter wind howled daily, whistling through the trailer's windows and doors. It was so windy, the snow didn't even have a chance to accumulate. Both the furnace and a space heater ran nonstop, but I was still cold. To stay busy, I sewed crafty things and experimented with new recipes for dinner. Jodi lived nearby, and I visited her occasionally. But with two toddlers now, she didn't have much free time. I'd never thought about having kids. It wasn't my thing, but she seemed to thrive as a mom.

Running errands, I picked up our mail and found a letter from the EEO Commission. No big surprise: Frank had denied the conversation took place. Now what? If I fought this, would it screw up my career? Afraid that it would, I let it go. *Someday*, I thought, *I'll get another chance to work on a hotshot crew. Maybe even his.*

Joe suffered through stacking brush in the brutal weather all week, so we stayed indoors all weekend. It was too cold to run, too cold to go anywhere. I had cabin fever, big time. Right before I went completely stir-crazy, Joe's job ended until next spring. To get out of the cold, we rented a cabin in Madera Canyon right before Christmas. It seemed almost tropical in comparison. It was also good to be back.

Second day, I hit the Nature Trail for a run. Winded at the first hill, I could tell I'd skipped two months of conditioning. When I awoke the next morning, my calf muscles were tight and my right knee hurt. Boy, was I out of shape.

To earn some money, I took on landscaping jobs. In early April, I woke Joe by bouncing on the bed, holding an offer letter from the Coconino National Forest on the Mormon Lake District. "Guess what I got!"

He sat up, rubbed his eyes, and scanned the letter. "Recreation crew? You won't like it." He handed it back.

Yeah, the fact that the job was on a recreation crew wasn't ideal, but I reminded him it was a job offer, and I wouldn't get another one unless my backup Bureau of Land Management (BLM) application came through. Besides, maybe I could switch over to the Mormon Lake Hotshots, who were stationed there.

He scoffed. "So what? All you'll do is stack brush. Alaska's the place to be."

I knew that, and had applied there, but I couldn't *force* BLM to make an offer. He rolled over, saying into the pillow, "Up to you."

His non-supportive response sucked the joy out of me. Why couldn't he just say he didn't want me to leave? Then there was the other half of my hurt feelings. What I'd wanted to happen, hadn't happened. Glenn had secured a transfer for Joe to Florida, but there was no job offer for me. More than anything, I wanted to matter to Glenn, and apparently I didn't. Hurt and angry at both him and the Forest Service in general, I thought, *I'll never have a Forest Service career. Men get all the breaks. I wish I'd been born a man.*

But, dammit, the clock was ticking. A week later, I decided I couldn't wait any longer for BLM to come through. I accepted the job on the Coconino. Recreation work at Florida hadn't been all that bad. We often did other things besides cleaning. Most likely it'd be the same up there. Additionally, with all of my fire experience, maybe they'd let me transfer to a fire crew. Why wouldn't they?

# TWENTY-SIX

## Summer of 1979: Lake Mary District, Coconino National Forest, Flagstaff, Arizona

ON A BRIGHT, sunny Saturday, I made the seven hour drive to Flagstaff. Only two blocks from the district office, I rented a 1950s trailer in an antiquated RV park snuggled among towering ponderosas. It wasn't as cheap as Florida, but it worked for me, especially because I'd have no roommate, except the furry kind. Before I'd left Tucson, Bev offered me a kitty she'd rescued from coyotes. I'd nuzzled Calley's short, brindle coat and immediately adopted her. My mom agreed to cat-sit if I ended up on a fire crew.

Monday morning I woke up way too early, excited about a new job, a new place, and new people. In the back of my mind, though, I still held out hope for a BLM position or a switch to a fire crew, but first things first.

"Oh, hi, Linda," the receptionist said when I introduced myself at the front counter. "Charlie's waiting for you."

She led me down a long corridor to the back of the building and stopped at a cubicle in the corner. A heavy-set uniformed man sat at his desk, occupied with paperwork.

"Charlie, Linda's here."

Charlie spun his chair to face us. "Well, hello Miss Linda," he said with a wide smile. He stood up to shake my hand. "Pull up a seat."

I slid a chair closer to his desk and sat down. Charlie's phone rang, and, raising a finger indicating a need to answer it, he lifted the receiver. I studied the framed photos on his wall while he handled business. The photos displayed many happy faces in outdoor settings. I assumed they were probably former crews.

Charlie hung up and faced me. "So, I see you've got a lot of fire experience." He leaned forward in his chair, resting his elbows on the armrests and interlacing his thick fingers in front of him. "What brings you here?"

His tone sounded genuine and friendly, so I answered honestly: I liked firefighting, but needed a change from the Coronado.

Charlie's laugh hissed through his teeth. "You actually *like* firefighting? Whoa, girl, that's too much for me. I don't give a hoot if I ever go on a fire again."

I smiled, not at all offended.

"Well, if it ain't Mutt and Jeff . . ." Charlie said to the figures who appeared behind me.

Jeff, the tall, skinny one with a bushy mustache, snorted a laugh. "This our new gal?" He extended his hand. "Welcome to our *wonderful* world of recreation!"

I grasped his hand and smiled tentatively, unsure if he was teasing.

Charlie laughed again. "Now, don't go scaring her away on her first day."

Hutch ("Mutt") chuckled. His eyeballs flitted between Jeff and Charlie, as though checking for permission to laugh. I kept a smile plastered on my face; as the newbie, laying low seemed like a good idea.

Up walked a rather scruffy, lanky guy, carrying a daypack with a large thermos poking out of the top.

"Hey, Walter," Charlie said. "You're the last of the suckers, ahem, I mean, *new hires*." He covered his mouth and snickered. Jeff bent over and howled. Walter and I exchanged puzzled looks and smiles. I liked these guys already.

Like on all first days on the job, I filled out tons of paperwork and retested to renew my government driver's license. I'd work weekends, something I'd learned to enjoy a long time ago. If anything, it meant fewer people in the grocery store when I shopped during the week.

After lunch, Jeff gave us a tour of the district facilities. Again, I sat in the middle, this time with plenty of legroom, with the truck an automatic. Walter poured himself a cup of coffee from his thermos. We started our drive south of Flagstaff.

"Over there's Lower Lake Mary," Jeff said.

A dry lake bed, with its silty bottom a mosaic of cracks and tall patches of decaying, musty grass on its edges, was holding not one drop of water. Hard for me to imagine it ever held any.

"Well, it's Lower Lake Mary when full," he said, maybe noticing my skepticism.

We continued to another long, narrow lake, this time holding water.

"This is Upper Lake Mary," Jeff said. "It'll only spill over the dam into Lower Lake Mary if over-full. Been dry this year."

We made a circle around a large picnic area with multiple tables and outhouses.

"This one's heavily used by fisherman, not that I would eat anything from this lake." Jeff wrinkled his nose. "Fish here taste funky."

"Can you swim in it?" I asked. So far I hadn't found a lake in Arizona I wanted to get into—I'd been spoiled as a kid by the sandy beaches of Lake Ontario. The murky water and slimy bottoms here gave me the creeps.

Jeff cringed. "I wouldn't."

We swung back onto Lake Mary Road, and soon Jeff again turned off the pavement. "Amherst is a rare natural lake. An improved recreation area with grills, running water, outhouses. No power, though. It's hysterical how some people consider that roughing it," he said with a laugh. "Campground-host-Bob lives here for free. Keeps an eye on everyone. We'll visit him often. He and Charlie are buds."

It was a much bigger campground than the one in Madera. *Might take a full day to rake around all those tables.*

Parked next to a rocky shore also not conducive for swimming, Jeff fished in the pocket of his plaid flannel shirt for a cigarette. Walter poured more coffee and lit a cigarette of his own. The cab filled with smoke, and my eyes watered. I used to put up with this, but not anymore.

"You don't mind if I smoke," Jeff asked with cigarette pressed between lips, "do you?"

I nodded, waving Walter's smoke out of my face. Jeff complied, and returned it to the pack with a frown. "Charlie said you fought fires . . ."

Delighted he brought this up, I expounded on how much I loved the excitement, the prestige. How I'd miss it this summer. Sadness smothered my heart for a few moments, constricting my throat. I missed Florida, the way things were. *Why did everything have to change?* A deep breath. *It'll be okay . . . give it time.*

"Don't worry, you'll like it here," Jeff said. "I've worked for Charlie a long time. You couldn't ask for a better boss."

Our tour continued through dense conifers interspersed with open, grassy meadows. Yellow, purple, and pink nodding wildflowers flourished among the grasses. Clean, cool air and pastoral scenery—no wonder the Coconino attracted big-city dwellers on vacation. How lucky I was to have a job where I could satisfy my "nature fix" simply by going to work.

The scenery changed from pines to water. "This," Jeff said, pulling off to the side of the road, "is Mormon Lake."

*Still not a swimming lake, darn it.* Swells lapped at the muddy, cattail-lined shore; the air fragrant with a mixed bouquet of wet plants, fish, and decay. A few sailboats skimmed across the surface effortlessly, taking advantage of the summer breezes.

"It's the largest natural lake in Arizona," Jeff said, beaming. "When full, it's six hundred acres. It's only ten feet deep, though, so no motorboats allowed." We passed an RV, waving back when a man raised his hand in greeting.

"Campgrounds here and at Pinegrove are the only ones on our district with flush toilets. Luxury, Forest Service style. I don't know about you," Jeff said, "but to me, one other camper means it's too crowded."

Nice to meet someone who shared my camping philosophy, but I felt a bit uneasy. There were at least a dozen campsites here.

We turned at a redwood sign for Kinnikinick Lake Recreation Area. *Another one?* What had I gotten myself into? Over the lake's rough road we bounced, with me gripping the dash, the rear tires struggling for traction. Jeff cursed. "Gutless wonder. I told Charlie not to rent automatics."

My thoughts turned worrisome. "Jeff . . . I have a question."

"Shoot."

"How long does it take to clean all these sites?"

"Oh, about seven days."

*Seven days?* I couldn't say Joe hadn't warned me I wouldn't like this job. This was not what I bargained for, but what could I do?

After a quick look at the last facility, we returned to the station for more orientation.

"Here's where we keep toilet paper, disinfectant, garbage bags," Jeff said, unlocking the supply room. "We keep the door locked so no one will steal the toilet paper. We also lock the outhouse dispensers."

"Isn't stealing TP kind of self-defeating?" I asked, incredulous.

"Oh, just you wait. You'll see just about everything imaginable around here."

That's what I was afraid of.

# TWENTY-SEVEN

AT HOME, I ate dinner in front of the TV, Calley curled up beside me. One thing about Florida—I could always find company whenever I wanted it. "What do you think, kitty? Should I take a class or something?" She purred her reply. I decided to sign up for a welding class at the community college. I'd always admired Joe's welding skills. This would be good for me.

On the first day of class, I arrived early. Three guys scurried in at the last minute, giving me the once-over. A scholarly-attired man dashed in, smiling. Four faces smiled back.

"There probably aren't enough of you to make the class a go," the instructor said, "but since you're here, I'll teach you as much as I can."

A woman in a welding class didn't faze him, and in no time, I'd welded my first piece. Fun—no wonder Joe liked to do this. With hopes high that somehow the class would continue, I returned the next week, but the note on the door said: "Class cancelled." It was too late to sign up for something else. *Rats.*

On Monday, I arrived at work to find everyone gossiping about a break-in over the weekend. What in the world would anyone want to steal? It wasn't like we had a safe full of cash.

"It's a real puzzle," Charlie said. "As far as we can tell they didn't take nothin'." With a thoughtful expression, he stared at the ceiling. "Funny thing, though. An amateur job. Made a mess with a cutting torch tryin' to get into the garage." A big grin spread across his face. "You know, it fits the M.O. of someone who might've taken just *one* welding class."

It took me a moment. "You don't think *I* did this do you?" Would I need to defend my whereabouts over the weekend?

"So. What *were* you up to this weekend?" Jeff asked, squelching a smile.

"I did *not* break into the office!" Although I laughed, they had me going there for a minute. They continued to whoop it up all the way to the trucks. Typical guys. But I didn't mind. Guys tease people they like.

On the way home, I stopped at the trailer park's office to collect my mail. My mom had written, but there was nothing from Joe. Disappointed, I hoped for a letter from him tomorrow.

ALTHOUGH I LIKED my coworkers, this job wasn't what I wanted. What to do . . . ? I wanted to fight fire. Could I ask, and not offend Charlie? I decided to go for it.

His eyes grew huge. "Whoa, I'll check, but I've never seen a woman on the hotshots."

That didn't sound promising.

Charlie had an answer the following day. "The foreman made some lame excuse why he won't let you . . . but, well . . . I've never experienced racism in the Forest Service, but being black has affected me in other ways, so I get how you feel. And, if you really want to fight fires, I'll do what I can, hotshot crew or not."

While I appreciated Charlie's offer, I wondered if I should file an EEO complaint. Then I remembered what had happened the last time with Frank. I had no support then, and couldn't trust I'd have any here. *Forget it.*

ANOTHER BUSY MORNING loading our trucks with the tools of the trade: disinfectant, garbage bags, toilet paper, rubber gloves, and foil pouches of the Forest Service's industrial deodorizer, which we poured down the holes of outhouses. The first time I emptied a package into the toilet, the updraft spewed it back into my face. Later, when I blew my nose, the tissue turned blue. Were my lungs blue, too? The experience was scary enough that I decided to wear a mask.

Amidst our activity, the hotshots gathered for their morning workout. I'd checked out the fitness trail they used in back. It was shady, with an easy-on-the-feet cinder track and a dozen exercise stations. I wanted to stay fit and keep my Red Card current, so I decided to ask Charlie later if I could use it.

Workday over, the hotshot bus parked next to us and the crew spilled out. I smiled and said hello. Not one returned my greeting. Embarrassed, I turned away. What in the world had I ever done to them?

"What's with those guys?" I asked Jeff, as we tossed bulging garbage bags into the dumpster.

He snickered. "They think they're too cool for the likes of us rec-techs."

"But, Jeff," I said, "there has to be more to it than that."

He shrugged.

Were they annoyed I dared ask to be on their crew? Now I wanted to use their fitness trail even more.

"Whoa, girl!" Charlie said, when I asked for permission. "You really *are* serious about this firefighting gig, aren't you? I don't care, but you'd better check with the crew foreman. It's kinda theirs."

Positive that the foreman noticed me waiting for him to finish his conversation, my jaw dropped when he turned to leave without so much as a glance my way. I called out his name, and he stopped. I managed to stay civil, despite feeling otherwise. "May I use the fitness trail after work?"

Lips tight, stare icy, he looked to be considering saying "no," but he couldn't think of a good enough reason. "Well. I guess. Just don't use it when my guys are."

"Okay, thanks. I won't." I gave him my best phony smile, thinking, *You're not God's gift to the Forest Service. Jerk.*

Incredulous that I wanted to exercise after working all day, my crew called me nuts when I changed into the shorts, T-shirt, and sneakers I'd brought with me. I laughed them off; but it tickled me that they hung around just long enough to see me change clothes. Men.

BY THE SECOND week, we had our cleaning routine down pat. I pulled up to the first outhouse on our circuit. Jeff ducked inside to remove the toilet paper so it wouldn't get wet.

"Whoa, Nellie!" he said, pinching his nose. "This is a ripe one. Get me a shovel."

Disgusting. No matter how hard we tried to keep outhouses clean, someone always refused to sit on the toilet seat. You'd think they were afraid they'd fall in.

Walter perched his cup of coffee on the tailgate and started the pump on the truck, while I unrolled a hose and dragged it over. Jeff held the door open and turned his head. "Let 'er rip!" With the nozzle on full blast, I sprayed the interior with disinfectant, its pine scent strong enough to knock down both me and E-coli. On to the next one. There, Jeff produced a wadded-up baby diaper held between two gloved fingers. "They stuck it behind the door. Better than down the hole, though. Plugs up the shit-suckers."

A crappy job required a good sense of humor. Jeff's huge repertoire of recreation jokes kept us in stitches so much of the day, you'd think we loved cleaning outhouses.

"WANT SOME OVERTIME?" Charlie asked me Friday morning. *Extra money?* "You bet I do."

"Aren't ya gonna even ask what you'll do?" he asked, chuckling.

"Okay, so what will I be doing?" I said, knowing I'd still say yes.

"Timber crew's got a Semi full of baby pine trees that need planting ASAP." Something besides cleaning outhouses. Let's go.

Although the timber crew shared the same office as us recreation folks, they were rather elusive, usually in the field by the time I arrived at work. I wondered about their job. What did timber crews do all day?

"Let's go talk to Jonas," Charlie said, rising from his chair.

Charlie introduced me to a cute coal-haired Ken-doll. His clear, blue eyes met mine for a moment, and he flashed a smile. My eyes gravitated to his left hand: no ring. How could this guy not be married? We exchanged pleasantries, and he said I should report Saturday morning at five a.m.

Brrr . . . it was downright cold at four-forty-five a.m., even dressed in three layers against the mountain chill. Hard to believe that later in the day I'd peel off all but one layer.

Jonas and I drove for an hour, got tossed around on a rutted logging road for another hour, arriving at the clear-cut harvest site about seven. Sadly, where a once great forest of tall pines had stood, were remnant stumps and orphaned pine boughs. In the process of dragging trees to waiting trucks, all understory plants were trampled into oblivion. One cleared area had been plowed into deep, reddish-brown furrows, fragrant with freshly turned soil. I took solace in the fact I'd be planting a new generation of pines.

"You'll be working with Ned, here," Jonas said, addressing the man of Navajo descent. I smiled and extended my hand. Ned offered a hint of a smile and a limp handshake. Jonas drove away, leaving me to my planting duty. *Darn.* I'd hoped he would stick around.

Ned asked, "Ever plant?"

I shook my head "no," not sure if he meant plant trees by hand or by machine, not that it mattered. I'd never planted trees before, period.

Ned motioned for me to follow him.

*Might as well be social.* "So, what's it like working on a timber crew?" I asked.

Ned gave me another meager smile, but said nothing. At this point, I assumed he didn't understand English very well.

Ned pointed at a trailer of sorts. "Tree. Plant. Machine."

Picture a low truck bed with a roof. Inside, a metal tractor seat faced a tiny Ferris wheel coming up through the floor. Ned motioned for me to climb inside.

*You want me to get inside this?* Self-conscious, I feared I'd look ridiculous towed behind the truck in this buggy-like contraption. Good thing Jonas left after all. I sat down with the wheel between my legs, facing backwards. Ned pointed to an open burlap sack behind the seat, filled with skinny little ponderosa pine seedlings—essentially a stem with needles and hairy roots.

"Place here," he said, indicating the clamps on the wheel.

I figured asking for further details might make him uncomfortable, so I just nodded. How hard could it be?

Ned watched from the sidelines as the driver started up the truck and drove down the first row, towing me behind. The planter rode furrows hard, tossing me from side to side, jarring my teeth when it hit a berm sideways. Dust churned and rolled, smothering me in a thick cloud. Loud squeals and squeaks hurt my ears, and I regretted I hadn't thought to bring ear plugs. All the while, the Ferris wheel turned, presenting me with open jaws, like begging baby birds. It took me a moment to focus. *Oh! I need trees!* I turned and grabbed a handful of seedlings, fumbling to untangle their roots. I managed to get one seedling free, then another, but the wheel was turning way too fast. I finally managed to stick one upright in a clamp, then one more, and one more—trying to find a rhythm to the madness. Movement caught my eye: Ned—jumping up and down, arms waving, yelling something—but I couldn't hear him. I turned from him to view the row I'd just planted. Roots, not tree tops, stuck out of the ground. I'd planted the trees upside down! Doubled over with laughter, tears streaming down my cheeks, I pointed at what I'd done. Hiccups prevented me from catching my breath to reply, so I nodded vigorously to assure Ned that I understood. I solved the problem by reversing placement, but Ned still watched me like a hawk.

An hour later, the silly image of upside down trees popped into my head again. Once I started giggling, I couldn't stop, tears running down my cheeks, blurring my vision.

Ten hours later my tail bone ached from the metal seat, my ears rang, and my whole body vibrated—even after I got out of the contraption. Ears still ringing, I rode with Ned back to the station, and then walked home, frazzled, exhausted, and still vibrating. I opted for a shower before dinner, taking off clothes so filthy that I left a trail of dirt all the way to the bathroom. I stared in the mirror: my face looked like I'd been doused with a bucket of water, followed by a shovelful of dirt—worse even than a week on a fireline.

The following Saturday, I endured more of the same. Weary, I trudged home, stopping by the trailer park office. Still no mail—but in my driveway sat Joe's gray Chevy—with Joe sitting on my steps! My arms wrapped tight around his neck, squeezing tighter just to make sure he was real.

"I've missed you so much," he said, squeezing me back.

In bed that night, I thought about how comfortable we were with each other. But, maybe, too comfortable? Was that a bad thing? I missed the romance and excitement we used to have. Was this what marriage would be like? If so, I wasn't sure I liked the idea.

Joe left in the morning, and I went back to tree planting. Ned never did say more than hello the entire month I worked with him, but he did finally trust me to plant trees right side up.

TREES PLANTED, I was back to a forty-hour workweek, which seemed strangely short after working several sixty-four hour weeks. But those fat paychecks made it worth every layer of dirt, a sore posterior, and ringing ears . . . times ten.

Somehow, we managed to get ahead on campground cleaning, so Charlie found other chores for us to do: fixing broken signs, slapping redwood stain on posts, and assembling outhouse kits. These tickled me. Who knew they came in a kit? Leave it to Jeff to have us in stitches during assembly, commenting that the "new car" smell would soon be gone forever.

A week later, volunteers from the Young Adult Conservation Corps (YACC) came to help for a day.

"How am I going to keep these yaks busy?" Charlie asked when we gathered around his desk. "Mormon Lake Trail needs work, but I don't know anything about trail maintenance. Do any of you?"

Bingo. "I spent eight weeks on a trail crew last summer," I said.

He beamed. I beamed. Another day of no outhouses.

Charlie said I would supervise "some" teens. When I met their bus at the trail head parking lot, and they filed off nonstop, I felt a ping of self-doubt. Twenty? Could I do this? Charlie thought I could. I paused to think: *Make the large group manageable. Assign teams.*

"Drag them out of sight when you're done," I told the strong-armed older kids who were sawing overhanging limbs.

"Dig out the toe-trippers," I told the team of sturdy boys and girls. Their enthusiastic activity raised clouds of dust and tools chinked against rocks. Talk and laughter accompanied their work—boys flirting and girls giggling.

I noticed some trail erosion. "Go get some flat rocks and I'll show you how to build a water bar," I said to a team.

They scattered to accomplish the mission. How satisfying it was to watch them have as much fun as I did on trail. At the end of the day, their faces glowed with sweat and pride for a job well done. Mine, too.

In the morning, Charlie walked the trail with me. "Good job, Linda. This looks great." At that moment, my not-quite-what-I-had-in-mind job felt quite worthwhile.

A few days later, Charlie made me suspicious when he placed fishing poles in the back of our truck.

"We're going fishin'," he said, grinning.

Jeff scowled. "Fishing? What are you up to Charlie?"

I didn't trust the way-too-wide grin on Charlie's face, either.

"Oh nothin', nothin'. I'm just gonna take you guys fishing."

An hour later we pulled up alongside a pond. A vile stench rose like steam from a hot spring. This "pond" was a sewage treatment lagoon.

Before we could utter a word, Charlie said, "I need you to fish out all the plastic bags, Pampers, and soda cans."

I so wanted to believe that at any moment, he'd bust out laughing and tell us it was all a practical joke. But he didn't.

"Oh, Charlie." Jeff's eyebrows pinched together. "You're gonna owe us big time for making us do this. You are staying to help, aren't you?"

Charlie hopped into his truck. "Tee-hee-hee. Nope. Got things to do. Toodles!" And off he went.

Jeff, Walter, and Hutch cast lines to snag the putrid trash, I held plastic bags open for them to deposit each disgusting, brown sludge-covered item. Although I wore industrial strength rubber gloves, I feared catching some despicable disease. I tried breathing only through my mouth, but that's hard to do for very long. Walter kept up with his many coffee breaks. How could he stand to do that? On the way back, we schemed and plotted our revenge. Charlie owed us, big time.

All my clothes went into the wash. Should I disinfect them? Should I disinfect me? I ran the hottest water I could stand and used so much soap I stood in a sea of suds.

Thank goodness back to normal chores the next day—which, compared to our fishing task, now seemed far less odious. Jeff and Hutch drove off. Walter watched them, turned to me, and complained that he never got to drive. At that moment, I forgot why I hadn't let him drive before, so I turned over the keys. No sooner had we hit the winding Lake Mary Road, did Walter turn to reach behind the seat for his thermos.

*Oh yeah, that's why.* "Let me get that." I said.

"Nah, I got it."

My alarm grew as I watched him hold the steering wheel with his knees, open the thermos, and, cup in one hand, thermos in the other, pour his coffee. My eyes darted from him, to the road, to oncoming traffic. Positive he'd run us into the ditch or cause a head-on collision, I braced myself with a hand on the dash. An upcoming S-curve was more than I could handle, though, and I reached for the wheel.

Defensive, he scowled at me. "I got it, Linda, quit worrying so much."

Coffee poured and thermos put away, Walter put one hand on the wheel and sipped. "See, I told you I could manage."

Gripping the armrest with leftover terror, I decided from now on I'd do the driving no matter how much he complained, to save not only my life, but everyone else's.

We managed to get in a few hours of work before a monsoon downpour sent us seeking refuge with Bob-the-campground-host at Amherst Lake. A wiry, withered old man with yellow teeth, tobacco-stained fingers, and a rattling smoker's cough—Bob could've easily been a poster child for an anti-tobacco campaign. Squeezed together at his tiny kitchen table, everyone but Hutch and I lit cigarettes. I coughed and waved my hand, but they ignored me. I thought about sitting in the truck, but I wanted to hear Bob and Charlie's hilarious stories about crazy summer visitors. Nobody could make this stuff up. But after a half-hour, feeling headachy and choking on the fumes from four chain-smokers, I had to leave.

Seated in our truck, I stared out the windshield at scenery blurred by sheets of rain. No book, no radio, and no fun. The passenger door flew open and Hutch jumped in.

"I don't like the smoke either." He wiped rain from his face. "You're the first to ever protest." He opened the glove box and produced a deck of cards. "Poker?"

At least it passed the time; but I could hear hearty laughs coming from Bob's trailer. I didn't like paying the price of feeling left out simply because I didn't want to suffocate from second-hand smoke.

When my mom pulled into my driveway Saturday, I dashed out to hug her. This was a big deal: her first road trip alone, and our first weekend together with just the two of us. We explored Wupatki National Monument, an Anasazi ruin, stared into the humbling Sunset Crater and ate tuna sandwiches under a park ramada. As I waved goodbye Sunday morning, homesickness tugged hard at my heart for the first time in a while. Lonesome, I decided to check my mail. Not a darned thing. Dejected, I went to bed early. My tiny trailer felt empty—missing both my mom and Joe.


MORNING ROUTINE: RALLY around Charlie's desk, check whether anything new was on the agenda, and go load our trucks. I was about to leave, when Charlie asked me to stay a minute. Jeff and Hutch glanced at Charlie, then at me. I shrugged; I didn't know what was up either. They left.

"Want to go on a project fire?" Charlie asked.

# TWENTY-EIGHT

"A FIRE? WHERE?" My mind raced in circles. I'd have to get a fire pack together, get a neighbor to feed Calley . . .

Charlie put up his hand. "Hold yer horses. They're looking for timekeepers in Montana."

The bottom fell out of my enthusiasm. *Timekeeper.*

"Hey, it's a chance to get outta here, make some overtime."

*And no outhouse cleaning.* "Okay."

My first fire without a crew—this would be different. At the Flagstaff airport, I boarded a Cessna and made brief conversation with a woman from another district. In Missoula, I took a seat on the bus and people watched. A twenty-something brunette just couldn't sit still, leaning over the back of her seat to talk to the people behind her, walking up and down the aisle, chatting with almost everyone. I've no idea why she fed my insecurity. Why couldn't I be outgoing like her? One of those people that everyone admired . . . didn't they?

Just outside of town, smoky haze turned the sun burnt-orange, and I felt that twinge: I wanted to fight the fire, not be a timekeeper.

Once at fire camp, resigned, I stood in front of a long table where women flipped through lists. More women sat at tables in the back, shuffling papers.

"Who are you, where are you from, and what's your assignment?" a woman asked, her tone clipped. I told her.

"Timekeeper? You're here as a timekeeper? Who the hell requested more timekeepers?" she asked over her shoulder.

A voice from the back said, "I haven't a clue. As far as I know, we have plenty."

An awkward moment passed. Without even looking up, the woman said to me, "We'll get you if we need you. Next."

I gulped. *Now what do I do?* A touch on my elbow made me turn.

"Don't mind her, she's overwhelmed," a kind-faced woman said. "Follow me, hon, and I'll get you settled."

Abandoned in a tent with no work and not so much as a book to read, an hour later I decided I couldn't just sit there. I returned to ask the same flustered woman if anything had come up. She snipped an impatient "no."

I wandered over to the mess tent, grabbed a sandwich, and sat alone. Two men talked loudly at the next table. One complained about being short-handed on the fireline, the other, about timing of relief crews. I debated. Should I say something? Why not? Be proactive. It was crazy to sit here and do nothing. I summoned up a considerable amount of courage.

"Excuse me. I'm Red Carded, and more than willing to work on the line if you need me."

Dead silence. One raised his eyebrows, reared back, and said, "Uh, no, we don't need anyone."

Humiliating. *Oh, God, I'll never do that again.*

Two days later I returned to Flagstaff. Charlie waited until everyone left to ask me what happened.

"It was awful, Charlie," I said.

"So, they didn't need any timekeepers, or what?"

"Not only that, but they didn't give me anything to do."

Charlie frowned. "We got our hands slapped for sending you where you weren't needed. Also, word is you asked to get on a fire crew."

*What?* Those men had actually said something to my district? That knocked the wind out of me. Why was my asking so wrong?

Charlie's mouth set in a hard line. "An official in Missoula told our office that you had no timekeeping experience, and that you sat around and did nothing."

This was beyond ludicrous. "Charlie, that's an out and out lie. You *know* I have timekeeping experience and I *pleaded* for something to do."

"Look, I'm sorry it all happened," he said. "For what it's worth, I'm on your side, but there's something else I think you should know . . ."

*What in the world is going on here?*

"Our district knows that you registered an EEO complaint on the Coronado," he said, his eyes lowered and his voice low. "They think you're a troublemaker, and . . ."

Words continued to tumble from his mouth, but what registered was, " . . . you're blacklisted from working in fire on the Coconino."

Every muscle in my body cinched tight. Blacklisted. EEO complaint. A troublemaker? *Me?* I blew up. "That's confidential information! How'd they find out?"

Charlie lowered and shook his head.

I jerked to my feet and stormed out. My boots pounded pavement, my tears flowed. *Would I lose my job over this? That's not fair!* I flung open the trailer door, fell onto the couch, and buried my face in a pillow. My sister Elaine, there on a visit, sat down next to me and asked what was wrong.

"I can't believe this place. I've been blacklisted," I said through heaving sobs.

Elaine listened to my story. "Why do you put up with this?"

My breath hitched. "Because I love my job. But why does it have to be so hard?"

She shook her head, sympathetic, but I sensed she didn't understand why I *did* put up with it. At that moment, I didn't either.

"You look really bummed out," Jeff said the next morning. He started to speak, paused, reconsidered, then said, "You should know, in case you try to apply for the hotshots here, they think you filed an EEO complaint against them."

I went ballistic. "Bullshit! I did not!"

Poor Jeff. He didn't know what to say. I wanted to quit that very moment, but then what? Here I thought what had happened on the Coronado wouldn't happen anywhere else. How stupid was that? What a way to start out the day.

Mid-morning, Charlie met Jeff and I at Pinegrove campground. They disappeared together, while I went about gathering supplies for the restrooms. A middle-aged couple dashed up to me, their faces flushed and concerned.

"Quick . . . over there," the man said, panting. "There's a fire!"

I stared where he pointed. No smoke. "How big?"

The woman wheezed, bent over with hands on knees. "An old log . . ."

There was no sign of Charlie, who carried the only radio. I grabbed a shovel. "Show me."

On the side of a hiking trail, a rotten, downed tree was indeed on fire. Confident I could manage, I smothered flames with dirt and scraped a line around it. Within minutes, it was contained. I thanked the people for the alert and tracked down Charlie.

"Is it out?" he asked, reaching for the radio on his belt.

"I think so. But it wouldn't hurt to have someone dump water on it."

Part of me wondered if I would get in trouble for putting the fire out by myself. The other part didn't care.


LATE SEPTEMBER, I escaped to experience the fall colors. A side road showed promise; I parked and entered an aspen grove. My favorite way to enjoy aspens? On my back, staring through the twittering, bright yellow leaves to a deep blue sky. Total autumnal immersion—there was nothing like it.

Joe arrived for a short visit. Up all night, we had a serious talk about my doubts, our problems, and how we'd resolve them. Would all be good now? It seemed so. We made plans to live together again after layoffs.

Performance reviews always gave me the jitters. Not sure why: Glenn had always checked the "satisfactory" boxes, and I never got a peek at anyone else's. I sat at Charlie's desk, prepared for a similar report. However, out of the seven categories, he'd checked four "excellent" and three "very good." It was tough for me to accept praise, but this felt great.

"You did good this summer," he said, his smile as genuine as they come. "I'm guessing you won't be back."

It was nice to be appreciated. But . . . "I want to be a firefighter."

Charlie still didn't get this, but I didn't mind. Years later, I'd still remember what Jeff said about him being a great boss, and I'd still wholeheartedly agree.

I left Charlie's office glowing with pride. I hopped into the truck with crazy-driver-Walter, who unfortunately had the wheel. In a good mood, I decided what the heck, let him drive.

"So how'd you do?" he asked.

"I got four excellents!"

Walter's smile faded. "No shit? Huh. Guess I would've gotten a better score if *I* had boobs."

That comment stung like raw whiskey.

Walter steered the truck out of the complex; I sat deep in thought. He deserved a bad review. C'mon . . . *two* accidents with a government truck? Wasn't that grounds for firing? Still, I replayed his nasty comment in my head all day. Wounded, I wondered if the others felt the same way about me.

At day's end I didn't even say goodbye to anyone before I left. A stack of empty boxes sat in my living room; I'd planned to leave Flagstaff in the morning. *Screw it.* In record time, I packed and hit the road by eight. Driving south on I-17, I played out the horrible day. *So what if they blacklisted me? I don't want to work on the Coconino again anyway. Jerks.* I'd have to find someplace else to work—where men didn't give me a hard time. For certain I wasn't going to give up.


JOE AND I rented a cabin in Madera Canyon for the winter. I took on landscaping jobs to tide me over. My clients loved hiring a woman: I knew this because they told me so. It seemed that not too many guys showed up on time, or, in some cases, at all. I always arrived early and did meticulous work.

In early November, I opened a letter from my mom. Inside, she'd tucked a newspaper clipping. I read her letter first, until I got to, "Isn't this Roy?" I unfolded the clipping and read it. Twice. The obituary was indeed Roy's: suicide at the age of twenty-three. Everything in the room blurred—my knees buckled, and I sank to the floor, crying in heaving sobs. *Noooooo . . .*

"Roy died," I said, my voice shaky, when Joe came home for lunch.

"Who?"

I reminded him. Joe didn't say a word. Granted, maybe he didn't know what to say—but I needed a shoulder to cry on; after all, I'd lost someone

I'd been close to. But his body language told me that wasn't an option. After lunch, thinking I needed to explain why Roy's death had hit me so hard, I said, "I used to love Roy as much as I love you now." He turned to glance at me and walked away.

On the couch, with knees drawn to my chest, I wrapped my arms around them and let the tears fall. Roy and I were *really* over now—not that I thought we weren't—but I guess I always thought I'd see him again someday. What tore at my heart was why Roy hadn't reached out to me if he was that depressed. Could I have done something to save him if he had?

RAW EMOTIONS EASED after a few days, although I never shared them with Joe again. Now I had an important decision to make: where should I apply for next summer? Should I try for BLM again, or stick with the Forest Service? Sick of the sexist comments and discrimination, I thought that BLM might be a better choice. Plus, the odds of getting picked up by BLM in Alaska were good: they offered more fire positions there than in any other state. In high school, I'd toyed with the idea of homesteading in Alaska, and then going there with Roy. While I'd since dropped the notion of living off the land, I still wanted to see Alaska. Therefore, just like last year, I applied to BLM and the Forest Service, and began the long wait.

IT WAS A lovely spring day, with cottonwoods budding a hint of bright green leaves to come. I'd already run the Nature Trail and would go to work soon.

"Breakfast is ready," I called to Joe.

"Are you going up to see your parents?" I asked, setting a plate of eggs in front of him.

"Yeah, be back later." He patted my rear.

Joe kissed me goodbye and started up his truck. From the window, I watched him pull away, only to stop, jump out, and run back in.

"What'd you forget?"

"My watch."

That's when I noticed his truck, moving on its own, heading right for a tree.

"Joe! Your truck!"

Too late; it bashed into the tree, denting the fender. He ran out, shut the engine off, and stormed back inside.

"Damn it, you stupid idiot," he yelled, punching and swinging at the air.

"Oh, I'm so sorry! It'll be okay, it's not that bad," I said, stepping close to give him a hug.

With both hands, he gave me a powerful shove, sending me flying backward. I hit the floor, hard, and sat there, stunned. He continued railing, chastising himself for being stupid. With my heart pounding and body trembling, I stood up while his tirade continued. Frightened by the thought of what else he might do, I threw some clothes into a suitcase, snatched up Calley, and left. I didn't think he even noticed, his rage was so blind.

Five miles down the road, I parked, sobbed, and trembled. *Why did he do that?* I'd only tried to hug him. Cried out, I wiped tears from my face and blew my nose. If I didn't go back and deal with him, I'd have to move back home with my parents. If I left, it would be for good. *Is that what I want? No, I love him.* Maybe my leaving had taught him a lesson, made him realize that he could lose me. I didn't believe he'd want that. After all, he loved me. I turned my car around.

When I lugged my suitcase into the house, he sat in the living room, his face still contorted with anger. He glared at me as I walked by. Reluctant to make a scene, I avoided him for the rest of the day. By evening, he acted like nothing had happened. My inner voice and I argued in an endless loop: You should leave. *No one else has loved me so much.* You shouldn't have intervened when he was so angry. *I'll do better next time.*

# TWENTY-NINE

## Summer of 1980: Wildwood Station, Kenai, Alaska

TWO JOB OFFERS came in the same week. How often does that happen?

Each time, I ripped open the envelope, thinking, *Where to? Where to?*

The first one was on the Coronado National Forest: tanker crew, at Columbine Work Center, in the Pinaleño Mountains, a glorious alpine forest one hundred miles northeast of Tucson. An unexpected, but tantalizing offer; only because I'd forgotten about this isolated gem. What made me pause? Tanker crew. Not my idea of the perfect fire suppression job. I wanted to be on the ground, digging line at the fire's edge, not driving around depending on water and truck access to put out flames.

Then the really exciting one: Bureau of Land Management, tanker and Helitack crew combined, on the Kenai Peninsula, Alaska. Same pay rate, but it included a ten-percent per diem increase on top of base salary. Again, a tanker crew, though. But we're talking Alaska here. The Last Frontier.

I made a list of pros and cons for each job, including the plane ticket expense. But it was a total waste of time. I knew what I wanted. I wanted to go to Alaska.

The letter said to call the head of Wildwood Station. My hands shook when I lifted the receiver to dial.

Gruff and curt, the man said, "You do realize that you have to pay your own way up here."

"Of course." *Does he really think I'd assume BLM would pick up the tab?*

"Kenai's two hours by bus from Anchorage," he said. "Best to use the local commuter plane. Takes only thirty minutes."

After discussing a few more particulars and learning my report date, I hung up. My hand rested on the receiver. *I'm going to Alaska!* Who to call first? My parents weren't home. I'd need to see if they would take Calley for the summer. My best friend Gail didn't answer either. Joe would be home from Florida soon. I paced, checking the clock in anticipation of his coming through the door. Seven o'clock, I called the station. Maybe they had a fire.

Pete answered, drunk, with loud music and voices in the background. "Yeah, he's here."

Again, Joe had left me out of another impromptu party. Those were my friends too, or so I thought. Maybe not anymore. Ever since I no longer worked at Florida—not by choice, which still hurt—no one who I'd considered a friend, or even the man I loved, ever asked me to join them. It was as though I ceased to exist. When Joe came home, late, we revisited that old argument.

"It never occurred to me to call you," he said, shrugging.

That always stung. I'd gone from coworker to girlfriend to nobody important. Did he not want me there? I loved Joe, and thought he loved me, too, but I didn't understand why he treated me this way. Well, I wanted to go explore a new place, get away from here. Maybe we weren't right together. Maybe I wouldn't live with him again when the summer was over. I began planning my trip.


WHAT TO PACK? For a cold and wet climate, I'd need my down vest, thermal underwear, and rain gear. Skip bringing shorts or sleeveless tops. And, time to face a reality I didn't want to face: mosquitoes. Who hadn't heard how huge, numerous, and voracious they were up there? My childhood was spent in mosquito-land Syracuse. The blood-suckers ate me alive. One friend insisted that vitamin B-12 kept them away, and another suggested garlic tablets. Willing to try anything, I bought both.

At daybreak on April fourteenth, my plane circled west over the Tucson Mountains, their shadows stretching for miles across the desert floor. Circling back again, I glimpsed the Santa Rita Mountains and felt a heart tug. Last, we flew past the Santa Catalinas, where I'd first met the hotshots. With a touch of unexpected sadness, I thought, *Goodbye, Arizona, see you later.*

Not a seasoned traveler by any means, I worried about the forty-five minutes between flights in Seattle, and whether I'd make it to Anchorage in time to catch the connecting commuter service to Kenai. In Seattle, I silently urged my fellow passengers to hurry up and get off the plane. I tore through the terminal and reached my gate as the last person boarded. I couldn't imagine how my luggage would have made it on the plane when I barely did, but there wasn't a thing I could do about it now.

My luggage did make it to Anchorage, but how could I possibly carry a backpack, large suitcase, duffle bag, small carry-on, camera case, and my purse? A man in a uniform came to the rescue and loaded my bags onto a dolly. We walked and walked, through seemingly endless waiting areas filled with weary passengers and families with crying, whining children. The crowds thinned. *Where the heck is he taking me?* A news headline flashed through my mind: *"Woman Abducted by Man Posing as Airport Employee."* When I saw the sign for the commuter service, I was relieved to be able to send him on his way. After unloading my bags at the ticket counter, he extended his hand, palm up. I stared at it, drawing a blank. What did he want? *Oh! A tip.* Oops.

All I'd brought were traveler's checks. He frowned and walked away. The man behind the counter seemed amused by the transaction. Not particularly amused myself, I asked him if the last plane had left for Kenai.

"Nope. That'll be sixty dollars," he said, containing a smirk.

Luggage stacked around me, I sat in a torturous orange plastic chair along with a half-dozen others, in the tiny, cold, drafty waiting room. I huddled in an effort to stay warm. It reminded me of the derelict Phoenix bus station, although much, much colder.

A half hour *after* the scheduled departure time, I wondered if I'd boarded the wrong plane: vinyl seats, cracked and peeled like a bad sunburn, windows fogged with scratches, threadbare carpet—more like a cargo plane than one for paying passengers. Plus, compared to the refrigerator waiting room, I now sat in a freezer. *Oh my God, I can see light coming in from outside!* Wide-eyed and apprehensive, I waited for a flight attendant's reassurance. But no, there were just us passengers on this low-budget ride. As the plane taxied to the runway, the pilot spoke over the loudspeaker. "Fasten your seat belts. Life preservers are under your seat. Thank you for flying with us."

Life preservers? Why in the world would we need those? I gripped the armrest. Propellers gathered speed, the plane rattling like loose fenders on an old pickup. A loud bang and thump under my feet startled me. *What was that?* I clung to the armrest, afraid to let go. Ten minutes later, I relaxed and decided we weren't going to fall out of the sky. I struggled to peer out my teeny window, where the formidable steel-gray Cook Inlet spanned for miles. Now I understood the life preservers, but my inner voice told me there'd be no survivors if the plane crashed into that arctic water.

Relieved to have arrived in one piece with all of my belongings, I huddled outside at a payphone and called the station, then sat down on a bench to wait. Snow fell, people scurried by in down coats, wool hats, mittens, and practical knit scarves. A white BLM van pulled up to the curb, and a guy in red high-top Keds bounced out.

"Hey, you must be Linda," he said, dancing a jig as though trying to stay warm. We shook hands and tossed my gear in back, snowflakes dusting my shoulders and hair.

Kenai's main street, lined with strip malls, gas stations, and grocery stores, could have been anywhere USA—except it was only seventy-seven feet above sea level. Two frosty mountains rose above the Cook Inlet like white Egyptian pyramids.

"So you braved the commuter plane," said my driver, Aaron, fingers tapping on the steering wheel.

*Bravery was necessary?*

Aaron laughed heartily. "Oh, man, locals don't use those puddle jumpers unless they have to. They're notorious for breaking down and getting in trouble with the FAA."

Okay, not a good first impression of my supervisor, who'd told me to take the commuter plane no local would use. Then I met the guy in person, and my impression worsened. He sported a wild beard, which connected to the bristly chest hair emerging from the open collar of his shirt. His bushy eyebrows didn't quite hide the furrows between his eyes, formed by a permanent scowl. His thick down vest, worn over a plaid, quilted flannel shirt, added bulk to his already-stout frame. He looked like a black bear in clothes. And the first words out of his mouth?

"You'll have to cut your hair. It's a fire hazard."

*Uh* . . . I stared at him, speechless. Could he make me do this? *No damn way.* In a voice braver than I felt, I said, "I always wear my hair braided and pinned up at work. My hair length has never been an issue anywhere else."

He puffed out his chest. "Well, I take issue with it."

Despite his intimidation attempt, I stood my ground. "I'm *not* cutting my hair."

He huffed. "Aaron will take you to your quarters."

Stand-off over. If I'd made a mistake coming here, there was no turning back now.

Aaron delivered me to one of the retired Air Force Base houses on the second block, identical to the ones on the first block. In fact, I worried about finding my place after I went out. The houses didn't even have numbers. *All the houses made of ticky-tacky, and they all looked just the same.* At the plain, white house, void of landscaping, or even a curtain in the window, the flat, sodden grass, muddy brown spots and dingy patches of snow, depicted a thaw in process. It brought back memories of early spring in Syracuse, lacking my mom's daffodils, tulips, and fragrant hyacinths, though. Snow flurries continued to spit like the dead of winter in New York. I was puzzled. Why hire fire crews now?

"So . . . when does it warm up around here?" I asked, following the bouncing Aaron up the sidewalk, toting half of my luggage.

Aaron turned, thoughtful. "Hmmm . . . July?"

*July?* I didn't bring enough warm clothes.

Aaron unlocked the door. "Take any room you want, you're the first one here."

It had always served me well to be first.

In the foyer, I faced a closed door. Curious, I opened it. Steep steps led into a dark basement, smelling of damp concrete. Basements always gave me the creeps—a childhood thing. I shut the door and moved on. To my left, a bright kitchen with modern appliances connected to a small dining room. The living room was sparsely furnished with a teal couch and two plush armchairs upholstered in camel velveteen. A rickety coffee table held a few magazines. Up the staircase were the bedrooms, where, just as Goldilocks did, I picked the one that was "just right." A steam radiator under the window filled the room with warm, moist air, which smelled suspiciously of wet dog.

Unpacking took all of fifteen minutes. What to do with the two hours before dinner? For the first time since I'd left, I was hungry. *Where* would I eat dinner? I considered exploring, but it was so bitterly cold out there. A woman's voice floated up from below.

"Hello?"

I trotted downstairs.

A cherub-faced woman straightened after setting down a huge suitcase. She smiled and extended a pink, chubby hand. "I'm Teresa."

We chatted, and I learned she'd work in administration. She struck me as a bit naïve, like someone fresh out of high school, which she was.

"We can get dinner at the cafeteria. Anyone tell you how it works?" she asked.

I'd planned on buying groceries, but let her explain.

"Just sign in before you eat, and they'll deduct four dollars from your paycheck. It's a pretty good deal. That being said, I'm cooking for myself." She tugged at the waistline of her jeans. "I'm on a diet. I eat grapefruit all day except for dinner, when I can have anything I want!"

I nodded politely, but thought, *Who'd want to eat grapefruit all day?*

She went to unpack.

Bored, I decided to venture out into the deep-freeze and check out the grocery store. I strolled down the aisles and priced various foods. Sticker-shocked, I left without making a single purchase. Everything here cost triple what it cost in Tucson. I couldn't afford to do that. Cafeteria food would have to do.

Wide awake before daylight, I stared at the ceiling, apprehensive. It'd been over a year since I fought fire. *Could I still do this? What if my crew had more experience than me? Would I fit in? Would they like me? Oh, just get up and go to work.*

After breakfast, I reported to the single story building, typical of city firehouses, with two extra-large garage doors to accommodate fire engines. These doors gaped wide open, so I walked into a bay, where I met a tall, slender man standing in front of a locker. Dark, curly hair extended below his wool cap, his face scruffy with week-old stubble.

"Hey, you must be Linda." He reached out to shake my hand. "I'm Rob. You're on my crew. Have you met the others?"

"No, just our boss."

I followed Rob past a window, where The Bear sat at his desk. At the back of the garage, a door opened into the lounge. Numerous windows kept the room bright on this cloudy day. Wildwood's fire crews sat on two orange vinyl couches or at the Formica-topped table. A small TV on a wheeled cart against the wall murmured the local news broadcast.

Rob ran through the who, what, and stationed where, of Wildwood's tanker crews. Most interesting to me, though, was that everyone came from outside Alaska, except Fred, a native. Sean, Karen, Fogie, "Ichabod Crane," and Rob, were all from the Pacific Northwest. Craig was from Minnesota. When Dan told me he hailed from Southern California, I felt an immediate connection. We had the west in common. Someone I could relate to.

Ron then said, "Everyone's up and running but us. Our boss is building our tanker."

The government allowed an employee to build a tanker? Apparently so. He had requested the unfinished Model 50 tanker chassis be delivered here for completion and customization.

Dan said that our boss worked secretively, and that he wouldn't let anyone see his progress. "We call him Strudel," he said, twirling his index finger around his ear. "As in having strudel for brains."

I laughed, but hoped The Bear didn't hear that. Heaven forbid anyone should get fired so soon.

At lunchtime, I found an opportunity to talk to Karen, the only other woman on the crew. "Did the boss say anything to you about your long hair?"

Karen's eyes widened. "No . . . why?"

"He told me I had to cut my hair."

Her jaw dropped. "He told you *what*? What did you say?"

What a relief I could tell someone. "I told him no way. For a moment there, I thought I'd be back on the plane to Arizona. But he didn't force the issue, so I guess I'm staying." I laughed. "I am *not* cutting my hair."

After lunch, everyone walked to the warehouse to pick up our gear. Fogie, the foreman on Wildwood's Model 20 tanker, strolled alongside me. An epitome of relaxation (or sloppiness, I wasn't sure which yet), Fogie wore his fire shirt with one tail tucked in, one tail out, and one pant leg stuck into a boot top, one not, his bootlaces untied and flinging as he walked. By the end of the week, I discovered that he always dressed this way. Here, I'd worried about my appearance, remembering what Glenn had said about how civilians saw us as "their tax dollars at work."

Hal, the warehouse supervisor and station custodian, supplied us with fire gear identical to what I'd carried with the Forest Service—except for the industrial strength mosquito repellent, DEET.

Hal roared, his beer-belly shaking. "Not that it'll do any good. The most effective mosquito repellent up here is a shotgun."

Everyone laughed but me. I felt a little sick. I hated mosquitoes. Plus, many insect-repellants caused an allergic reaction, and the last thing I wanted to do was experiment to see if this kind gave me itchy red blotches. But I didn't want to spend my own money either. Still counting on vitamin B-12 and garlic, I put the bottle in my pack to use as a last resort. So far, the mosquito situation hadn't been too bad. Then again, that could've been because it was still snowing.

Hal's smile turned diabolical. "You foreigners will also need these."

I held the headnet as though he'd given me a bag of venomous snakes. *But I don't want to have to need one!* After a moment, I decided he must be exaggerating. It would *never* be that bad.

# THIRTY

"LET'S GO CLAMMIN'!" Rob said in front of the gang Friday afternoon.

Just the distraction I needed to alleviate that pang of homesickness. I stood in front of my closet Saturday morning, debating on what and how much to wear. It was hard to imagine being cold, since my bedroom radiator chugged steam nonstop, overheating the room. I found no way to regulate it. *Must ask Warehouse Hal.* Outside, dark, angry clouds loomed heavy and foreboding. Temperatures couldn't have been much above freezing; the dirty patches of snow hadn't budged all week. I dressed in multiple layers and rushed out the door before I began to sweat. I rode with Craig and Sean, straining to see through Craig's shattered windshield.

"Windshields have a short life on the ALCAN Highway," Craig explained. "No point in replacing it, it'll just get broken on my way home. I went through this every summer with my salmon cannery jobs. Worth it though. I made a fortune in a few months, if you don't mind working until you drop dead."

I had to admire anyone who'd drive three thousand miles to take a summer job.

We parked at the shore of the Cook Inlet and unloaded shovels and buckets. One shade darker gray than the sky, the inlet no doubt rivaled the frigid temperature of the salty off-shore breeze.

"So how does this work?" I asked, shovel ready.

"I'll show you," Rob said, taking off at a brisk pace. At the water's edge, he slowed, stepping like a cat stalking prey. He stopped where a wave had just receded, squatted, pointed to a dimple in the sand, and whispered, "Clam." Shoveling like a madman, he flung sand everywhere, sending me leaping out of the way.

"Aha! Gotcha." He flipped out a clam and proudly dropped it into the bucket. "They can sense you coming."

"Oh, come on, Rob." Sean didn't believe him, and I wasn't sure I did either.

"You've gotta be fast, because as soon as you start digging, they use their foot to pull themselves deeper."

Wet sand made for heavy shoveling—hard work for one lousy clam. It took two hours for me to half-fill my bucket. We headed back to the station and arrived before the heater could thaw my icy toes.

At home, I tugged off my wet boots. *Damn, I just oiled them.* I propped them by the radiator to dry out. After a suggestion to buy a pair of Army boots as spares, I'd checked them out. They were flimsy and ridiculously expensive. I'd passed. *My boots better dry out fast; I'll need them tomorrow.* I headed upstairs to take a nap and found my bedroom stifling. Ironic, after being so cold. I opened the window. *No screen? That won't do.* I'd have to ask Warehouse Hal about that too.

Knocking woke me up. I padded downstairs in sock feet and opened the door to find Rob, Craig, and Sean, buckets in hand.

"You're the only one home with a kitchen," Rob said, grinning.

We sat at the dining table; Sean explained what they did. "We soaked the clams in cold water so they'd spit out sand. Now, we just need a skillet to sauté them."

I found a sixteen-inch fry pan. "Will this do?"

"Perfect," Rob said. "I'm starving. Let's cook these puppies."

I watched from the dining table while the guys huddled over the stove.

"So how long do we cook them?" Sean asked Rob.

"Heck I don't know, fifteen . . . twenty minutes?"

I'd never cooked clams, so didn't have anything to offer. They stirred them around and around, making a tremendous racket as shells rattled against the metal pan. Soon the kitchen smelled like the sea. A half hour later, they declared them done.

I poked at a clam with my finger. "How do you eat these, anyway?"

"Pry the shell open, and scoop them out with your front teeth," Craig said, demonstrating.

I chewed and chewed, finally swallowing it whole. Like eating a seaweed flavored eraser. Why did people go to all the trouble to catch these things? They were awful!

Sean finally said something. "Are they supposed to be this tough?"

Craig pulled a clam out of his mouth with his fingers, examining it. "No, they aren't." He placed the uneaten clam on his plate. "Maybe we didn't cook them long enough."

Rob shrugged. We tossed them in the trash.

I woke the next day itching with numerous mosquito bites. I'd forgotten to close the window. I slammed it shut. *Need to talk to Warehouse Hal.*

In the lounge, Rob had splayed the newspaper in front of him. He laughed and pointed out an article for me to read.

*Clams: How to Find, Catch and Cook them.* We'd harvested and soaked them correctly, that much was encouraging. *Cook clams for two or three minutes until they open. DO NOT overcook. Overcooking turns them into shoe leather.*

WITH NOT MUCH to do, we hung out in the lounge in the morning. So far, BLM had provided no fire, safety, or first-aid training. I found it odd, if not scary. I decided to bone up on the tanker operation manual, so made myself comfy on the couch. Might come in handy should I need to use the equipment.

Dan sat down next to me. "So what are we doing today?"

Rob changed the channel on the TV. "Strudel hasn't said. I don't think he's even put together a game plan for the summer yet."

Fogie scoffed at BLM's disorganization. "To them, we're just a bunch of tanker dogs."

Dog? Not sure I liked being called a dog. I assumed he meant firefighters as grunt labor, but still . . .

"So what's it like fighting fire in Arizona?" Sean asked me.

"Oh, about the same as anywhere," I said, wondering why he'd ask.

"But doesn't it get kinda hot there?"

*Oh yeah, he's from the northwest. Maybe he doesn't know.*

"Over one-hundred degrees in the summer," I said. "Everything in Arizona sticks, stings, or stabs." A little exaggerated, of course, but this was fun.

"I'm guessing you don't have water to put fires out, so what do you do?" asked Rob.

"We use dirt. It's hard enough carrying drinking water, let alone having enough to put out a fire."

They thought for a moment about what I'd said.

"What in the world is there to burn in a desert?" Craig asked.

Many people didn't know Arizona had plenty of forests, including the largest stand of ponderosa pine in the world.

"Oh, I didn't fight fires in the desert. I worked in the forests of Southern Arizona, near Tucson."

"Forests in *Tucson*?" Sean asked, incredulous.

My first chance to brag about Arizona. Almost as much fun as telling people what I did for a living, always getting a kick out of their disbelief, awe, and confusion as to why would I want to do such a thing.

On Monday, Strudel sent Fred, Ichabod Crane, and me to the main complex in Anchorage to test and tune up Mark 3 submersible pumps. Any other time, I'd have been thrilled to have the government put me up in a motel and pay for meals. The problem? Fred and Ichabod Crane.

Ichabod Crane, not the literary version of course, fit in with us like someone who misread the party invitation and mistakenly showed up in costume. An off-kilter sense of humor didn't help either. He dissolved into hysterics when things weren't funny, oblivious to the fact that no one else was laughing, and he regarded us with a puzzled expression when everyone else was cracking up at a joke.

And handsome Fred, studying me with those dark shadowy eyes. Did he do this because I was a woman, a woman firefighter, or because as a native Alaskan he found me an oddity coming from the desert Southwest? He made me self-conscious.

We spent the night before work in a motel and met for breakfast, but I might as well have dined alone. Fred stared at his food. Ichabod Crane gawked at the other patrons. I studied the two of them, wishing I'd ordered room service. I dreaded fourteen more meals like this one.

At the district's cavernous, unheated warehouse sat dozens of Mark 3 submersible pumps, used to draw water from lakes and rivers; if your fire happened to be near such a thing. Not surprisingly, I'd never used one; Arizona had few rivers and even fewer lakes. However, saws and pumps had similar engines, so my chainsaw experience came in handy. It didn't take long for me to get the hang of tuning, and soon Fred and I had a nice assembly line going. Ichabod Crane didn't catch on. Not sure why. I could have sworn he'd said he spent two fire seasons on a tanker crew.

By midday, I decided why not make the best of the situation? I teased Fred, trying to make him laugh. But with Ichabod's lack of social skills, and Fred speaking no more than two words at a time, I spent most of the day listening to myself talk, at least when pump motors weren't running at full throttle.

After work, the subject of meeting for dinner came up. I hesitated. Would it be as awkward as breakfast and lunch? However, I didn't much feel like being alone all evening, either. We took a booth, and I ordered a glass of wine. Fred dittoed my order. Ichabod passed. Soon Fred and I were engaged in jokes and laughs as though we sat alone. My outlook for the week improved. By Wednesday, I was enjoying Fred's company. It was ironic to think that now, Friday had come too quickly.

We returned to the station in early afternoon, so I stopped to ask Hal about the radiator and my missing screen. He exploded a loud laugh. "What the hell do you need screens for?"

"Mosquitoes!" I said, incredulous.

Hal shook his head, but said he'd take care of it. However, he couldn't do anything about the heat. It was either on or off, and he wasn't about to turn it off.

*Yeah,* I thought, *it could snow at any minute.*

Every morning at nine o'clock sharp, dispatch radioed fire personnel for service status. Rob responded with "ten-eight," (in service), and this time he turned to us with a grand smile. He knew who was coming up next. Strudel's voice, muffled and slurred, also responded "ten-eight." Yet we hadn't seen him all morning. Where the heck was he?

"Let's go find him," Rob said with a mischievous grin.

We climbed into a tanker and drove past Strudel's home. His BLM truck sat in the driveway. Dan burst out laughing. "He's still in bed!"

Sean launched into hysterics and had to pull over to prevent a collision. I laughed so hard, my stomach hurt.Dan wiped tears away with his sleeve, saying, "Hey, it could be worse. At least he's not bugging us."

Nobody could argue with that.


BLM HAD NO fitness requirements, but I accepted Rob's suggestion that we all run two miles through the woods behind the station. Dan's and my pace matched, so we ran together.

"I worked on a tanker crew in Ojai last summer," he said.

California, the land of brush fires. "Geez, Dan, that's scary." I'd never wanted any part of those intense blazes, wildly more dangerous than a forest fire.

"Yeah," he said, "Those dry Santa Ana winds send deranged pyromaniacs into action. Add volatile chaparral, which explodes when it burns, and you've got a real-life version of hell."

A herd of animals started across the road ahead. *Reindeer?* But wait. Are reindeer real, or imaginary? Funny, but I didn't know. They looked like reindeer to me.

"Hey, caribou," Dan said.

They stared at us; we stared at them. Captivated by their grace, I resisted the urge to speak so they would stay. Their ears twitched, tails swished, as they evaluated the potential threat. Several minutes later, we pushed on, getting remarkably close to them before they trotted off.

That weekend, I awoke early, ate breakfast, and wondered what I'd do all day with no car, no TV, and no music. I'd never run on a beach, and thought doing so had such a lovely connotation, as in: I'm going to run the beach barefoot today, catch some rays, splash through waves. It was only a short jog to the Cook Inlet, where a sharp wind changed my mind about the barefoot part. But sand invaded my sneakers, rubbing my feet raw. I took them off. Firm, cool sand gave a little under my soles and squished up between my toes. A wave sloshed toward me, and I veered over to splash through it. Yelping, I dashed back to shore. *Man that's cold!* In that one brief moment of contact, thousands of icy needles pierced my skin, arctic cold penetrating bone deep. I put my shoes back on.

On my next run, Dan joined me.

"Just don't take off your shoes," I said with a laugh.

Our sneakers thumped on the wet sand, leaving momentary footprints that would disappear when the tide swept in. Solar rays pushed the thermometer up to a balmy sixty degrees, tropical by Alaskan standards, and felt warm on my skin. A gentle surf lapped; the air stirred salty and clean. We jogged up to a commotion on the shore.

Dan paused to take a breather. "What's going on?"

"I'm not sure." I stopped beside him. A figure emerged from the sea, dressed in nothing but shorts, taking long, splashing steps. In his arms, he carried an armful of a wiggling salmon.

Dan's jaw dropped. "How can he *do* that? Water's got to be, what, thirty-five?"

"He's either really brave, or really nuts."

The strapping man jogged up the beach, dropped the fish into a large bucket, and waded back out.

"What's he using to catch them?" I asked.

"I think he's using just his bare hands," Dan said.

Sure enough, moments later, the fish-catcher splashed back to shore carrying another salmon. Dan and I watched the man wade out for another fish, amazed by his Alaskan fortitude. *Wow!* We returned to our run and our conversation.

"You mentioned you live with someone back in Arizona," Dan said.

"Yeah, Joe and I have been together a few years now."

Dan sensed my wistful tone. "You guys talking marriage?"

"Joe asked me once, but I wasn't ready. I still don't know if I'm ready. We've had problems."

Dan's forehead creased. "Relationships are tough. I still haven't found the right girl."

Our sneakers pounded sand, in sync for a few minutes while we gathered our thoughts. Confused, uncertain, and tired of all the heartache, I couldn't make a decision whether Joe and I were meant to be or not. One thing for sure, he always waited for me to come back. His love was constant and unwavering. Didn't that count for something?

"I refuse to settle for something less than I deserve," Dan said.

We continued jogging in silence. His last comment hit home. If I married Joe, would I be settling? I wished I knew the right thing to do. Maybe this time apart from Joe would help me figure that out.

"We have a phone call scheduled tonight," I said.

So far, I'd stayed in touch with Joe. I wanted to. Once a week at a prearranged time, I waited in the empty office for him to phone, excited to tell him about Alaska and my new job. Never good on the phone, Joe let me to do most of the talking, and soon I ran out of things to say. I often listened to long staticky silences between us.

"Weren't you going to join Fred and me for Poker tonight?" Dan asked.

Maybe I'd miss Joe's call this time. Next week I'd say something came up.

After dinner, we sat at Dan's table with stacks of poker chips and a bottle of Southern Comfort.

"Watch your facial expressions," Dan said. "Don't let on you've got a good hand."

I nodded, holding my cards close to my chest. Three of a kind . . . not too shabby. I sipped my drink, savoring the sweet, pleasant burn as I swallowed. Fred shoved a tall stack of chips to the middle of the table.

Dan studied Fred's face. "Are you bluffing?"

Not a muscle twitched. He might as well have been made of wax.

"Okay, I give. I'm folding." Dan tossed his cards on the table and the last of his drink down the hatch.

"Me too." I threw my cards in with Dan's.

Fred confidently showed his hand: Two tens.

Dan slapped the table. "That's it? I had a pair of kings!"

A tiny smile crept up at the corner of Fred's mouth. A complicated guy in many ways, but I admired the way he played the game.


OF ALL THINGS, someone knocked on my door at six a.m. on Mother's Day. *Who'd be coming over this early?* Dan stood on my porch with a giant handmade envelope under his arm.

"Happy Mother's Day!" he said, beaming.

I laughed at his grand gesture. "But I'm not a mother! Okay, come on in."

Inside the envelope I found an equally huge homemade Mother's Day card, signed by the whole crew.

Slightly embarrassed, I said, "Geez, thank you, Dan, this is so nice . . . Was it your idea?"

"Well, yes, but Craig and Sean helped me last night. We all appreciate how you look out for us."

*They do?* I'd no idea. My self-esteem inched up a notch.

From outside the station Monday morning, I noticed a distinct lack of activity. *Where is everyone?* I discovered the entire crew in the lounge, glued to the TV.

"What's going on?" I asked.

"Mt. St. Helens erupted," Karen said, her voice filled with dread, eyes transfixed on the screen. Her face paled. "I hope my house is still there." She jumped up. "I've got to call home!"

Somber, Rob said, "I think I lost my Christmas tree farm."

Unsure what to do or say, and stunned by the images, nobody spoke again. Footage of the exploding mountain, billows of smoke and ash churning into the sky, replayed over and over, while reporters, standing in front of ash-covered houses and cars, told of evacuations, damages, and fear. The whole broadcast was surreal to me, as though a Hollywood movie, not a real-life event. Karen couldn't get through on the phone, so she sat down again to wait. Rob fretted and paced over his farm. When we watched all we could stand, everyone went about their business, their faces still showing worry. I kept quiet, wishing I could find the right words, but knowing nothing I could say would make a difference. Not until the next day did Karen find out that her home and family were fine, and that Rob had indeed lost his farm.

"WHAT SHOULD WE do today?" Rob asked as he steered out of the station for another day of cruising. Yesterday we watched wildlife, so I suggested we take photos of wildflowers. We had nothing better to do.

"There's another bald eagle on top of that tree over there," Dan said, pointing. "If I'm keeping count right, that makes twenty-four this week."

"Should we go to Skilak Lake?" Rob asked.

Again? We went there the other day. With only sixty miles of pavement in our patrol area, this was getting old. Not much to do after work either. Entertainment outside of Wildwood included bar-hopping, (Dan's idea of fun, but never mine), or the movie theater, where flicks showed for a dollar.

That night, Dan suggested a movie. "They're playing *Friday the 13th*," he said, as we walked to the theater. "Should be fun."

We bought sodas and popcorn, and relaxed into our seats. Dan discretely doctored our drinks with the Tequila he'd snuck in. It didn't take long before we were moderately drunk. Creepy music played, giving me goosebumps.

Dan whispered in my ear, "Watch out!" but it didn't help.

Caught by surprise when someone got impaled, I jolted, flinging popcorn everywhere, screaming, then laughing at my reaction. Dan chuckled, picking my popcorn out of his hair.

"Geez, Dan, next time give me fair warning," I said, my voice raspy, as everyone filed out.

"Sorry 'bout that, Linda. I didn't know how bloody it was."

Dan walked me home. Ten o'clock and still light out. I just couldn't get used to twenty-two hours of daylight.

"What's going on with you and Fred?" he asked as we approached my door.

*Me and Fred?* I laughed. "Nothing, why?"

"Just a sense I get. I think he really likes you."

"That's ridiculous, Dan." Based on Fred's comment last week about girlfriends being too demanding, I couldn't imagine him having an interest in me.

"Doesn't matter," Dan said, opening my door for me. "Something's up."

I crawled into bed, mulling over Dan's comment. Stubborn rays peeked around the drawn window shade. How could anyone sleep around here?

In the morning, I asked around about the light-at-night problem. Suggestions included "What light?" (Fred), tying a scarf over my eyes (Craig), or covering the window with a blanket (Teresa). I opted for the blanket. Warehouse Hal gave me one, saying, "That's what all the other lower forty-eighters do"—as though us "lower forty-eighters" had some kind of defective gene that didn't allow us to sleep when the sun wouldn't set.

Army blanket, hammer and nails in hand, I walked back to my place. I positioned the gray wool over the window and tapped in a few nails to hold it in place. That helped the sleeping problem. A little. But I still missed *real* night. Something was just not right about daylight at midnight.

# THIRTY-ONE

THANK GOODNESS STRUDEL finally finished our tanker. About time. He'd painted the truck himself, in BLM's custom color, a vile shade of chartreuse, or as we fondly called it, "baby-shit green." Talk about dedicated, or maybe obsessive, rumor had it that Strudel convinced the government to buy the painting equipment, too—what we referred to as one of his "special purchases." The tanker now waited in the station garage for final detailing.

Cold, drizzling rain fell from an overcast dawn sky outside my bedroom window. I didn't even have to be outside to feel the chill. When I dashed to work, I held my coat over my head to keep my hair dry. Even in the garage, I shivered despite thermal underwear, a flannel shirt, down vest, and wool-lined denim jacket. It was hard to imagine, but I missed the blazing Arizona sun.

"Strudel wants the storage cabinets labeled," Rob said to me. "Can you cut stencils so we can spray paint them?"

*Thank you, Rob.* I made them inside the nice, warm lounge. When we were done, Strudel inspected our paint job, complimenting us on the professional workmanship. *Huh. Maybe he'll be an okay boss after all.*


*WELL, THERE YOU are!* I thought when the muted sun greeted the morning. More customization on tap today.

Fred and I spread a canvas tarp over the equipment and installed snaps to make removal easy.

"Here, stretch this tight while I secure it," he said, handing me a corner, allowing his sturdy body to get closer to me than he'd ever dared before.

"Want to go camping some time?" he asked, inserting a pop rivet.

What brought that on? Before I could answer, Strudel marched into the garage, and opened and closed each cabinet.

"You've got all of 'em filled already," he said in a disapproving tone.

"Was there something else you wanted to store in one?" Rob asked.

Strudel scowled. "Of course! You need Scott Air Packs."

Rob's eyebrows arched. "Scott Air Packs? What in the world for? We aren't trained to use them."

"You guys might come up on a structure fire and be asked to help," Strudel said.

Rob's tone heated. "That's nonsense! We aren't trained for structure fires."

I'd never heard of Scott Air Packs, so I listened while Rob and Strudel argued the point.

Finally, Rob gave in. "Okay, fine, I'll set a cabinet aside, but no one on my crew will ever use one. Period."

After Strudel left, I asked Rob, "So what was that all about?

"That idiot wants us to carry Scott Air Packs. We aren't trained in structural firefighting, so we don't need them."

I understood the basic differences between fighting forest and structure fires. Burning buildings could collapse at any minute, and often have the dangerous backdraft phenomenon. In an enclosed space, fire uses up all the oxygen, creating toxic fumes—which is why structural firefighters carry oxygen. Forest fires have their own unique characteristics, like the ability to create their own weather. Fire storms were the worst. I'd met men who'd fought structure fires, and they told me that never in a million years would they tackle a forest fire. And I'd sure never enter a burning building: we respected each other's expertise, but we had no desire to trade places. The more I thought about Strudel's outrageous demand, the madder I got. This man was insane.

"HOW ABOUT WE camp near Hope?" Fred suggested the next day.

Well, this would be interesting. But always game for a chance to explore, I agreed to go. Camping gear loaded in his weathered Oldsmobile, we saw Dan on our way out. Fred stopped and backed up. I rolled down my window.

Fred leaned over me. "We're going camping. Wanna come?"

Dan hesitated, his eyes flitting from me to Fred. "Nah, I'll pass. Our rainy hike last weekend was enough for me."

"Okay, see you Sunday!" I waved. For a moment there, I thought Dan might be jealous. *Nah, we're just friends.*

Thirty minutes of silence passed between Fred and I while scenery breezed by. What in the heck was I thinking? What in the world would Fred and I talk about for the next two days?

Fred broke the silence. "It must be quite the challenge for you to be working in a place so different from Arizona. What do you think of Alaska so far? How did you get into firefighting?"

Eager to respond, soon we were talking nonstop about everything and anything. Could this be the same guy I'd started out with? Had I completely misjudged him?

A light mist fell in Hope when we arrived mid-afternoon. Fred pointed out the historic buildings, including a Russian church, with its domed roof and tall spires. Alaska once belonged to Russia, he reminded me.

We agreed to avoid a regular campground, not that there were many around. With public land so prevalent, you could camp just about anywhere. I'd learned long ago that locals always knew the best places, so I let him pick a spot. A short hike later, I pitched my tent at the top of a yawning valley. Tall, snow-covered peaks fed a turquoise whitewater river below. The stubborn sun dipped toward, but not below, the horizon. Campfire built, we passed a bottle of wine between us.

"This feels good," I said, warming my hands near the flames.

Fred placed an arm around me. Another surprise. Had I misjudged him again? I thought he didn't want a girlfriend. Using two fingers to lift my chin, he explored my eyes with his. "You're a puzzle."

*Me?* Funny. I thought it was the other way around. "How so?"

"Well, for one, seems you like to fly solo."

How'd he guess that? Was it that obvious? I admitted I wasn't ready to settle down.

"I respect that. I've spent a lot of time watching you and wondering what made you tick. Now I think I know." His arm squeezed me a little tighter.

So he *was* studying me all this time. I laughed lightly. I didn't know what made me tick, so how could he?

Eyes lowered, he kissed me, his lips tender on mine and tasting of wine. My body responded, but my mind said, "*no.*" Our kiss ended. I rested my chin on his shoulder.

"We don't have to do anything," he said close to my ear. "I mean, I think it's best we don't get involved, since we have to work together."

What a relief. I didn't want anything more either. I also assumed this wasn't going anywhere. Girlfriends weren't on his priority list. I slept with his arms wrapped around me and awoke the next morning to a typical overcast day. A bald eagle soared on air currents, eying our camp, its high-pitched screech echoing in the valley. Fred took my hand and led me to the river below, where the frigid, churning water teamed with salmon. We half-joked about competing with grizzlies for breakfast. An hour later, we tore down camp and hiked out.

Fred grew quiet again on the way back to Kenai, but I didn't mind. Comfortable with him now, I enjoyed the ride. What would everyone think when we got back? Let 'em talk. I didn't care—I liked Fred and enjoyed the lingering pleasure of knowing that he'd let me into his very private world.


SOMETHING NEW HUNG on the cork bulletin board next to Strudel's office the next morning. I fingered the cardboard cutouts of Dalmatians wearing fire helmets and comical faces. *How adorable.*

Fogie walked up behind me. "Hey, that's us. The tanker dogs!"

In no time crew nicknames adorned each tiny tag around the dog's necks. Not sure who first called me "Mom-dog," but "Papa-dog" soon followed for Rob. Dan had earned the name Barfly early on. Only a few guys called me Mom-dog, and even that bugged me. I still didn't much like the dog reference.

Strudel later called a meeting of the entire Wildwood staff. *What now?* I walked outside with everyone to find the shiny new tanker parked next to a fire hydrant. Dan and I stood next to each other amidst the crowd of twenty.

He whispered in my ear, "Oh boy, a dog and pony show!"

Strudel beamed like a kid on Christmas morning unwrapping his first toy fire engine. He expounded on all of the special features he'd added to this truck. Not particularly interested, because I'd already crawled in, over, and under the truck for weeks, I only half-listened while Strudel bragged about these features, including the controversial Scott Air Packs. Yawns and eye rolls were sprinkled through the crowd. At last, Strudel stopped talking. He rolled out a length of hose and attached it to the fire hydrant in order to fill the tank. I paid more attention.

With his hand on a lever, Strudel said, " . . . and *never, ever* fill from a hydrant with this valve open." He opened it to demonstrate. "It must be closed or you'll blow out all the seals."

Dan and I both rolled our eyes. Strudel was exaggerating—again. Listeners exchanged grins.

Strudel cranked open the fire hydrant. Rumbles and gurgles came from deep inside the truck's bowels, until water erupted from every orifice like a Mt. St. Helens reenactment, showering everyone. Dan instinctively grabbed my sleeve, and we darted away from the waterworks. Others hollered and yelped, running in every direction, trying to get out of range as the ice-cold water spewed everywhere. In the meantime, Strudel, frantic, shut off the hydrant.

No need to say a word—Dan and I held onto each other and laughed and laughed. Forever etched into Wildwood's history—the first official Wildwood Dog and Pony Show.

Finally, though, my crew was mobile. This was my first time behind the wheel of such a behemoth truck, which carried more than twice as much water as the Model 20 we used at Florida. It took me a while to get the hang of double-clutching to change gears, but soon I shifted like a pro.

"I want to stop at the bank," Rob said. "Pull over here."

Parallel park? That would be like trying to park an elephant. I pulled straight into the shopping center parking lot, taking up two spaces.

On the following day, Ichabod Crane drove.

"Turn right at the second stop light," Rob said.

Ichabod nodded and immediately flipped on the turn signal. It blinked and blinked and blinked. Minutes went by. When he finally turned, a car horn blared, the driver shaking his fist at us as he sped around. My patience thinned.

"So where to, guys?" Rob asked.

"I want to see Craig and Sean's station at Skilak Lake," I said. They bragged about the place all the time. Made me curious.

Rob turned to me with a grin. "Strudel won't like that."

Strudel insisted we stay spread out to protect more area.

"So?" Dan said. "He'll never know."

Off we went.

Love at first sight. They lived my homesteading dream in a real log cabin. A gravel path, edged with a profusion of colorful wildflowers, led to the rustic, weathered gray door. Inside, a field-stone fireplace warmed the room, casting amber shadows onto wood furnishings. Out back, a large vegetable garden, the plants heavy with fruit, could easily feed a family of four.

"We're living off the land," Craig said. "I killed a bear yesterday, and the meat's on the grill. We've also got salmon in the smoker."

They served up lunch: just-picked garden vegetables and slabs of bear meat and salmon. I ate the fish and vegetables, but bear meat—no way. None of those guys could convince me it didn't contain Trichinosis.

On the way back to Wildwood, I thought about the time I'd wanted to homestead here, and how different my life would be. Could I still do that?

When I arrived at work the next day, I found Rob taking apart the door panel of our truck.

"Window won't go down," he said.

I admitted I didn't know much about electricity (the incident with Tom wiring the emergency lights had proven that), so I stood by, ready to help if I could. Rob fingered the intricate maze of wiring, talking to himself. A truck pulled into the driveway. Door slammed. Strudel headed toward us.

"Trouble at twelve o'clock," I said.

"What seems to be the problem here?" Strudel elbowed his way between Rob and the door. "Let me see."

Rob rolled his eyes and stepped back.

Strudel ripped out a handful of wires which resembled a pile of rainbow spaghetti. He glanced at his watch. "I don't have time for this, you'll have to finish up." He jumped into his truck and drove away.

We stared at the disaster left in his wake.

Rob leaned against the truck, hand on forehead. "Oh, brother, it'll take me forever to figure out how to put those wires back."

In case Strudel returned, I posted myself as lookout. I planned to tell him we'd already fixed it so he'd leave us alone.

On Saturday, I joined Rob, Craig, Sean, and Dan, and after squeezing into Fred's car, we were off to Homer Spit, a tiny fishing community eighty miles south of Kenai. All the way there it sleeted, and it continued to do so after we arrived. We sat in the car, watching the windshield wipers slap back and forth. No point in just sitting there, I pointed out.

We walked the pier, misty white vapors appearing when we spoke. Menacing clouds loomed low in the sky, matching the color of the ocean, suggesting dusk, even though it was barely noon. Subtle activity took place on the colorful fishing boats. Pale-yellow lights glowed from cabins and decks. Fishermen huddled under plastic awnings near portable heaters, busy mending nets with fingerless gloves. How could they not be freezing to death? What a hard life. It made me appreciate how fish got on my plate.

Undeterred by a week of wet, I accepted Craig and Sean's invitation to Russian Lake the next weekend. Although not a fan of hiking in rain, I decided I had to get over it. If I waited for the rain to stop, I'd never go anywhere. So far, only wispy horse-tail clouds streaked the sky, but I still added a poncho to my daypack. One could almost guarantee it would rain at one point or another. Craig opened the camper shell door and removed his hiking gear. He reached in again and produced a rifle.

Carrying a weapon on a hiking trip? I didn't like hunting and hoped that wasn't his plan.

Craig noticed my wide eyes. "This is serious grizzly country."

My enthusiasm waned. "So . . . is it safe to go?"

Sean laughed and pointed at Craig. "We don't have to outrun the bear, we just have to outrun you!"

I laughed nervously, not at all comforted. Staying behind wasn't comfortable either, so I joined them. The narrow path led us through acres of downed black spruce, scattered like a game of pick-up sticks. Powerful storms often blew over the shallow rooted trees, which were unable to penetrate the permafrost. But nature had a plan for the newly opened meadow. Tall, hot-pink fireweed, purple monk's hood, and Alaska cotton, with its cotton-ball top begging to be touched, sprouted amidst the fallen.

Entering dense woodland, Craig froze, raising his hand for us to stop. "Did you hear that?"

An urge to flee kicked in, but I couldn't make myself move.

Craig placed a finger on his lips. "Shhh . . ." He took the rifle off his shoulder.

More rustling. *Please don't let this be a grizzly.* Sean's joke aside, should I run? Craig had never said. Then velvety antlers appeared above the thick brush—it was a huge moose, at least eight feet tall. Craig lowered the gun. I let go of the breath I held, but still didn't move. I wanted the moose to leave first. My first week in Kenai, I'd snapped moose photos like crazy. Then I discovered they were as common as cotton-tailed bunnies at home, often wandering Kenai streets. About as threatening as a herd of dairy cows: until I heard about one that trampled a man to death when he got too close.

Mr. Moose went on his way; our partly-sunny day vanished. Light mist dampened my jacket, and I felt the chill seep through my layers of clothes. Even though I wasn't too keen on getting wet, I didn't want to turn back alone, either.

By late morning, we reached the frozen lake. Craig inched out onto the ice. "C'mon, Sean, let's toss in our lines and see what bites."

"Are you *sure* it's frozen solid? I can guarantee I'm not diving in to save you," I said, laughing, but completely serious.

Craig assured me all was good. They found a place to drop their lines. I waited for them on a cold rock, slightly preferable to the wet ground, and watched. They finally gave up, one degree before my posterior suffered frostbite. Halfway back, Craig admitted that using the trail would take us too long.

"I know a shortcut," he said. "We'll follow the Russian River."

I didn't like not knowing exactly where I was, and shortcuts made me nervous. But what could I do? I followed them.

The Russian River blasted its way to the Kenai River, and eventually the Cook Inlet, with roaring whitewater drowning out a voice right next to you. Glacier melt colored the river an odd, iridescent green.

"Watch out for grizzlies," Craig yelled over the tumbling rapids.

*Oh, just great.* Super-vigilant, I strained to see animal movement, ankle-twisting rocks, and downed trees, in the waning light.

"Are you *sure* this will come out at the truck?" Sean asked for the third time.

Craig marched ahead with determination. "Yes, yes, we're almost there."

How he knew where to turn, who knows, but we walked up on a much-welcome view of Craig's truck. Not sure how far we hiked, but my feet were frozen, and I couldn't tell if I had ten toes or two. Craig cranked the heat up full blast, and we started the drive home. Exhausted, I leaned against the headrest and closed my eyes.

"Uh-oh," Craig said.

I sat up straight. "Uh-oh, what?" I hated uh-ohs, and late-night ones were the worst.

Craig stared at the dash. "I forgot to buy gas."

Sean leaned over from the back seat. "You're kidding. Right?"

The gas gauge pointed to "E," and the "low fuel" indicator light glowed.

Craig offered a sheepish smile. "What's worse, there aren't any gas stations open."

Sean groaned. "Craaaig."

"Maybe we'll find someone open late," Craig said, ever the optimist.

A confirmed pessimist, I envisioned a long, cold night sleeping in the truck. We drove for a long time, finally cruising into a gas station on fumes. There were no lights on, and a "Closed" sign hung crooked on the door.

"This is just great. Now what?" Sean sounded exasperated.

"I'm gonna go to the house next door. Maybe they'll let us buy enough to get home," Craig said.

"Be my guest," I said, sliding down into the seat. I *so* did not want this to be happening.

Craig banged on the front door with his fist. No response. He knocked again. A light came on in an upstairs window, and the sash flew open.

"What?" a man hollered.

Craig turned on a polite and contrite voice, asking if we could buy five dollars worth of gas. The window slammed shut. *Oh great, he's not going to help us.* But then the front door opened, and the man came out with a set of keys.

"See, it all worked out," Craig said as we drove away.

I slunk down into the seat and frowned. *That'll teach me. No more hiking with these guys without a map and a full tank of gas.*


AS HE OFTEN did, Dan came over after work, and together we walked to the cafeteria for dinner. We read the posted menu.

"Oh no. Mystery Meatloaf again," he said. "I shoulda known it'd be meatloaf, since yesterday they served hamburgers. I just know they're grinding up leftovers to make meatloaf."

At least with C-rats, I knew what I was getting. Here, everything was a mystery.

The next morning at breakfast, Rob, Dan, and I stood in line, watching the cook, Woody, prepare Rob's order. Woody had that hard-life look about him. We swore he'd just been released from prison. Bones poked through his sallow skin and bloodshot eyes stared above a perpetual five o'clock shadow. Black tattoos ran up and down both arms. Then there was that filthy, stained apron he tied on every day—it was enough to warrant a health department inspection in itself. Woody dipped a miniature string mop into a bucket of oil and slathered the grill. He cracked Rob's eggs into the sea of grease, where they skated across the hot griddle. Woody flipped them over once, slid them onto a plate, and shoved it so hard at Rob, the eggs glided to the rim, nearly spilling onto the floor.

Dan gave me a look of disgust.

Woody glared at Dan. "What'll ya have?"

Dan deferred to my order. I shook my head, "no."

"Well, c'mon, I ain't got all day."

Dan raised his voice. "Two eggs, over-easy, and hold the grease."

I giggled.

Woody stared at us for a moment, then, mumbling unintelligible words under his breath, defiantly grabbed the mop, smothered the grill and cracked two eggs into the oily mess. Dan rolled his eyes. My stomach rolled. I couldn't take this anymore. I didn't care how much it cost, I would not eat this awful food one more day.

After work, I bought the least expensive groceries I could find—but still far more expensive than the four bucks a meal at the cafeteria, but hey—this was necessary. I set the bags on the kitchen counter and opened the fridge to put away perishables. *What in the world?* Packages of crab filled every shelf.

"Teresa? What's with all the crab?"

She joined me. "It's that new diet I read about. You can have all the crab you want, and you'll lose weight. Plus, it was on sale! I stocked up."

"Crab? Just crab?" Certainly there was more to this diet than just crab. After all, how much crab could one person eat in a day?

I tried reasoning with her. "But, Teresa, do you really think you can stand to eat that much crab? Plus, won't it go bad in a couple days? I mean, seriously, you've got enough here for twenty people."

She looked thoughtful. "Well, yes, I suppose. But it was on sale." Her face fell.

I hugged her. "I'm sorry. I hope this works."

Sighing, I rearranged the shelves so I could put my food away.


STILL NO FIRES, and still no projects. I worried I'd get so used to not working, that if we did go to a fire, it would kill me. I missed trail work, fence building, station maintenance, even cleaning outhouses. (Okay, not really.) We all were unhappy, but I probably complained the most. Rob appealed to Strudel for something constructive to fill our days.

"You need to be fire-ready at all times," Strudel said. "If you're on a project when we get a fire call, the whole forest could burn down."

Outside the lounge window, steady rain fell in visible sheets. *Yeah. Right.*

Maybe Rob finally got through to Strudel, or maybe a coincidence, but our boss finally gave us something to do. It sounded a little suspicious, though. Strudel wanted us to harvest a large quantity of trees. Not one word about why or what for. Maybe Rob pinned it: "I'll bet he's building himself a log cabin. This has nothing to do with BLM."

A couple hours later, I stood with my crew in front of the thickest forest growth I'd ever seen. How in the world would we *walk* through this jungle, much less tote a chainsaw and gear? What lurked in these impenetrable woods? *Lions and tigers and bears, oh my!* Me and my big mouth.

# THIRTY-TWO

WITH A CAN of orange spray paint and a cloth tape measure in my daypack, I turned to Fred. "Join me?" Not that I couldn't work alone, but I didn't want to get lost, and Fred looked like the kind of guy who didn't get lost.

We waded through thick grass, some of it over my head. Unable to see the ground, I evaluated each step for secure footing. One step my foot landed on nothing but air, and I plunged three feet downward with a shriek. After mentally checking for injury, I climbed out. Hummocks were giant grass mounds that rose like tiny islands above the forest floor, and I'd just stepped off of one. My choices were to hop from plant to plant, or to walk around. Coming from snake country, I feared sticking my appendages into places I couldn't see, even though Fred had told me Alaska had no snakes. I decided to step in between the hummocks, the lesser of two evils—maybe. I was still jittery about unknown, scary, biting things, though.

Little sunlight shone through the canopy of dense woods, so when a cloud shadowed what little light there was, I turned to look up. *Oh no.* It wasn't a real cloud—it was a storm cloud of mosquitoes. I waved my arms to disperse them, swallowing the dread rising in my throat. I tore through my daypack. *Where is that headnet!* Although the net kept them from biting my face, they still bit through my pants. Desperate, I fogged DEET on my clothing, hoping for no allergic reaction.

At the end of a long, bug-infested day, we met at the trucks. Fred asked something I hadn't thought to ask. "So how are we going to get those trees out of there?"

Rob paused. "Hmm . . . Good question. I don't know."

We speculated that either Strudel didn't want to share his secret plan, or he didn't know either.

Two days later, we loaded up our chainsaws.

"Are these brand new?" I asked Rob.

Rob swung one into a side box on our truck and nodded with a smile. "Another one of Strudel's 'special' purchases."

*Ah, yes, one of those.*

At the harvest site, I strapped on heavy chaps, required safety gear for sawyers to protect their legs from injury. Staying ahead of the game, I also donned my headnet, as mosquitoes were already searching for a backdoor entrance. Fred and I again teamed. I walked around the hummocks, while he leapt from one to another.

Over the next hour, we searched and searched, but couldn't find one single marked tree.

"What do you think, Fred?" I said. "This one looks good."

I set the saw down and removed my gloves to fill the gas tank. Within milliseconds, mosquitoes zeroed in, inflicting multiple bites, including, unbelievably, around my cuticles. I put my gloves back on. So much for B-12 and garlic—what a waste of money. Not one mosquito buzzed around Fred, and he wasn't wearing a headnet.

"How come you aren't wearing a net?" I asked, waving my hand to disperse the swarming vampires.

"They don't bother me."

"They don't bother you as in . . . you don't care, or as in they stay away from you?"

"They don't bite me, never have."

"Well, lucky you," I said, sarcastically. *Ah-ha!* I actually got a smile out of him.

With a pull of the starter cord, the saw roared into life, puffing blue smoke. I revved the engine to keep it from stalling and studied the angle of the tree, which dictated the most likely direction of fall. I made a horizontal cut, feeling the weight of the saw, then the easier cut, at an angle downward to meet it. Fred and I dashed out of range. The tree groaned, swayed slightly, then toppled with a swoosh, crashing out of sight.

"You know, Fred, the minute we walk away from here, no one will ever find this tree. *We* would probably never find this tree, even if we came back in five minutes."

That actually earned a laugh.

We felled six trees, none of which were marked. At the trucks, I asked Rob what they'd found. Like Fred and I, they'd cut trees without markings.

"No one is ever going to find those trees," Rob said, storing away our gear.

I figured he was right. How terrible to cut down trees for nothing.

STRUDEL WALTZED INTO the lounge with a big grin slapped on his face. "I've got a big surprise." Glances with raised eyebrows passed between us. *What now?*

"I'm gonna take you guys out on the Kenai River in my new boat," he said with marked enthusiasm. No one said a word. "Oh come on, you guys, this'll be an adventure."

Somehow, Strudel talked Rob, Dan, Fred, and Fogie to go for a ride. Not wanting to appear a poor sport or miss anything fun, stupid me joined them. In retrospect, I blame severe boredom.

Forty minutes later, we pulled up to the boat launch. The Kenai River, cast a glacial-green, churned wildly before me. White caps formed on its surface, hell-bent on reaching the Gulf of Alaska, like a horse galloping top speed for the barn after an all-day trail ride. It looked like pretty rough boating to me.

Strudel handed us orange life vests. "Wouldn't want to take any chances."

Rob cupped his hands around my ear. "Five minutes in that frigid water, and we'd be dead of hypothermia long before we drowned."

My eyes widened with alarm. Now, wasn't that reassuring?

While I watched Strudel prepare the bucking boat in the choppy river, my apprehension rose like a mercury thermometer on a hot day. My boating experiences were relegated to a rowboat on Lake Ontario as a kid.

Strudel sat at the rear by the outboard motor, while the rest of us settled in the seats toward the front. I sat next to Dan, closest to the bow. A frantic check for seat belts proved futile, so I grasped the cold metal railing along the side. With the engine at full throttle, Strudel pointed the boat upriver, fighting the tumultuous current. Rising up and over a wave, the boat went airborne for a moment, and crashed down with a jolting *smack*, landing with such force, I thought for sure the hull would rip open. My arms hurt from the impact, and frigid water splashed in my face. I refused to let go of the railing to wipe my eyes clear, for fear of being thrown overboard and sucked down into the churning water, never to be seen again. Behind me, his eyes maniacal and his mouth frozen in a determined, ghoulish grin, Strudel was on a mission to conquer this river. *Not with me in this boat! I want to turn around!*

When we did turn around, I realized in terror that the return trip was even worse. Now we rode the wild river on its terms. Each time we tipped to one side, arctic water sloshed inside, filling the space around our feet. The choppy water tossed us at will—up, down, here, there—threatening to turn the boat sideways. If we did get turned sideways, we'd flip, tossing all of us into the glacial water for an icy death. Fred sat frozen, his jaw clenched tight. Fogie's eyes were wide, and his mouth gaped open. Dan appeared to be praying, head down and lips moving. Rob glanced nervously around, first at the water, then at the wild man at the outboard motor. After a ridiculously long hour, Strudel steered toward the boat launch.

*Get me outta here!* Bypassing the guys, I clambered out of the boat with wobbly, trembling legs, toes numb from soaking in the freezing water. I could've kissed the ground.

"So what did you think of that?" Fogie asked me, nonchalantly removing his life jacket.

"What did I think of that? Terrifying!"

"Yup, that was a bit over-the-top." He chuckled, giving Dan's arm a playful punch. "I was positive there for a moment we were all going for a swim."

Dan glared at him. "No shit."

Strudel acted like nothing had happened, chatty, excited, and smiling like a crazy man. Rob just stared at him. Fogie rolled his eyes. Fred's perfect poker face betrayed no emotion. Angry and trembling, I glared at Strudel. *You could've killed us.*


"HELICOPTER'S COMING TOMORROW for six weeks," Rob said the next morning.

At last, a break from our dull routine, aside from the terrifying experience aboard Strudel's boat. It would be valuable Helitack training for me, too. When I walked into the lounge, someone new was sitting at the table with Rob. *Who's this?*

"This is Monte, our pilot," Rob said.

My jaw dropped. *Our pilot?* Okay, I didn't drool, but knew the summer would be dull no longer.

# THIRTY-THREE

MONTE AND I could've started our own science experiment. I felt the chemistry between us from the moment he said, "Hi." Not only was he younger (and more handsome) than any pilot I'd ever met, but his casual bell-bottom-jeans and polo shirt attire, tousled, sandy-blond hair—requiring frequent sweeps to keep it from his eyes—and the simple gold chain around his neck, radiated masculinity to me in a way I'd never encountered before. This guy must have to fight women off daily.

Adding to all of those sexy attributes, Monte was not ex-military, like most Forest Service pilots. I'd soon learn it was his father who'd taught him how to fly. Curious about this captivating pilot and his privately owned aircraft, I walked over to the helipad on my day off, to find him tinkering with his Jet Ranger—just like a guy with a fancy car. How I hoped his delightful "sweep you off your feet" smile was meant only for me. Here was a perfect opening to ask the question I'd always wanted to ask a pilot. How did helicopters fly anyway?

Monte's face glowed with pleasure at the chance to share his passion for flying. "Here," he said, motioning me to get into the passenger seat. "I'll show you how they work. They aren't that complicated."

That comment didn't fool me. I'd heard they were incredibly difficult to fly. Interested both in his explanation, and in him, I soaked up every word he said.

With an instructor's voice, Monte explained, "Top rotors create downward air pressure for lift. Rear rotor steers it left and right. Weather conditions are far more critical for a helicopter's ability to stay aloft than for a plane. Planes can soar, helicopters can't."

This confirmed in my mind that the crazy pilot who auto-rotated with me onboard a few summers ago was nuts.

Later, Monte asked me if I'd like to go play some pool. In high school, guys with his good looks would've walked over me in the hallway rather than go around, if that was possible. That's how invisible I'd felt back then. For a guy like Monte to show an interest in me made me want to throw myself at his feet. I said I'd love to. Now, my billiards experience amounted to maybe, four games? But this wasn't really about playing pool. At the billiards table, he had me so flustered, I couldn't think straight. *How stupid of me to accept. He'll think I'm an idiot.*

"Let me show you the best way to hold the cue," he said. Positioning himself behind me, he wrapped his hands around mine, arranging my fingers in the proper position. My entire being illuminated from his touch.

In the morning, Monte invited me for a jog on the beach. The sun's meager rays warmed the cool day, but his presence warmed me even more. Alternating running with sitting on the sand talking, I enjoyed the surf and his company. I'd never met anyone like him. Hours passed easily—so many that when the tide came in, it boxed us against the cliffs, creating a challenging return trip. Inside Monte's car parked at the top of the bluffs overlooking the beach, I snuggled into him while the sun made a brief disappearance below the horizon, feeling safe and comfortable in his arms. He suggested we go for a drink.

Live music pulsed inside the smoke-hazed bar. When a sultry song played, he asked me to dance. Lost in his arms and the music, I tuned out everyone in the room but the two of us. We stayed until the bar closed, then returned to the bluffs, parking and making-out in his Malibu's backseat like high school kids. For the first time, a guy had to tell *me* to slow down.


HAVING A HELICOPTER at our disposal put cruising on hold so we could train. Morale was higher than I'd ever see it. Even Fred became Mr. Chatterbox.

Because there is so little room inside, helicopters use sling-loads to transport cargo. Stability is easily compromised on takeoff, so they hover while the slings are attached to the underside. Today I'd learn a hover-hookup, and I'd get to spend time around Monte. My heart and mood soared.

Our instructor filled a cargo net with gear so we could practice. Monte's helicopter hovered, waiting to start the training exercise.

Dan, lucky dog, got to go first. Eyes huge, he crouched low onto the landing pad and picked up the hook that lay on top of the load. My pulse raced as the helicopter hovered right above his head. He swung the hook, trying to latch a ring, and missed. He swung again. Got it. In an exaggerated crouch, he returned to my side. Even as a spectator, I tingled with excitement as if I'd done it myself.

"How was it, Dan? Were you scared?"

"It was harder than I thought it'd be. Plus, I got a static-electric shock when I touched the hook to the ring."

*What?* "How much of one?"

He grinned.

Rope pulled taut, Monte lifted the parcel slowly off the ground. Cargo sailing underneath, the ship circled and returned to drop the load on the helipad for the next person to try.

From the radio inside our truck, I heard Monte hailing us. "Wildwood Tanker five-five-oh, Helicopter two-three." I dashed to answer, pushing the call button. "Go ahead."

"Ready for the next one?"

"Ten-four," I replied. Did he notice the smile in my voice?

Okay, my turn. Underneath the ship, my heart raced, as a powerful downdraft from the thumping blades threatened to blow me over. Surprised by the hook's substantial weight, I used both hands to hold it steady. Down the ship came—lower . . . lower. It hovered above my head, but the darned ring wouldn't stop swaying. On my first attempt, I missed. Annoyed, I tried again. An electric charge zinged from my fingers to my toes as metal met metal. I dashed off to join the others and watched Monte fly away. That did it: I wanted more helicopter training.


"YOU SOUNDED SO damned sexy today on the radio," Monte said, smoothing my hair behind an ear. "It was hard for me to focus."

Thank goodness Teresa was out for the evening, leaving us alone. My entire body sparkled with desire, passion, want, and need. Using both hands to surround my face, he kissed me, deep and full. I responded in kind.

"I love you," I whispered, the words feeling true and real.

"I don't feel that way yet," he said, stroking my back. "I could, though. Our relationship doesn't have to include sex to make it better."

That sounded so obscenely crazy, I didn't respond. He took my hand and escorted me upstairs.

At the end of August, after spending time with Monte every single day, his assignment at Wildwood ended. Crushed, I asked when we'd see each other again.

"I'll try to come see you, sweetheart, but I have contracts elsewhere."

What could I say except, "okay?" But it wasn't okay. He'd tossed me off a cliff, and the water below churned and frothed, awaiting my arrival.


ALASKAN WEATHER RIVALED that of my hometown, Syracuse: cloudy, cold, wet, and dreary. All of the reasons why my parents had moved us to Arizona. And, for someone who wanted to fight fires, it didn't appear that Alaska was the place to be. Morale dipped lower than the daily high of fifty degrees.

Seated in the lounge one gloomy morning, I listened, and contributed to, the gripes about the lack of fires. A steady drizzle blurred the view outside the windows like a watercolor painting left out in the rain. Dan clipped his fingernails. Rob scratched his now full-grown beard. Sean sharpened his penknife. Fogie dipped a carrot into a jar of peanut butter, and crunched. Funny, I couldn't remember ever seeing him eat anything else.

Strudel must have overheard us complaining, because he stormed into the room and wagged his finger, saying, "Just remember. The Swanson River Fire started on a day like this." He turned on his heels and went back to his office, muttering and slamming the door.

Strudel brought this up often, prompting Rob to check into the details. The district records showed that a major fire had broken out on the banks of the Swanson River in 1969.

"But did it really start on a rainy day?" Fogie asked, leaning back in his chair and propping his boots up on the table. "I mean, seriously, can a fire become a major-rager with this much rain?"

He had a good point. Everyone sat silently contemplating. Dan's face lit up. "Every place I've ever worked had custom T-shirts made. We should do that! It'll be fun."

That night, as requested of me, I sketched my idea out at the dining room table.

Before work, Dan held up my drawing for everyone to see. A pony, its head down and forlorn, stood with a Dalmatian at its feet, holding an umbrella over both of them. In a semi-circle around the scene I'd written: *"Just remember, the Swanson River Fire started on a day like this."*

Everyone voted to have T-shirts printed with my artwork above the pocket. What an honor . . .

Two weeks later, Dan swept into the lounge with a box.

"They're here?" I asked, immensely curious to see how they turned out.

Laughter and joking accompanied the distribution of the shirts, with some of the guys trying them on. The commotion drew Strudel's attention, and he blasted into the room. "What's going on here?"

My smile faded, worried about what he'd do.

Dan pointed to the emblem on his shirt. "Our new motto."

Strudel studied it and frowned. "I don't like this. I forbid you to wear them around the station." He stomped out.

I glanced around the room to gauge reactions.

"Oh, who cares what he thinks," Dan said.

"What should we do?" I asked.

Everyone grinned. We wore them anyway.

A week later, Dan walked into the lounge, chuckling. "You won't believe this. Strudel just told me he wants to order not one, but *two* of our T-shirts."

The room ignited with raucous laughter.

Only days later, an honest-to-goodness fire call came in.

# THIRTY-FOUR

"WHERE IS IT?" I asked Rob as we scrambled to collect our fire gear. Anxious, I realized that I hadn't even *looked* inside my fire pack since April. Did it have everything I'd need?

"Some place west of Anchorage."

Sean had shared many cool maps of Alaska with me, including a fascinating topo map of the ocean floor, depicting submerged, unexplored mountains, so I knew there wasn't much west of Anchorage. In fact, I couldn't think of any civilization west of Anchorage.

A chartered plane delivered us to the Anchorage airport. Chartered. So even Strudel didn't trust the commuter service. On the tarmac, to my surprise and delight, Monte readied his helicopter for flight.

"I'm your pilot, ma'am," he said, with his brilliant, sexy smile. "Get in front with me."

Before I climbed into the cockpit, I noticed pontoons on the skids. Were we planning to land on water? If so, then what? Would we get into a boat?

"What are those for?" I asked Monte as he hopped into his seat.

"In some places the tundra's deep and boggy. Sure wouldn't want to land, only to have the helicopter half-sink into the ground." He swept his hair back and slipped on the helmet. "That might be a bit of a problem."

I laughed a little with him, but the thought of it actually sinking sounded like a real problem. Monte handed me a helmet. "Here, put this on. Then I can talk to you in private." This special treatment felt quite grand. *The guys in back must be jealous.* Deep in concentration, Monte flipped switches and monitored gauges. Off we sailed toward Kenai's two active volcanoes, Mount Iliamna and Mount Redoubt, still wearing stark white blankets of snow.

"This fire's been difficult," Monte said, his voice sounding tinny over the headset. "It's overrun fire camp three times."

Three times? Sure, winds play havoc, but fire camp burning up three times? What was up with that?

"Grizzlies raided the camp, too, twice. I've brought rifles."

Burned up camp. Bear raids. Rifles. Welcome to firefighting in Alaska.

Our flight took more than an hour—the longest I'd ever spent in a helicopter at one time.

"Have you ever been to Hawaii?" Monte asked, beaming that stunning smile.

*Hawaii?* What I wouldn't give to go to Hawaii! I shook my head "no" and felt pleasant tingles all over as I wondered if he was asking me to join him.

"Someday I'd like to take you, sweetheart. We'll walk the beach, eat great food, watch sunsets."

I'm sure I glowed from the warmth spreading inside me. "When do we leave?" I gave him my best smile to convince him to take me there.

Monte's helicopter didn't have the windshield wrapping underfoot, so I gazed out the side window. Isolated pockets of black spruce floated amidst marshy tundra. Despite all that water, a bank of smoke in the distance spread out low and flat. We buzzed over Fire 4617, now nearing a thousand acres. *How in the world did it get so big?* At the same time that raindrops speckled the windshield, trees burst into bright orange flames. Unbelievable. I stubbornly refused to admit, though, that Strudel might have been right.

Monte expertly landed us with nary a jostle. I hopped out onto tundra, marveling at its foam-pillow softness. Away from danger, four of us crouched low and watched the chopper take off for more crew. Instead of going to work, though, the fire boss told us to settle in for the night.

"Well, that's different," I said to Rob, while we searched for a place to pitch our tents. "I've never arrived at a fire and not been sent out right away."

"Yeah, who knows what that's about." He tested the ground with his feet. "Nothing's worse than finding a lump in the middle of the night."

*Just like The Princess and the Pea*, I thought.

Tent spread out and ready to secure, I realized that the tundra offered nothing for me to pound stakes into. I tied the tent to bushes instead. Pleased with my ingenuity, I crawled inside. *Nice.* Tundra made a superb mattress. Maybe I'd get a decent night's sleep.

For dinner, I ate tuna C-rat and trail mix. That darned, stubborn sun refused to go down, so I crawled into my tent with the sky still light and placed my watch within easy reach. During the dark-less night, I awoke twice, disoriented, as often happened in a strange place, but also because light messed with my internal clock. When I jarred awake for the third time, I sat up with a start. *What time is it?* I snatched my watch. *Seven o'clock!* Mortified, I thought I'd overslept and the crew had left without me. *Wait.* I heard Rob snoring. If they forgot me, they forgot him too. Not likely. Now wide awake, I listened for camp activity. *What's that steady hum? A generator? It couldn't be, not loud enough.* Tiny shadows zigzagged a bizarre dance above my tent. *Oh no.* Millions of hungry mosquitoes waited for me to unzip the tent door so they could have breakfast: me. I'd need heavy artillery. I sat up and fished the DEET out of my pack. Blood-suckers hovered at the screen door, waiting patiently for me to come out. *Bastards.* What to do. If I unzipped the door, they'd swarm in. Later, I'd lose sleep with all the high-pitched whining and anticipating mosquito bites, then getting mosquito bites. I read the label: "Warning: Product will melt nylon." *If it'll melt nylon, how could it be safe for skin? Wasn't the tent made of nylon?* I couldn't tell. *Now what?* The steady hum continued. *Damn, there's probably a gazillion of them now. Well, if it melts my tent, so be it.* I sprayed my clothes and then the tent door. Could I do this fast enough? Only one way to find out. I unzipped, scrambled out, and frantically zipped the door shut. I half-expected the tent to melt like the Wicked Witch of the West, but it looked fine to me. I set the can outside the door. I'd need to do that in reverse when I returned.

For breakfast, I ate more tuna, and more than twelve hours after arriving, we went to fight fire.

"Winds are calm, so there's no danger of being overrun," the crew boss said as we walked toward the blaze.

That was the understatement of the year. Looking behind me, I noticed water filled my footprints in the spongy tundra, leaving boot-shaped puddles. That didn't bode well for dry feet. Too late now to regret not buying spare boots. Finally we reached the fire, which blazed with a surprising amount of vigor, considering that it literally burned on top of water. There was no digging good old-fashioned fireline here. We stomped the ground hard, bringing water up to the surface, to make a "wet" line. In drier spots, we cut tundra with our Pulaskis, peeling it back to expose the permafrost. Curious, I knelt down and tapped the frozen ground with my knuckles. It was solid as a rock. *How in the world do plants grow here?* Later, we'd have to replace the tundra to keep the permafrost from melting, protecting the delicate arctic ecosystem.

About noon, we took a break. Out came C-rats and handy-dandy P-38 can openers. Sour faces and silence accompanied the meal. I'd had tuna for breakfast, and wasn't in the mood for more. After a few bites, I set it aside.

Hoping to sleep well, I flew into my tent after the repellant application and snuggled into my comfy tundra mattress. I slept so soundly that a bear could have raided camp and I wouldn't have noticed.

For the next several days I worked with wet feet. I built fireline for who knows what reason and watched it rain. Oh, and did I mention I ate nothing but tuna? There was no excitement, and no thrills or feelings of accomplishment.

"What I can't figure out," Fogie said, "is that if there's no threat to anyone or anything, why are we here? Kinda takes the fun out of it."

Dan pulled a deck of cards from his pack. "Anyone for poker?"

Too funny. In past fire assignments we never had time to play cards while *on* the fireline. Annoyed with bugs, rain and wet feet, not to mention hungry beyond belief for something other than tuna, I still passed. I sat on my poncho to watch them play. Huddled together with a tree stump serving as a table, Dan, Fogie, Fred, and Rob, looking like little old church-going ladies in their headnets, clutched the cards dealt to them.

"Damn bugs," Dan said, waving his hands in a vain attempt to discourage mosquitoes that couldn't be discouraged. "This non-stop whining has the potential to induce temporary insanity."

How I wished he hadn't said that. It ruined my own ability to ignore the whining.

"So when are we going to get some real food?" Fogie asked. "I just can't eat barf-beef-stew again." He sorted his cards.

I laughed. "I'm pretty sick of Typhoid Tuna."

With a faraway look in his eyes, Dan said, "I'd give anything for a *real* cup of coffee."

Rob discarded. "I don't think I'll ever eat salmonella-spaghetti-with-meatballs again. Hit me with two." Tongue in cheek, he studied his hand. "I'll bet two sticks, raise you three. I heard a paracargo shipment's coming tomorrow."

What a relief. Real food.

Fred tossed in three sticks. "What've you got?"

Rob splayed his cards on the stump. "Two pair, aces high, kings low."

Fred laid down a full house. Everyone else threw their cards down in disgust. I grinned. I knew that was coming.

That night at camp, we forced down more bad fare. It was a little hard for me to care about food, though—I had something more important on my mind now. I removed my boots and socks and propped them near the fire. *Dry. Please, dry.*

Because of the former bear attacks, we always posted a lookout while the crew manned the fire, and took turns taking care of camp. Dan and I were assigned camp duty today.

I saw the plane first. "Dan! It's here!"

Dan turned from his conversation with our bear lookout, who'd earlier scared off a grizzly. "What? Oh!"

I trotted to the edge of camp to watch. Dan ran up beside me, shielding his eyes from the weak sun. "He's getting into position."

The two-propeller aircraft, coming in loud and low, returned to align itself with the drop zone. From the cargo doors spilled a large crate, then two more. Two parachutes opened, but not the third one. That crate plummeted and hit the ground with a *smack*, disappearing from view. The others floated gracefully, tumbling a few times before they stopped. We laughed at the irony of one chute not opening.

"I can't wait to see what they sent," Dan said, as we made our way to the crates. "I've got first dibs on coffee and Danish."

"I wonder if there's any fresh fruit," I said, salivating at the thought.

"After I put coffee on, I want bacon and eggs to go with the Danish."

Soon we realized retrieving the boxes wouldn't be easy. We'd have to cross boggy tundra. Each of us picking a different route, we searched for stable footing. At first I found solid ground. But on my next step, one leg sank clear up to my crotch. *Oh my God! Quicksand!* Terrified, I clawed at the ground, desperate for something to hold onto. But there wasn't anything! In a few moments, all Dan would see was my hand poking out of the ground.

Panicking, I screamed, "Ah! Dan! Help!"

"What?" he asked, without turning around.

"I'm stuck!"

He turned and chuckled at my predicament. "Well, get unstuck."

"I can't!"

He folded his arms. "What do you mean, you *can't?*"

When I didn't sink any further, overwhelming relief turned my fear into silliness. One leg on top on the ground, the other one deep in the bog—I must look completely ridiculous. I exploded into a fit of laughter.

Dan screamed. "Argh! Hey, now *I'm* stuck."

That struck me as even funnier. "Well get unstuck!" I managed to spit out.

Annoyed with me, Dan said, "Hey, this isn't funny!" Then, "Bwah-ha-ha!"

He threw his arms on the ground as though in homage to the tundra god, rolling on his side, tugging hard at the sunken leg. I tried that, too. But like a giant suction cup, the tundra had no intention of letting go that easily. Cold water seeped into my buried boot. *Damn it.* I tugged harder, worried my boot would come off. Now that would be bad. No boot would be worse than a wet boot. I finally got it out with a sucking *thwop* and stood up. *Thwip.* My other leg sunk. *I don't believe this!* After several attempts, I managed to get both legs out at the same time, and immediately sat down. Dan also managed to pull both legs out.

"Hey, I've got an idea," I said. "Try crawling on all fours."

"You're kidding, right?" He wiped a few stray tears with his sleeve.

"I learned that as a kid in Syracuse, when the snow was too deep to walk in. It spreads out your weight."

Dan grinned at me, shaking his head. "Now we're really tanker dogs."

We crawled to the crate which had augered into the tundra. Dan stretched out on his stomach. He reached down to lift the lid. "What've we got here? Hey, a coffee can." He held up a flat piece of metal. A few specks of coffee flittered off in the breeze. "Wait, but where's the coffee? I don't see any in the box."

I pulled out a plastic bag, turning it over a few times. White and flat. "What could this be? Oh, I know what this is; it's a loaf of bread!"

Dan laughed. "You mean *was* a loaf of bread. Now it's just a giant cracker."

I threw it back in the box, where it landed with a thud. Nothing in the crate was worth salvaging. Every item was either squished, or just plain missing, like the coffee.

"We'll have to leave it here," Dan said. "We'd need a hoist to get it out."

"Yeah, what a shame to lose all that food. Let's go check the rest."

Fortunately, the others had landed on firm ground. We dragged, pushed, and cajoled our prized supplies back to camp.

Dan pulled with the rope looped over his shoulder. "I feel like a sled dog!"

"We must look ridiculous," I said, tugging a crate.

"Good news," Dan told the crew later. "We got food today!"

"Oh, please tell me they sent something decent," Rob said.

"Yup." Dan winked at me. "We only got two of the boxes, though. There's one more out there with chocolate—any volunteers to go out and get it?"

Rob and Fogie jumped up and dashed to the drop zone. Dan and I dissolved into hysterics.

That night, Monte taught me the trick of roasting potatoes, vegetables, and steak in an aluminum foil pouch. How I wished we were alone on a camping trip. Again, I propped my boots by the fire, desperate for dry feet.

"PUMP WATER TO put out a fire burning on top of water?" I asked, the next morning when I heard the new plan. Were they kidding?

I despised the term "learning experience," because it alluded to an unpleasant one. *This will look good on my next job application*, I thought, to convince myself that I wanted to do this. I slung a fifty-foot bundle of canvas hose onto my shoulder, and traipsed through swampy tundra, taxing my muscles and testing my balance, following others doing the same. We unrolled and connected hoses to form a hose-lay several hundred feet long. Fred set the pump alongside a deep pond and tossed in a hose end. He pulled the starter rope, and the engine kicked in, sucking water to charge our line. Back to the nozzle we trudged, where we stood, aghast. A wind change had already sent the fire out of our reach.

*I don't believe this.* All that work for nothing. A very unhappy me rolled my length of hose inch-by-inch, pressing out the water, uneven terrain fighting every attempt to make a neat bundle. I hoisted the now heavier load onto my shoulder and joined the others to lug the rolls back to camp. I mentally added a new reason to why I preferred working on a fire suppression crew versus a tanker crew—no hose-lays.

Two days later I awoke to steady rain doing what rain *should* do: put fire out. But no one mentioned leaving. We passed more time playing cards when the mist let up and huddled under ponchos during brief, heavier rain. Not sure what prompted our release, but it finally came. There was no mention of mop-up. If they had, I would've doubted their sanity.

Once back at Wildwood, I picked up Teresa's note off the dining room table. "It was fun being roommates! I'll write and fill you in on my new diet." I smiled and sighed.

Upstairs, I flopped spread-eagled on my bed. *Ahhh.* My poor sodden feet burned something awful, though. Too bad getting clean required getting wet again. The hot shower was great, clean clothes were great, but most wonderful of all was slipping on dry socks and sneakers.

Days later, I wondered why my feet still burned. Too many days of wet boots, I guessed. Stubborn, I suffered for a week until the tingling quit. Years later, curious, I researched the symptoms. I'd had trench foot. I could've lost my feet to gangrene. My jaw dropped. *Oh my God, gangrene?*

Several letters from Joe awaited me. Each one tore at my heart. Since I'd met Monte, I still wrote Joe, but not much. Our phone calls had ended months ago. Did I still love him? I wasn't sure. Maybe? But I did wonder if I could ever love only one person. It didn't seem so, I mean, at one time I was in love with both Glenn and Joe. What an emotional mess I'd created.


MID-SEPTEMBER: WINTER would descend on Alaska soon. I recognized all the signs: a lower angle to the sun, that unmistakable early-morning scent, and a different kind of nip in the air. Strudel gave us the option of working for two more weeks or taking the layoff starting that Friday. Two more weeks of this place? It was not like me to turn down the extra earnings, but I couldn't stand it here anymore.

I'd come all this way to The Last Frontier, and there was so much more to see.

I shipped all of my belongings home, except my camping gear, 35mm camera, and a change of clothes. I wouldn't need anything else.

# THIRTY-FIVE

TRAVEL BROCHURES SCATTERED across my living room floor, I had to quell my longing to visit every single place. Not possible in seven days on a limited budget. One thing for sure, I wanted see Mt. McKinley. A narrow-gauge railroad trip from Whitehorse, Canada to Skagway would be fun. From there I could ride the ferry to Seattle, and then fly home. It seemed wonderful on paper, but when I made reservations, I began to get nervous. Could I do this alone?

"I'm a little scared, Dan. I've never done anything like this before."

"You'll be fine," he said, then paused. "I just have to say, though, that I think this trip smacks of avoidance. You don't want to deal with Joe. You know that song by Supertramp? Makes me think of what you're doing."

*Take the Long Way Home.* I knew the song, and now I'd never hear the lyrics in the same way again. It surprised me that Dan thought this. Avoidance had never crossed my mind.

A few days later, Dan again surprised me. Stretched out together on the living room carpet, talking, he dropped a bomb. "I like you a whole lot."

"I like you, too, Dan," I said. "You're a great friend."

"Well, maybe I like you too much."

*Did I hear him right? How did I miss this?* For the first time, we discussed our friendship and our feelings for each other.

"Do you think we're in love?" Dan asked. "I mean, look how great we get along."

Were we? I liked Dan very much. Could it be possible we were in love and didn't know it?

"Is it okay if I kiss you?" Dan asked, blushing.

We kissed. But I couldn't deny it. There was no romantic spark. I told him so.

"Yeah, that's okay, I didn't feel anything either," he said.

Wounded, now I wished I *had* felt something. Would that have changed his response?

As my last day approached, I reminisced. I'd formed a kinship with my coworkers here at Wildwood, especially Dan, but I'd miss everyone. Monte had asked for my itinerary, saying he'd try to meet up with me. What would happen to our relationship after my trip? Would he come to see me in Arizona? I didn't ask. Probably because a week earlier, he'd said he'd "love to be with someone like me someday." I wrapped the sharp sting up with layers of denial to keep it from hurting so much, believing he'd find a way to be with *me*, not someone *like* me.

Stoic Fred acted like he didn't care. I expected this from him. I wondered if he regretted us not getting involved. Not that I thought it would've worked— it was one of those little "what if" moments.

Hours before I'd catch my ride to Anchorage, I sat with Dan at my dining room table. Our special friendship had formed an emotional closeness that's rare in life. The "rescuing the food box" episode still made me laugh, as did all of our adventures. I'd miss him so much.

"Will you write?" I asked.

"Sure." Deep in thought, he stared at his folded hands resting in front of him.

I placed my hand on his arm. "Did you find a job in California?"

"Angeles National Forest. Leaving tomorrow." A deep breath. "I'm so impressed that you're going off on this trip, alone." His eyes were moist.

It gave me a boost of confidence to know that my traveling alone impressed him. I could do this. We hugged.

"You've been a great friend," I said, choking back a sob, my face pressed against his neck. He broke the embrace. We exchanged our final words—not quite goodbye, but not "maybe we'll see each other again," either. From the kitchen window I watched him walk away and felt a few tears trickling down my cheeks.

AT THE ALASKA Railroad station, I hopped aboard, excited about my first train ride. *Wow, it's a double-decker!* I bypassed seats on the first level and scampered up the stairs to snag a roomy window seat. Soon the train zipped along at a steady clip through picturesque scenery on its way to Fairbanks, my take-off destination.

Late afternoon, I sat down inside the bus to McKinley Park, when a woman with a friendly smile asked, "Is this seat taken?"

Delighted to have the company of someone my age, I welcomed her to sit. We shared the same first name, which added to our connection.

"I'm from Juneau," Linda said. "I took time off to see Denali, something I've yet to see. It's always hidden by clouds. This time I'm prepared to stay two weeks."

The possibility that I'd not see the peak in one day hadn't even occurred to me when I made my travel plans. I'd need to think about that . . .

Linda and I pitched our tents side-by-side at the visitor's center campground and built a fire to keep warm.

"What did you bring to eat?" she asked, unloading supplies from her pack onto the picnic table.

"All I've got is peanut butter and bagels," I said, laughing. Hey, they were cheap and portable.

"Oh my, that will never do."

She heated up some chili and offered me a steaming bowl. It smelled delicious. Famished, I dug in. While we ate, we talked as though we'd known each other for years, not a few hours.

Morning greeted us with low gossamer clouds floating a mere twenty feet off the ground. I rubbed my arms to warm them. "Well, this doesn't look good."

"It might lift," Linda said, hopeful.

Once on the tour bus, Linda explained we'd not be allowed to get off.

"Not at all?" I couldn't believe I came all this way and couldn't get off the bus.

"Disturbs the wildlife. But they'll stop whenever we want to take photos."

Still disappointing.

"Grizzly!" the driver announced over his shoulder, pointing straight ahead.

I jumped from my seat to join everyone up front. The cinnamon-brown bear, unfazed by our presence, lumbered across the road. Zeroing in with my telephoto, I finally captured a grizzly photo, the ghost of which had shadowed me all summer; though not necessarily a bad thing. Especially now that I saw how huge and formidable they were. Another mile down the road, the bus stopped again.

Linda pointed to a herd of white animals. "Dahl sheep. They don't look real, do they?"

They didn't. With hooves tucked underneath them, curled horns held up high, they posed, contrasted against the indigo clouds like white marble statues.

Linda's comment about the difficulty of seeing McKinley got me thinking. Should I change my plans and stay longer? Maybe I should find out if I could backpack into the park. Then I remembered my budget, and the weather. Those snowflakes out the window could mean business. A couple of nights in this cold was one thing, but a week? Better to stick with the original plan.

"So where's McKinley?" I asked, seeing nothing but clouds and swirling mist.

Linda sighed and pointed to my left. "It's over there. Socked in."

Linda prepared to revisit the elusive mountain in the morning, while I readied my gear for the bus to Whitehorse, Canada. She zipped up her parka against the frosty air. "You'll call me when you get to Juneau, right?"

I tied my tent to my backpack. "I sure will!"

A full day passed on the bus, with an overnight stop on the Canadian border. I arrived in Whitehorse and skipped down the steps, eager to explore. I also needed to find the youth hostel I'd read about. Backpack slung over one shoulder, I strolled down the main street, meandering in and out of shops identified with carved wooden signs dangling from chains. Tentatively, I opened the door under the sign "Youth Hostel—Vacancy," and entered, my boots echoing on a plank floor. A coffee can and sign sat on the counter. *Please deposit $5.00 per night.* Fee paid, I smiled at the group of people sitting on the floor in the center of the room. I heaved my backpack onto a vacant top bunk and accepted the invitation to join them.

A bearded man with long, stringy hair had a woman draped across his lap, her head resting on his crossed legs. He told me they'd hitchhiked all the way from California, and had been on the road for months now.

"Wouldn't have it any other way," he said, stroking the woman's hair.

She smiled up at him. "Yes, we love being free spirits. We've camped in such beautiful places. People are so kind; we've made tons of friends."

What would it be like to see Alaska that way? Maybe the weather would improve, and I could camp overnight in Skagway.

A cold and damp morning greeted me as I tiptoed out early to explore the streets of Whitehorse before departure. Bright and sunny, at least by Alaskan standards, only a few wind-whipped residual clouds from last night's rain streaked the sky. Quaint, historic railroad cars painted bright canary-yellow with black trim, awaited boarding. There was no sign they'd let me on yet, though, and with my empty stomach reminding me that I hadn't eaten, I sat down on a bench next to an interpretive sign, fished peanut butter and a bagel out of my pack, and read:

*This trail, the longest of its kind, winds through the steep Chilkoot Pass, following the route of the historic Klondike Gold Rush that took place from 1897 through 1899. Over one hundred thousand people walked the Chilkoot Trail. So many horses and mules died, their remains left where they fell, the route became known as the "Dead Horse Trail."*

How tragic. No wonder it's called gold fever. And all of those poor animals, just left there.

Before I boarded, I asked at the ticket counter if there were any messages. Monte's note apologized for not making this stop. Only slightly disappointed, I thought maybe I'd see him in Skagway.

On the train, I discovered a small group of people standing on a platform outside the caboose. With no windows to get in the way of photos, and plenty of fresh air, this was the place to be. Smiles greeted me. So far, traveling alone was far from lonely. With a toot of the train whistle and a sharp jerk shaking the caboose, off we went, the clicking of the train over the tracks rhythmic and reassuring.

"Excuse me," a middle-aged man said with a gentle smile. "Would you mind giving me a hand so I can lean over the railing to take some photos?"

If this meant my making a mistake would have him falling off the train and dying a horrible death, well, I'd have to pass. Hesitant, I asked him to explain.

He grinned broadly, his eyes crinkling at the corners. "Oh, don't worry. I've done it before. You can get great shots of the train as it turns corners if you lean over and point the lens down the track. I just need some help."

"Well, okay," I said. "What do I do?"

My right hand gripped his belt, my left kept a tight handhold on the caboose to counter his forward lean. Pictures taken, he asked if I wanted to try it. Heck, why not?

"I've got you," he said confidently. I leaned over, my heart racing. *Whatever you do, don't drop your camera.* I squeezed it so tight that my hands cramped, and I took photos so fast, I could only hope they'd turn out. What a thrill, though.

A startled cry made me turn to a woman staring at the camera clutched in her gloved hands, her face horrified. "Oh my God! It's jammed!"

After determining that it was broken, everyone came to her rescue, including me, offering to send her prints. Another man even said he'd let her use his camera.

The woman wept from the outpour of support—making me tear up, too. Then I realized I was missing some great scenery and returned to the railing. In the distance, folded shadows defined the jagged snow-covered mountains and autumn had turned the tundra into a patchwork of turquoise, gold, and rust. Between two prominent peaks, an iridescent blue-green glacier spread out like an alluvial fan. Glaciers were plentiful, but I never tired of seeing them. I'd visited Portage Glacier with Fred and Dan a month earlier. We'd stood together on the shore, hushed by the utter silence, deep space coldness, and glacial patience. Fred had impressed me again that day, in the way he stood there, honoring the icy monolith.

Our train plunged into a dark, narrow, hand-built tunnel. Gasps and murmurs of riders echoed inside. It was dark in there. Very dark. *Okay, I want out now . . .* Just in time before I got claustrophobia, the train emerged from the tunnel and clattered across a wooden trestle—spanning easily a thousand-foot-deep gorge. My breath hitched, and I clutched the railing. Not only because of the precarious height, but from noticing the trestles were original, made of wood, and therefore over a hundred years old. No point in questioning if they were sound, it wasn't like I could hop off the train and walk.

At the halfway point, we stopped at the Bennett Lake depot for our free lunch. My legs wobbled when I stepped off the train, a side effect from compensating for the sway of the caboose. After regaining my balance, I detoured to the shoreline to take a photo of the lake. Clouds shaped like white, woolly sheep, and the fall-colored mountains beyond, mirrored in the lake with such perfection, I couldn't differentiate the reflection from the real thing. I momentarily forgot I was starving, and took so many photos, I had to scurry to catch up with everyone heading to the dining area. Seated at a long wooden table, I quivered with delight at the hot meal set before me. Not one speck of peanut butter in sight.

Upon arriving in Skagway, my perfect weather became a rainstorm with a wintery bite. So much for my camping plans. Another youth hostel provided shelter, and after dropping off my backpack, I ventured outside to explore. Lined with weathered, wooden buildings, main street Skagway still had the character of its rowdy mining days, and held an amazing number of saloons. I took refuge from the glacial temperatures inside a historical museum, reading the displays about Skagway's gold rush days while soaking up the warmth. Reluctant to go outside, I took my time, but eventually I couldn't procrastinate any longer. I dashed through the deluge to the hostel, longing for hot soup, a grilled-cheese sandwich, and a steaming mug of tea—with brandy—none of which was on my menu.

Rising early, I shouldered my backpack and slipped out the door. A damp, misty morning greeted me, with feathery low-lying clouds wrapped around the mountains like a shawl. Each breath suspended as white vapors in front of me for a moment. Before boarding the ferry, I stopped at the ticket counter to see if Monte had left a message. He had not. I frowned. *Whatever.* So far, I hadn't missed having a traveling companion.

The ferry's travel brochure said I could either book a stateroom or camp free on deck. Free was much better. On deck, I discovered there was not only a cover, but ceiling-mounted heaters. Perfect. I wouldn't have to worry about being cold. At first, I thought I wouldn't bother to set up my tent, but as the area filled with passengers, I opted for privacy. Within an hour, I'd made acquaintances with six travelers on their own unique adventures. Shy Eileen latched onto me first. I didn't mind that she seemed to need a friend and invited her to set up her tent near mine.

After a brief stop in Haines, the ship anchored in Juneau late afternoon. Linda had said to meet her at the Red Dog Saloon, easily identified by the large red sign sporting not a red dog, as one might expect, but a gun-toting "Yosemite Sam." A rowdy place in Alaska's gold rush days; that evening I also found it filled elbow-to-elbow with rambunctious locals and tourists.

"Only took two days for clouds to lift," Linda said over loud music and voices.

"Wonderful!" A pang of regret that I hadn't stayed longer to see it with her hit me.

"I used to live in a big city with so much crime," she said, taking a sip of beer. "We've got practically no crime. Everyone knows each other. Plus, we're landlocked! The only way in or out of Juneau's by boat or plane." She threw her head back and laughed. "We have *zero* car thefts. There's no place to go with one! Heck, you're looking at a city with only a few miles of roads. Authorities would be waiting at the ferry, the only way out."

Imagine a life where everything you needed was within a few miles, and no car theft . . . I glanced at my watch. Darn. Time to leave. Linda promised to stay in touch.

Eileen and I talked and played Rummy the following day while we sailed on open ocean, heading to Sitka. Her job as an executive in Seattle paid well, she said, but she didn't much like it. This solo trip was her once-a-year treat. She'd never married.

"Do you regret that?" I asked.

She twirled a lock of curly hair with her finger. "Sometimes I'm lonely."

I understood lonely, having felt that way, even in a room full of people I knew. I told her about Joe, our problems, my dilemma. And . . . about Monte, my other problem, my other dilemma, who was supposed to join me on this trip, but so far, hadn't.

"Wow. Conflicted?" she asked.

"You bet."

Eileen suggested we eat dinner together at the cafeteria. Even though I couldn't afford to buy anything, I joined her. Just thinking about real food made my stomach rumble, despite downing a peanut butter sandwich earlier. She loaded a plate with macaroni and cheese, steamed broccoli, and a slab of sourdough bread. My mouth salivated. God that smelled good. Not only that—it was *hot*.

"Aren't you eating?" she asked, when I didn't grab a plate.

I faked a smile. "No, I'm good. I'll visit with you while you eat."

Not having enough money was my own fault. I hadn't budgeted for meals. Did I think I'd crave something other than peanut butter? Obviously not. By the time this trip ended, I wouldn't be able to eat peanut butter for over a year.

Curled up in my sleeping bag, I felt waves rock the ship with Chinese water-torture precision. My stomach protested. *No, no, no* . . . I chanted, willing myself not to get sick. At daybreak, I staggered to the railing, fearing I'd throw up at any minute. The sharp breeze tasted of the sea, easing my queasy tummy. Eileen joined me, holding the hood of her faded green sweatshirt snugged tight at her throat. She gave me a knowing smile, and patted my back.

Abruptly, she pointed to the water. "Oh look! A whale!"

A humpback broke the surface, its shiny gray skin glimmering in the soft light. After blasting forth a fountain, it dove back under with a grandiose tail flip. My nausea vanished. *Damn.* Of all the times to not have my camera handy. An older couple joined us to watch, and I smiled at them.

"Did you know Sitka doesn't have any hoofed animals?" I overheard the guy say. Right away, I assumed he meant horses, possibly because of the difficulty of getting them on a boat?

"It's the rainfall," he told his companion. "Ninety inches a year. Causes hoof rot."

*Ninety?* Tucson averages eleven. How could it possibly rain that much and not float the town away?

Eileen and I scurried down the gangplank to explore Sitka after the ship docked. Who could've imagined a city like this? The houses perched on stilts over shores and marshes, with bridges connecting the many islands. At first, I marveled at the residents' resourcefulness, then I wondered where in the world they parked their cars. *If I chose to live here, I'd pick that house,* I thought. Maybe I could work in a gift store, or be a tour guide. It was fun to daydream.

"Let's go to the totem pole park," Eileen said.

We hitched a ride to the park, where I stared up at the exotic, colorful carvings. Although intriguing, I found the sinister grimaces carved on half-bird, half-human faces ghoulish enough to give me nightmares.

That night, a loud *bang* and a violent shake jolted me upright from a sound sleep. *Did I dream that?* Unsure, I crawled out of my tent to see people milling around, wide-eyed and confused. *Oh my God, are we sinking? Where are the lifeboats? Why didn't I pay more attention?*

A crewman rushed to the deck, making calming hand motions. "It's okay, folks, we bumped the dock in Petersburg a bit too hard. We'll be shoving off soon, so don't get off."

It took me a while to go back to sleep after the rude awakening. Groggy, I emerged from my tent to a hazy day in Wrangell. I forced myself to nibble a PB-bagel once again while Eileen and I strolled down the gangplank.

"Still no word from Monte?" she asked.

"No. And you know what, I'm to the point where I don't care. I thought I needed him to join me, but I discovered I'm doing just fine on my own."

I *was* doing fine on my own, but it hurt like heck that he'd blown me off.

Mist swirled around deep-green conifers in the mountains surrounding the tiny community. Everything sparkled with dew, the air so saturated that it felt like rain without it actually raining. I couldn't get over all of the water here: waterfalls poured from gashes in steep cliffs, filling streams and street gutters.

"Any more thoughts on what you'll do when you get back to Tucson?" Eileen asked.

"Not really."

I wished she hadn't asked. It was too hard to think about how to solve the love triangle situation. Was this love I felt for Monte one-sided? I refused to go there. For some stupid reason, I kept justifying the fact that Monte had never outright said he loved me with: *He does love me, he just hasn't realized it yet.* It did cross my mind however, that maybe neither he nor Joe were right for me. Then what? Good thing I had plenty of distractions on this trip.

Eileen and I strolled past another row of bright, primary-colored houses. Such a dramatic contrast to Tucson, where homes were often painted in muted earth tones. I envisioned living in this town, too. Curious about those magical waterfalls, the first thing I'd do was hike to the top of one to find its source.

"Let's get some lunch," Eileen suggested.

I finally admitted I didn't have much money.

"Fast food is okay by me. C'mon, you need to eat something other than peanut butter."

She had that right. Standing in a Kentucky Fried Chicken, I searched the menu board for the cheapest item that constituted real food. Four-fifty *for one piece of chicken and a biscuit? No way.* Eileen passed too, probably because she didn't want to eat in front of me again. What a pal.

One block later, I couldn't stand it. "Eileen, I have to go back."

I wasn't sure which was worse—spending the money and getting Canadian change—not realizing I couldn't spend it in the U.S.—or the greasy chicken that sat in the pit of my stomach like a brick for hours.

Our final stop: Ketchikan. Eileen and I stood on the pier, where brilliant fishing boats danced at their moorings, the briny air rich and brisk.

"Monte might be waiting for me in Seattle," I said.

She glanced down, then back to me. "If he isn't, how about staying with me a couple days?"

"Thanks, Eileen. I might just do that."

Way too soon, our ferry tooted its horn, signaling that it was time to return to our campground on deck.

Our ship headed south, easing between the San Juan Islands, where red buoys delineated the safe zone so we wouldn't run aground. Leaning on the railing, I studied the closer islands, thick with evergreens right up to the water's edge, some no bigger than a house and yard—all begging to be explored. What would it be like to visit one? *Hmmm . . . with no shoreline, how could you even get out of the boat?*

Over the loudspeaker, our captain announced that we'd have to move over to let a cruise ship pass. *Look at the size of that thing!* When I first boarded the ferry, I'd thought it was big. But compared to that Princess cruise ship, we were on a dinky tugboat. Passengers waved at us. I waved back. It must be nice to sail in style.

Soon the channel filled with speedboats, sailboats, and cabin cruisers—we were getting close to Seattle—and the end of my adventure. Never for one moment had I worried about traveling alone, not just on this trip, but during my entire time in Alaska. I would never feel that way again.

"The Emerald City" inundated my senses with dazzling greenness, like Oz's Dorothy, opening her door to a Technicolor world. It even smelled green. Crowds gathered at the railing, searching for faces of loved ones, including me, scanning for Monte. But there was no sign of him. My heart fell surprisingly far, considering I hadn't been very disappointed the other times he hadn't shown up. Then I recognized the handsome man with sandy-blond hair in bell-bottoms and a green polo shirt. I waved wildly to get his attention. Eileen's disappointment showed, but I hoped she understood.

"Hey, sweetheart," Monte said, sweeping me off my feet in a twirling bear hug. "I couldn't get away. But we'll have two whole days together."

*Two whole days.* Maybe now he would tell me he loved me. However, I'd need to play it cool—not let on that it mattered to me one way or another. Wouldn't playing hard-to-get work? I refused to think about how I might never see Monte again, or how I'd deal with Joe when I got home. Who hasn't floated down the "Denial River" once in a while?

Our time together played out like scenes in a romance movie, with me the lucky heroine. Monte and I dined atop the Space Needle, the restaurant revolving like a lazy carousel. We sampled delicious food at Pike Place Fish Market, strolled hand-in-hand through the Seattle aquarium, acting like a couple of teenagers, sneaking kisses in public, touching each other at every chance. By the time he dropped me off at the airport, though, his demeanor had changed. We kissed goodbye, and he again told me he wanted to be with someone like me some day. This time I knew he meant someone *like* me, but *not* me. I turned to wave one last time from the gate, but he'd already moved on and didn't look back. Boy, did that hurt. But you know—I'd seen this coming and chose to deny it. Stupid me. I had no right to expect more.

When I stepped off the plane in Tucson, a white-bright sun blinded me. My eyes adjusted, and I stared up at a sky that didn't seem real. How could I have forgotten how intensely blue the sky was here? I felt the need to imprint that blue into my brain forever. My heart jumped when through the throngs of people, I glimpsed Joe. Even though his body felt familiar against mine, I'd been away a long time and could tell. I wanted this moment to end all of my doubts, to make me forget Monte, to be the perfect reunion. It shouldn't have been so hard. After all, Joe loved me and Monte did not. What concerned me was that I thought I loved two men at the same time. Would one man ever be enough? Could he be?

That night, knowing I couldn't hide my conflicted emotions, I confessed to Joe that I'd gotten involved with someone else.

"I knew it!" he said, eyes glinting with tears. "You've just been waiting for someone better to come along the whole time."

My God, how much that hurt. I'd never intended to hurt him. I'd never wanted him to think I needed to keep looking. I hated myself at that moment. As much as his anguish pierced my heart, I didn't cry.

Detaching my emotions for the moment, I explained how he'd hurt me. How unimportant he made me feel when he didn't write. How unwanted he made me feel when he didn't include me in the stupid drinking parties at Florida, and especially how he made me feel undervalued when he was insensitive to my fear of his blind rages.

The silence was so charged with emotion, it was almost unbearable.

Tears tumbled down his cheeks. I'd never seen him cry, and the fact that I'd made him cry crushed my heart.

He swiped those tears away. "I'm sorry." After a deep breath, he said, "I need to know . . . Are you staying or going?"

I have no idea how I kept my composure, but I did. *No need to make a decision right now.* "Can I have some time to think?"

He gave it to me.

We fell into our routines. He continued to work at Florida; I took a job at a local plant nursery.

Early morning, I dressed in light layers, tied on my running shoes, and jogged down to the Nature Trail for my daily two-mile run. At first the trail had a bit of a climb, then the grade eased. It was shady and cold in the deep canyon, which wouldn't see the sun until mid-morning. White puffs accompanied my heavy breathing; patches of snow required careful maneuvering. A deer scared the wits out of me when it dashed across my path—a sharp pain twinged in my right knee at the sudden stop. *Ouch!* I continued, taking it a bit easier.

The next day that knee hurt a bit about halfway into my run. I changed my stride, and the pain quit. *Well, that was an easy fix.*

That weekend, Joe and I went backpacking in the Santa Ritas. After huffing and puffing for hours, we took a break. From a vantage point, he identified the various peaks surrounding us.

"That's Jack Mountain," he said, pointing to the forested mound. "Beyond it is Josephine Peak."

"What's that one?" I asked, indicating the jagged form to the north.

"McCleary."

Always proud of how he knew this area inside and out, I studied the shape and location of each one, determined to learn, too.

There was nothing like cold spring water to quench thirst. Of course Joe knew where to go. He also took me to old mines, with nothing left but caved-in shafts and tailings—remnants of someone's broken dreams. We pocketed some interesting rocks, examined abandoned equipment. What fun we had! Our interests were so much alike, and in many ways we were quite compatible. I'd never had this kind of connection with anyone else.

All of this time together rekindled my earlier love for Joe, or maybe it'd been there all along. One night, after a nice dinner in Tucson, we sat in my car, talking. I apologized for hurting him, for not knowing what I wanted. He sat silent, listening.

"I'd like us to grow old together," I said.

Another few moments of silence from him. Then he said, "That's all I've ever wanted."

In mid-November, a manila envelope arrived in the mail. It contained an eight-by-ten color photo of Mt. Denali, in all of its snow-covered glory. Linda's note said, "I thought you'd enjoy this!" She was right.

# THIRTY-SIX

## Summer of 1981: Bureau of Land Management,
## Durango, Colorado

WHAT A THRILL to have a job offer from BLM in Colorado! But not on a fire crew. Should I go for it? I wanted to fight fires. But why not try timber management? It'd look good on my application next year, and further enhance my qualifications. Another step up on my career ladder. A big plus was this job offered a pay raise. An even bigger plus: I'd be working in the small mountain community of Durango. Long ago I'd dreamed of going to Durango. Was this an omen? Joe and I would be far apart again, though. But darn it, he already had a secure job—while I still wanted, and needed, to follow my own career path.

Early Saturday morning, I walked outside and stared at the brand new Datsun pickup parked in the driveway. *So I wasn't dreaming. I did buy that yesterday.* Happy, proud, and optimistic, that afternoon I called my best friend, Gail, to tell her about my new job and my new truck, describing the color as "roadway-center-stripe-yellow." We whooped and hollered at all of my good news.

On the way to Durango, I stopped in Prescott to see my parents. When I swung into their driveway, my mom scurried out to greet me.

"Let me take a picture," she said, darting inside to get her camera.

I leaned against my new pickup as she snapped the photo, beaming at the prospect of a brand new job in an exciting new place.


AMIDST ALMOST TWO hundred miles of reservation land, with no visible civilization between Flagstaff and Cortez, a *Twilight Zone* episode, the one where a couple breaks down in a desolate place with menacing tumbleweeds, crossed my mind. Good thing I'd bought this new, reliable, truck. Calley stretched out on the dash, unfazed by car travel.

"Wait 'till you see where we're going sweetie," I said, scratching her chin. "Lots of trees up there." She held eyelids half closed over vivid green irises, contented and purring.

Positive that two days would be plenty of time to find an apartment, I settled into a Motel 6 and bought a newspaper. Several phone calls later, I realized this was going to be harder than I thought. I couldn't afford a week in a motel. What was I going to do?

A slender, tanned man with sun-streaked hair smiled at me from across his desk on Monday morning. "Have you found a place to live?" my new supervisor, Ron, asked.

I bit my lower lip. "Not yet. I'm still in a motel."

Brows drawn together, he said, "Hmm . . . You know, I think Scott has an extra room. When we're done here, I'll introduce you."

The twist in my stomach unwound.

Ron explained that I'd be collecting tree-plot data for use in future harvesting.

*Data? Am I in over my head?* But it also sounded challenging, and I liked challenges.

Ron grabbed a set of keys off his desk. "I'll introduce you to a few folks around here, and then we'll go out in the field for some hands-on training."

After passing through a maze of cubicles, Ron paused at an office door to introduce the two women inside. Petite and pretty Kristy was a geologist. She wore my favorite style of jeans and sturdy hiking boots, with a blue-plaid flannel shirt and rolled up sleeves. Kristy offered a shy, but friendly smile, and stood to grip my hand. Heidi, a towhead-blond and an archaeologist, smiled and nodded at me from her desk.

We walked to the next office.

"This is Randy and Dee, two of our fire crew," Ron said. "Jerry's off today."

*Fire crew?* For some reason I hadn't expected there to be one here. Dee sported the half-tucked-in-shirt look just like Fogie did. Randy was neater, and heavier, than Dee. They both raised their hands in greeting. I shared my fire experience—after all—that's what fellow firefighters do.

Dee twirled his chair around to face me. "Where 'bouts?"

"Arizona, Alaska."

That caught Randy's attention. "Alaska? Cool! Did you like it there?"

Always fun to get a reaction, I smiled. "Yes, but I fought more mosquitoes than fires."

They laughed. For a brief moment I forgot they hadn't hired me to fight fire. I couldn't resist. I had to drop a hint. I turned to Ron. "Do you ever need help? I'm Red Carded."

Ron hesitated for a second, then nodded. "If we're shorthanded, I'll have the guys give you a call."

On the way to the exit, Ron raised his hand to stop a Mark Spitz look-alike, asking him if he still needed another roommate. Scott folded his arms, dark eyes assessing me, his smile hidden by a thick black mustache. "Yeah, I do."

Problem solved: a place to live! What a relief. But two men for roommates? This would be interesting . . . but heck, as a liberated woman, I could handle it. Joe wouldn't care. I couldn't tell my father, though—he'd have a fit.

Ron and I drove out of town and soon pulled roadside, where he removed a briefcase and a leather bag from the cargo box. The open tailgate created our outdoor office. I sat next to Ron as he spread out a square, aerial photo on the make-shift table. "I'll give you a photo and the USGS topographic map of each inventory plot."

Aerial photos, captured by a camera attached underneath a plane, contained an amazing amount of detail, even more once Ron pointed out objects. This work was going to add a whole new dimension to my love of maps.

"Learning to read an aerial takes practice," Ron said. "See the diagonal clearing and parallel lines here? Shadows show it's a power line." He reached into his cruiser-vest pocket. "How are your compass skills?"

"I carry one hiking, but mostly for fun." I smiled and shrugged.

"This is a little different." He held the compass so I could see. "The arrow points to magnetic north, so the declination—the degrees off true north—needs to be set. I've already done that for you." He handed it to me.

I listened intently, wanting to learn more. Another critical motivator was at work here—I didn't want to get lost!

"To find your plot, determine the direction you want to go and get the compass bearing," Ron said. "To avoid having to recheck the compass often, find a landmark in the distance. A rock outcropping or a tall tree. Then walk to it. Take your time. I need you to be accurate. All your field data goes in here." He handed me a yellow logbook. "For each plot, you'll record the number of trees, their height, trunk diameter, and age."

Portable office closed up, daypacks loaded, we headed into the forest to practice. Sun-warmed pine needles, the scent reminiscent of cinnamon and cloves, crunched underfoot like potato chips, bringing on a memory of playing records in my humble trailer at the forested Palisades Ranger Station: Jerry Jeff Walker's "London Homesick Blues," Jackson Browne's "For Everyman."

A half-hour later, Ron set down the pack and removed a small instrument resembling a telescope. "We'll find the plot boundary first. Look through the scope and find the two vertical lines in your field of vision. Count only the tree trunks wider than the space between the two lines."

Trees counted, he taught me how to use each of the other instruments and how to enter the data. My head spun with everything I had to remember, but I couldn't wait to get out on my own. However, my conscience also nagged at me.

"Ron, will the trees be clear-cut?" I asked as we walked back to the truck.

"Hmm? We're looking at selective harvesting. Why?"

I hesitated a moment. Should I say this? I decided it would be okay. "I've seen clear cutting and think it's hideous."

He nodded. "It bothers me, too."

Ron and I would get along great.

Bright and early, I was off to my first solo assignment. A uniform would have made me feel even more official, but BLM, like the Forest Service, gave those out sparingly. Having a government truck at my disposal made up for no uniform, I decided. I tossed my daypack filled with the data collecting instruments behind the seat and headed out to locate my first plot.

Everything was going good until a "Private Property—No Trespassing" sign stopped me cold. *That must mean me.* How to bypass this? After trying several routes without success, I gave up and moved on to a different plot. At five, I asked Ron what to do.

"Oh, I should've told you. You need to ask the property owner for permission to cross," he said.

"So they don't mind?" I really didn't want to knock on a stranger's door.

He shook his head. "They just like to be asked first."

Why didn't BLM have access to their own land? But I knew logic and the federal government rarely coincided. I wished I could figure out how to do my job without approaching a stranger, though. In the morning, I drove beyond the sign and pulled up to the house, only to be greeted by another problem sign: "Beware of Dogs." Plural. *Great.* I listened. No barking. I stepped out of the truck. Still no barking.

A man walked out onto the porch, greeting me with a "who-the-hell-are-you" stare. Frantic dogs now barked menacingly from inside. In my most professional tone of voice, I introduced myself and asked for permission to cross his land. The man rubbed his eyes with both hands, drawing one hand down his unshaved face. Barefoot and clad in only blue jeans, he lazily scratched a hairy chest and eyed the blond BLM employee before him. Killer dogs continued their tirade. His brow furrowed, the man turned around sharply to address the source.

"Shuttup!" Whimpering came from within. He turned back to me. "Yeah. Just close any gates you open."

"Thank you." I rushed to my truck, relieved it was over, and completed my plot.

A few days later, I needed to get permission from another property owner. Feeling more confident, I pulled up, jumped out, marched up to the door, and knocked. An elderly woman answered. I made my request, obtained permission, and wished her a good day. I could get used to being my own boss.

"Our next project is out of town," Ron said, two weeks later. "There are many plots out there, so I reserved a motel room for you in Pagosa Springs. You can work as much overtime as you want, 'cause we need to get these done."

Staying in a motel, with no supervision and all the overtime I wanted? Way different from my fire crew experiences—more independence and even more responsibility. Ms. BLM Employee was feeling pretty darned self-sufficient.

Tiny Pagosa Springs had more billboards advertising their hot springs than they had motels, or even roads. A 1950s motor lodge would be my home for a few weeks. I set my suitcase inside my room and drove off to find my first plot. From the winding highway, I steered onto a narrow, rugged dirt road. It took me a while to find a place to park where I could turn my vehicle around. It was no fun driving backward for long distances—I'd done that once, and once was enough. Map and compass in hand, gear on my back, I headed out into the wilderness. Insects buzzed around my head, forewarning a warm day, but nothing compared to desert heat. Easy for me to get swept away by the pleasurable walk, but I needed to keep my wits together. *Time to consult my compass and find a landmark.* I picked a large rock outcrop in the distance to be my westerly guide. More walking, more checking. I took a water and map-reading break. As I sipped from my canteen, a rock squirrel paid me a visit. He scampered halfway up a tree, tipped his head, and twitched his feather-duster tail.

*How cute!* "Sorry squirrel buddy, no peanut butter today."

I still couldn't eat the stuff. On the aerial, I recognized a fence shadow near my plot. The topo map showed a section corner near it, too. Now that would be the ultimate find. In-ground brass caps marked land section corners. If I found that brass cap, I'd be more than lucky; I'd know my inventory site's exact location. Encouraged by a rusty, sagging barbed-wire fence, I followed it for a short distance until a glint of metal caught my eye. I squatted down and brushed aside pine needles. *Brass cap!* Akin to finding that darned needle in a haystack. My plot boundary was just a few steps away.

Like a kid with a bag full of new toys, I eagerly fished out the inventory tools from my daypack. Determining the plot boundary and counting mature trees came first. My ingenious tape measure converted circumference to diameter, and I recorded the data in my field book.

Ever since Eric had taught me how to pace a chain (sixty-six feet in length) during fire training in 1976, I wondered if I'd ever use the method to measure distance. Today would be the day. To estimate tree height, I counted thirteen steps (my one chain) from the trunk and pointed the hypsometer at the tree top to read one angle. A simple trig formula calculated a height of eighty-four feet. When Ron took me out for training, he estimated heights accurately just because he did it so often. Could I do that? I decided to practice on each tree.

Next, to find the tree's age. Before I did so, I remembered something I'd heard, but never tested. Did ponderosa bark smell like vanilla? I pressed my nose against the bark and inhaled. Nothing. I sniffed again. It smelled like, well . . . bark. So much for that.

Using an increment borer, a long, slender metal tube with a T handle on one end, I twisted it into the tree's center and removed a slender core. Using my pencil, I counted ninety-eight growth rings. I leaned back to see the top. *Wow. A grandpa tree.* Ron said a dark ring depicted a forest fire event. No sign of fire here. I replaced the core sample. Although Ron had read otherwise, he expressed concern that boring might injure the tree. I patted the bark. "Be okay, Mr. Tree."

Mission accomplished: I'd found my plot, located a brass cap, and best of all—I didn't get lost! I retraced my steps and drove back to my motel just as the sun set. After a quick shower, I was hungry. Apprehensive, because I'd never eaten alone in a restaurant before and felt self-conscious doing so, I cruised main street for an unassuming place where I wouldn't be, umm, noticed. The Mexican restaurant appeared quiet. Seated inside, I ordered a bean burrito; an easy meal that I figured I could eat fast and zip back to my room. In no time, the waitress set the plate in front of me. Starving, I took a bite. Bland. I mean, really bland. *Needs doctoring.* Condiments circled the napkin holder: salt, pepper, ketchup, and sugar—but no hot sauce I caught the waitress's eye and asked her if I could have some Tabasco sauce.

She pursed her lips. "Gee, I'll check."

Unbelievable. A Mexican restaurant with no hot sauce? My food grew cold while I waited, so I gave up and ate, and was finished when she returned with an unopened giant economy-size bottle. "Will this do? Oh. Sorry."

"That's okay." The last thing I wanted to do was make a stink and have people notice, and speculate on, the girl eating alone.

Before dawn the next morning, I bought breakfast-to-go from a convenience store. I parked in the same spot as yesterday, only today I headed in the opposite direction, again working until dusk. On the way back to my room, I considered a "to go" dinner too, but wanted a hot meal, so I endured another bland burrito.

On days three and four, I repeated the routine, parked in the same spot, and headed in different directions. The afternoon of day four, a helicopter buzzed over my head, made a circle, and passed over me again. *Huh, is there a fire?* I didn't smell smoke, though, so shrugged off the thought.

Headlights illuminated a note taped on my motel room door when I swung into the parking lot that night. "Call Ron ASAP." A bit alarming—but there wasn't a thing I could do until morning.

"Oh, there you are!" Ron said, when I called at eight.

"Is something wrong?" His concern worried me.

"Someone reported your truck hadn't moved for several days, so we sent a helicopter out looking for you."

*A helicopter? Oh! That's what they were doing.* A bit embarrassed, I explained how I'd parked in the same spot, dawn to dusk, and had seen the helicopter, but didn't know they were looking for me.

Ron's voice calmed. "We're going to get you a two-way radio. You check in every day."

Although I appreciated their concern, it also crossed my mind—why hadn't they thought of this sooner? And why hadn't I thought of asking for one? Because I never worried about being alone in the forest—being alone in a city scared me much more.


MY WORK IN Pagosa Springs completed, I again asked Joe when he could come up. This time, he agreed to meet me halfway in Flagstaff for a weekend. It was way too short of a visit, considering that we'd both spent eight hours on the road getting there. One night only served to make me miss him more.

That quick trip left me with the Monday blues. Adding to it, Ron sent me out to check on a logging site. *Ugh.* The last thing I wanted to do was to visit a logging operation. I liked my forests pristine. This was my job, though, so off I went.

Ribbons of orange flagging waved from a tree branch, marking my turnoff. I eased onto a rough road. No big deal, I'd encountered many of these. After a few miles, though, the ruts turned serious, and I slowed to a crawl. *Easy does it, no hurry.* After twenty minutes at a snail's pace, the road turned to squishy mud and the truck's tires struggled for traction. "Come on, truck, don't you dare get stuck." *Should I turn around?* I slowed down to think. *Heck no, I can do this.* I pushed on. Up ahead, heavy equipment spewed diesel fumes, fouling the clean forest air. Engines roared, metal clanked and squeaked, and a skidder dragged the downed trees to a waiting logging truck. Awful. *Let's get this over with and get out of here.* A group of men turned when they saw my truck—just like loggers in the movies, too, with plaid flannel shirts and red suspenders.

Midway up the hill, I lost traction and the truck stalled. *Oh, great. Just great.* I restarted the engine and gave it some gas. The rear wheels spun uselessly, spraying mud everywhere. *Darn it. Darn it. Darn it.* I hopped out of the truck and landed with a splat in muck up to my ankles. *Lovely.* After a few squishy steps, I saw what I dreaded. The rear tires were stuck hubcap-deep in the holes made by the spinning wheels. *Darn it. Darn it. Darn it.* Were the men watching me? Thank God, no—at least not yet. Determined not to ask for help—*would they think of me as an incompetent little girl?*—I set my mind to finding a way out. I needed traction. What to use? The truck bed held nothing useful, but . . . boughs would work. Lots of those around. More wading through sloppy mud to collect an armload. Hands sticky with pine sap, I jammed branches in front the tires. *Oh, man, I hope this works.* I started the engine, slowly gave it gas, rocking the truck gently forward and back. The wheels kicked up a little mud, but then grabbed, and the vehicle lurched forward. *Thank you, Providence.* I drove back down the hill until I found a turn-around spot and parked with nose down. Mud globs collected on my boots as I slogged up the road, my feet gaining weight with each step. A burly man with a scraggly beard met me halfway. He stopped, turned his head, and spit tobacco juice onto the ground.

"Hey, missy, I see you had a little trouble back there." Burly Man grinned, revealing brown, crooked teeth.

I nodded coolly. "Ron wants to know how much longer you'll be."

He unfolded his arms and hooked thumbs under his suspenders. "Tell him 'bout one more week."

Burly Man kept grinning at me. I left after a nod, hoping he'd lost his bet with the others for how long it'd take me to ask for help. My step had a bounce in it, even as I slogged back to the truck.


A NEW ASSIGNMENT was on tap today—patrolling firewood cutting areas. Would I be catching illegal woodcutters? Writing citations? I guess I could do that.

"Oh, no," Ron said, shaking his head. "We don't give tickets. We do want people to get permits, though. Heck, they're even free."

"So if they're free, why do you even give them out?" Seemed unnecessary to me.

"We just like to keep track of who's getting wood and how much. If you see someone cutting wood and they don't have a permit, fill one out for them on the spot."

Off to explore new territory—which turned out to be not worth exploring. BLM's bulldozers had dragged chains to rip out cedars for more grazing area. Dirt-covered trees ruined a saw chain and spoiled the "free" aspect of cutting your own firewood. Unlike in Kenai, at least I had more than sixty miles of roads to cruise. In fact, miles and miles of roads to cruise; and every mile looked the same as the previous mile.

Day ten. I couldn't believe it. There was no sign of any woodcutters. No sign of *anyone* the whole ten days I was out here. I didn't get it. Where were all the people? Miles clicked by, and I began to feel drowsy. My eyes closed for a split second, then popped open. *Oh my God, I fell asleep! For how long?* Terrified I'd have a wreck, I sang out loud, tapping my hands on the wheel, but that didn't last long. I pulled over, splashed my face with cool water, but my eyes still wouldn't stay open once on the road. Finally, I decided to give in, pull over, and a take a nap. When I did, I wasn't sleepy anymore.

I thought five o'clock would never come. *Boy, do I need a run.* I changed into running clothes and sped out my door to log a couple of miles. Once I gained my second wind, I ran faster and with less exertion. When I hit my best speed, a sharp stab in my right knee hitched my breath. I switched to my alternative stride, and the pain eased. Long ago I'd accepted pain as the price I had to pay for my chosen career. This was a minor annoyance. I decided to invest in elastic knee braces, thinking all I needed was some support.

Sweaty and less stressed, I passed through the kitchen on my way to take a shower. There, I was greeted with dirty pots on the stove, and dried-on food clinging to plates in the sink. *Damn roommates. What pigs!* I picked up a saucepan crusted with burned spaghetti sauce and wrinkled my nose. Inside the refrigerator, I discovered an equally-blackened pot, growing some kind of science experiment. *Oh, this is so not going to work.* Frustrated and fuming, I washed the dishes. The stomach-turning mess ruined my appetite, so I skipped dinner, took a shower, and went to bed early.

My other roommate, Len, worked nights and I rarely saw him, so I confronted Scott again about housekeeping. "You know, I pay rent here too and would appreciate it if you guys cleaned up after yourselves. I'm not your maid."

Scott's dark eyes narrowed and his mouth curled into a sarcastic smirk. "Nobody asked you to be."

"Well, I don't appreciate coming home to mounds of dirty dishes and spoiled food."

"Len lives here, too."

"Then tell *him* to clean up."

Scott pivoted on his heels and walked away. A wretched gut feeling told me this wasn't over.

Saturday morning, Kristy and Heidi squeezed into the cab of my Datsun so we could explore the mountain community of Ouray. Alaska undeniably cornered the market on wildlife, but here spectacular peaks in the jagged, zigzagging San Juan Mountains pierced the sky at well above fourteen thousand feet, earning the nickname "fourteeners." Add in crisp mountain air, deep blue lakes, gushing rivers, aromatic pines, and you've got the best nature fix that anyone could ask for. If I could bottle it, I'd be rich.

"Let's see where this goes," I said after spotting a dirt side road carved into a deep canyon. I craned my neck to look up . . . way up . . . at the tall mountain on my left. I hit the brakes. "Hey! Can you see this? Unbelievable."

High on the side of the mountain clung a group of rusty metal and wood buildings. Beneath them, a plume of gray mine tailings sprawled for hundreds of feet down the nearly vertical slope. Using my binoculars, I counted three intact structures.

"How'd they build them way up there?" Heidi asked, peering into the lenses. "I don't see any roads."

I grinned at them. "I think we need to investigate."

Kristy's skeptical face told me she thought I needed to have my head examined. "I dunno, Linda . . . looks pretty treacherous."

Common sense was overruled by the need for adventure. An hour of crawling up the talus slope and sliding down half the gain, got us, at most, fifty feet closer. Those buildings were not only much farther away than I'd thought, but reaching them from the road was flat-out impossible.

On the drive back to Durango, Kristy thought out loud. "We have aerial photos back at the office. I bet we could find a way up there."

Kristy shared those photos with Heidi, Randy, and me on lunch break. "An old mining road goes at least part of the way. It veers off in the wrong direction about here, but if we take this bighorn sheep trail, we'll come out above the buildings." She leaned away from the photo and against the back of her chair. "Probably the only way."

In spite of the obstacles, we agreed to try it the following weekend.


ANOTHER LONG PATROL day was finally over, and I hung up the truck keys, ready to head home. A commotion came from Randy and Dee's office. Curious, I walked over.

Randy rushed around his office, frantic. "Fudge! Where the heck's my radio?"

"What's up?" I asked from the doorway.

"We've got a fire!"

# THIRTY-SEVEN

"WE'VE GOT A fire, Dee took the day off, and Jerry's out sick. We finally get a fire, and no one's here!" Randy said, flustered.

Adrenaline had kicked in the moment he said "fire."

"I can go."

"Hey! That'd be great."

"Your radio is over there next to the window."

Randy frowned. "What's it doin' there?" He snatched the radio, then the tanker keys from his desk. I trotted downstairs behind him to the parking lot.

Randy pushed the tanker's gas pedal to the floor and raced down the main drag of Durango. My eyes darted from the speedometer to traffic. I debated whether or not to play backseat driver.

"So, what kind of fire are we talking about? Big? Little?" My eyes stayed glued to the road in case I needed to warn him of a pending accident.

"Snag." The traffic light turned red, and he slammed on the brakes.

I braced against the dash. "Hey! Take it easy, Randy. A snag fire isn't going anywhere fast. Plus, it looks like rain."

He sighed. "I know. We don't get many fires."

Safely at our destination, we parked the tanker next to a barely discernable two-track road, which hadn't seen a vehicle in a long time, evidenced by grass creeping into the tread. A display of horizontal zigzag lightning flashed, and distant thunder drummed. A whispery breeze carried the scent of rain, but that didn't mean it would rain *here*. Summer storms were fickle that way.

Our snag glowed far away as a red speck. Unsure of the road condition, we decided to hike in. Randy balanced the chainsaw on his shoulder; I carried a shovel and a canteen.

Gray, dusky light turned gnarled cedars into looming, spooky shapes; perfect for a Halloween scare-fest. An owl hooted; even more perfect. About a mile later, we stood next to the forty-foot snag, where flames flickered in and out of cracks, playing a bizarre game of hide and seek.

I'd never felled a burning tree before and wanted to. "I'd like the honors, if it's okay by you," I said, hoping Randy would say yes.

"Go for it."

Serious decay at the base would be a problem, and it made for a dangerous felling operation—a "widow maker." But there was no decay here. Randy positioned himself as spotter to warn me of falling branches, or if the gas in the chainsaw caught fire. I placed the saw on the ground and stuck my boot in the handle to hold it steady. Despite a good yank on the starter rope, the engine sputtered and died. Two more pulls, and the engine roared to life, sending out an acrid puff of blue smoke. I gave it full throttle and began the horizontal cut, vibrations tingling through my arms. The saw's teeth chewed into the dense, dead wood, spitting out cedar-scented sawdust. Earplugs merely muted the mind-numbing noise.

I turned toward Randy to see if all was good to go. He nodded. I made the second cut, angled downward, to meet the first. At the first creak, Randy and I dashed out of range. The tree teetered, snapped, and fell in slow motion, with a crash and a shower of sparks, right where I'd planned. Randy dug in with the shovel, smothering the flames with cool soil. Fire now subdued, I offered Randy the canteen.

"Now, that was pretty darned cool," he said, taking a swig.

Satisfied with how everything went, I had to agree. Mission accomplished, I offered to carry the saw. The awkward weight tugged on my shoulder muscles and my arm soon tired but I didn't want to ask for help. I could do this. Excitement over, I remembered something we'd forgotten. Randy did too.

"Damn. We should've brought headlamps."

Fortunately, unlike at the Box Fire with Eric and Tom, the moon was out and the terrain was easy.


A TASTE OF fire excitement made the next day's patrolling unbearable. Sitting behind the wheel all day wore me out more than hard work. Afterward, in need of a run, I started out at a slow jog around my neighborhood, passing a home with a dad washing the car, kids playing kick-the-can. A lawnmower buzzed, the air scented with fresh-cut grass. Exercise always helped me sort out my thoughts. Just a little knee pain today, which I easily ignored. I decided the brace must be helping, and I was getting better. What a relief.


"LET'S GET THIS show on the road!" Randy said, early Saturday morning at our appointed meeting place. Heidi climbed into his truck; Kristy rode with me.

"According to the map," Kristy said with it spread out on her lap, "the road should be coming up on our left."

"And there it is." I pulled off and parked.

After hiking for more than an hour, Randy recognized a narrow path as the sheep trail we would use. We opted for a short break before pressing on. A bold, dark cloud drifted over the sun, casting a cool shadow. Goosebumps prickled on my arm.

"Hey guys, we might need to turn around."

"What, you afraid of getting wet?" Randy said, teasing.

"Struck by lightning is more like it," I said.

Thunder grumbled; rain-scented wind swirled around us. I felt a wet drop. Then more thunder boomed, much louder and closer this time. Everyone donned rain ponchos just before the clouds released.

Randy dashed off. "Last one to the truck . . ."

Whooping at the top of our lungs, we ran all the way back. Naturally, when we reached the vehicles, the rain stopped and sunshine broke through the clouds with strong chords of light. I always thought Mother Nature played that particular trick just to remind us that she was in charge. We agreed to try again next week.

Lesson learned, the following Saturday we left much earlier and hiked faster, reaching the sheep trail in less than an hour. Steep slopes meant nothing to sheep, but were much harder for humans. Although we were fit, the high altitude made us short of breath. We'd already passed the timber line, the boundary above which trees won't grow. I rounded a bend and gasped. No wonder the buildings appeared reachable from below. They were huge!

Randy caught up with me. "How in the heck did they get everything up here?"

"That's why I'm here. I want to know!" I frowned at our downhill route— mine tailings of loose, golf ball-sized rocks. "You guys realize, don't you, that if you start sliding, there's nothing to stop you from going all the way down." A rational person would have feared sliding thousands of feet to certain death—but we weren't rational.

"Tally ho!" Randy plunged ahead, sliding several feet with each step.

I inched my way down, determined not to slide. Kristy and Heidi followed. Randy reached a manmade terrace, where a massive beam cantilevered over the thousand-foot drop.

He walked out, tight-rope style, sat down, and straddled the beam. "I've figured out how they built this."

After a brief, terrifying moment, fearing he'd fall, and warning him to please *not* fall, I asked him how.

"A tram," he said, pointing to a rusty ore car with a pulley at the top.

Those persistent and dogged miners of yesteryear . . .

While we were preoccupied, ominous clouds had formed—rumbles of thunder echoed in the valley below. We needed shelter, and fast. To reach the structures, we carefully maneuvered around rusty, sinuous cables partially hidden in the grass. I shuddered at the precarious way wooden stilts supported the buildings stuck onto the mountainside. Knees quivering, pulse racing, I approached the largest with an intact roof. The old wooden floor creaked as I entered, announcing my arrival to the ghosts of these ruins.

"Seems solid . . ." My voice echoed in the musty, cavernous room; dust motes danced in the shafts of light spilling through windows and cracks. The floor moaned with each tentative step. My eyes widened with wonder. *What a place this must have been in its day.*

Randy stuck his head out a glassless window overlooking a decrepit porch, under which there was nothing but air. "Can you imagine? You wake up in the middle of the night to take a pee, then one wrong step . . . and . . . whoops! Adios, amigo!"

Heidi's voice floated from the back. "Over here, guys, you won't believe this."

I eased over to her. Against the wall stood a gigantic cast-iron cook stove—rusty, but still serviceable. I could picture it in full operation: coffee perking, bacon sizzling, eggs crackling. How in the heck had they hauled it up here? I guessed it weighed a half-ton.

Randy stepped forward to enter the room—and Heidi grasped his arm. "Don't. The floor doesn't look good. Stove's probably still here 'cause nobody could carry it out."

Randy chuckled. "Makes you wonder what else used to be here."

More booming thunder, then a few pieces of hail pinged overhead. Seconds later, we cowered and covered our ears from thunderous vibrations of marble-sized hail pounding the tin roof. Amazing, how fast it turned icy cold; I could see my breath and needed my sweatshirt. With the hailstorm over, but still rainy, we ate lunch, exuberant over our discovery.

Once the clouds were momentarily wrung dry, we got out while the getting-out looked good. I slid a little less crawling up the wet tailings than I had going down. Still exhilarated when I reached our vehicles, I suggested finding out what we could learn at the Ouray historical museum. A short time later, we strolled among the display cases and studied the old photos lining the walls. The center of the room displayed a few mining relics, including a rusty ore car, much like the one we saw up there.

"May I help you?" asked the matronly woman behind the counter.

"Maybe." I smiled at her. "We just came down from that mine outside of town. The one perched on the side of the mountain?"

She removed her reading glasses. "Ah! The Old Hundred Mine. They hauled all the materials and the workers up by tram . . . oh, let's see, mid-1800s? Crazy miners. They did all that work, never found much silver or gold . . . oh, and there's a club. People who go up there often register with them."

We didn't register, but over the summer I wondered about the ruins. How long would they last? Would they be a pile of rubble if I decided to return some day?

ANOTHER PATROL DAY, searching for the ever-elusive firewood cutter, I was about ready to give up ever seeing anyone, when I noticed a middle-aged couple loading wood into a pickup on the side of the road. *Oh boy! Someone to talk to.* I parked behind them. The guy tossed a chunk into the bed and walked over to me, his face concerned.

"Good morning," I said. "Just checking to see if you have a permit."

"Permit? We need a permit?" Eyes wide, he glanced back and forth between me and his partner, who shrugged with palms up. "Are we in trouble?"

I explained that he needed one, but that we could resolve the issue on the spot. "You're limited to one cord, okay?" I said, handing the permit over.

He tucked it in his shirt pocket. "No problem. There isn't much here for the taking, anyway."

I never saw another soul.

*GRRR . . .* ANOTHER BLACKENED pot on the stove, dirty dishes heaped high in the sink, an empty milk jug, soured, on the counter, and an overflowing trash can. Flies buzzed around the detritus. *Enough of this.* Livid, I stuffed the whole kit-and-caboodle into grocery bags. I set half in Len's room, half in Scott's. I emptied the trash and wiped the kitchen down with disinfectant. Too late to go for a run, instead I made a sandwich and took it to my room to watch TV. An hour later, my door flew open. Scott glared at me, face flushed and eyes blazing.

"You can't do that!"

"The hell I can't. You guys are disgusting."

A screaming match followed, quite unlike me, but I was angry and sick of putting up with these guys.

Scott pointed toward the front door, furious. "Get out! Now. Or I'll throw all your stuff outside."

Worried he'd make good on his threat, I packed while he continued to scream at me the whole time, placed poor scared Calley into her carrier, and left. Huddled in a phone booth, shaking from the confrontation and sudden upheaval, I called Ron at home and told him I'd have to quit early. No way could I find another place for the two weeks I had left there. Ron insisted that I not quit and offered me his family's furnished basement.

"Now don't you fret," his wife said a half hour later. "You just make yourself at home and don't be shy about asking for whatever you need."

Downstairs, I found the hide-a-bed made up and clean towels on a chair. Did I ever need a bit of pampering at that moment. Although exhausted, sleep took a while to arrive. Amazing how Calley took this all in stride. She curled up with me, offering the reassurance I needed that all would be okay.

At breakfast, I brought up paying rent, but they declined. To offset the free room, I contributed groceries and helped fix dinner. After washing dishes, I joined their kids in a game of Monopoly.

When I arrived at work, the nightmare continued. Scott gave me a nasty, evil look as he walked by, and Ron worried about my safety. "Are you sure he won't retaliate?"

Would he? I owed him money for utilities, but I figured we were even because he'd thrown me out a week after I'd paid that month's rent.

"Just to be on the safe side, park in back of my house instead of on the street," Ron said.

The two of us stood in disbelief the next morning at deep tire tracks in his lawn, and a flattened mailbox. Coincidence? I didn't think so. I felt guilty exposing Ron's wonderful family to this, even though he'd told me not to worry.

Because I spent too much time avoiding Scott, my last two weeks dragged. Finally, on my last day, I sat down in front of Ron to go over my performance review.

"Good job!" he said. "You finished the inventory early and under budget. The district manager offered commendations, too."

"I had fun here," I said, both smiling and embarrassed. Compliments always threw me. I usually found it easier to pretend I didn't hear them.


AT THE DURANGO airport, I waited for Joe, pacing. The night before, I'd patiently twisted pink foam curlers into my hair. I rarely fussed like that, mostly because it was a royal pain in the neck, but the resulting soft waves pleased me. When he stepped off the plane, my heart leapt. Always handsome, that day, Joe was even more so. How long since I'd held him? Too long.

"You look great," he said, touching my hair.

I felt great. First thing, I took him to see the Old Hundred Mine, but from down below. He stared at me in disbelief. "You went up *there*?"

I grinned. I had the photos to prove it.

There weren't many campers out after Labor Day, and to make it even more perfect, canary-yellow aspens and fiery-red big-toothed maples, rivaled the autumns of my childhood. We pitched our tent, hunted for firewood, and dragged a log over to sit on. Dinner simmered on the open flames. Wine, nature, and good company. What could be better? I snuggled against him.

"BLM was okay, but it's not what I want," I said.

"So, what do you want?"

"Catalina Hotshots."

Joe frowned. "You know they're nothing special. The Florida crew did the same things they do."

Yes, I knew that. But hotshots went to more fires than we ever did. They had a reputation I wanted to lay claim to.

# THIRTY-EIGHT

## Summer of 1982: Palisades Ranger Station, Coronado National Forest, Mt. Lemmon, Arizona

*February 11ᵀʰ, Tuesday*

*The rain is falling outside the windows of our new home. Next Monday, it'll be 2 weeks since Joe and I moved into our 14 x 64 mobile home on 2½ acres. We've been happy since I've been back from Durango . . . looking back over what I have written— seems like I only wrote when times were bad. Joe's and my relationship has improved greatly—maybe we've become more patient with each other.*

BY LATE APRIL, I wore a modest diamond ring, with the plan Joe and I would marry in the fall. I also had high hopes I'd be spending the coming summer on a hotshot crew. To earn money until then, I worked at a local plant nursery, schlepping heavy plants out of delivery trucks and then into customer's trunks. Every time I felt ice-pick stabs of pain under my knee caps, I tuned them out. They'd go away. Of course they'd go away. My shoulder got better, so my knees would too.

In early May, I stopped at the Post Office to pick up our mail. Flipping through the envelopes, I recognized the one I'd been waiting for: the Coronado National Forest offering me a position on the Catalina Hotshots. I stared hard at that letter, hesitant to believe what I read. The offer registered: *I got it!* Excited, I sped home to share the great news.

But Joe didn't share my enthusiasm. "So how are you going to pull this off?"

Okay, so I'd ignored the logistical problem of living ninety miles from my new job. How *could* I manage a home and a long commute? Even if I could commute. With a busy fire season, I wouldn't be home at all. But darn it, I wanted Joe, a home, *and* my career. Other couples managed. Everything would work out.

The trip to Mt. Lemmon brought back memories—both good and bad. I'd come a long ways since 1975. Heck, even farther since the trail crew in 1978, when Frank had said he'd never hire a woman on his crew. If only he could see me now in the position he wouldn't let me have. At seven-thirty, I pulled into Palisades Ranger Station, a redwood building nestled among tall, stately pines. Smokey the Bear stood outside the front door, his wooden paws holding a sign reminding people that only they could prevent forest fires. *Good ol' Smokey.*

Inside, a twenty-something woman with an exuberant spring in her step greeted me. "Need help?"

"I'm Linda, a new hotshot," I said, secretly reveling in those words.

"Hey! I'm Sharon, your roomie. C'mon, I'll show you our quarters."

Sharon led me across the parking lot to one of the cabins. "Hope you don't mind; I took the lower bunk." She tossed her long raven hair back and laughed. "I'm afraid I'll fall out of the top!"

No kidding! That worried me, too. Not only that, but I'd have to remember not to abruptly sit up at night, whacking my head on the ceiling. I unpacked while Sharon sat on her bed.

"This is my second season here. Where've you worked?" she asked.

"A number of places." I opened a dresser drawer and placed jeans and T-shirts inside. "Three summers in the Santa Rita Mountains." I pushed the drawer shut. "Flagstaff, Alaska. Last year, Durango."

Sharon jumped up to stand in front of the wall mirror. She tucked an elastic hair-tie in her mouth and gathered her shiny tresses into a high ponytail. Mumbling, she said, "Alaska? Wow! What was that like?"

"I'm sure we'll have plenty of time for me to bore you with my Alaska stories." I smiled at her. Finished with my unpacking, I sat down on the couch.

Ponytail secured, she turned to me with a radiant smile. "I must warn you, the guys think I'm a threat to their manhood."

I laughed. "They do?"

"Yeah, I'm a professional weightlifter. Scares the hell out of them. My granny is embarrassed. She thinks I'll never marry as long as I compete."

I'd never met a professional weightlifter, much less a professional *woman* weightlifter. By the looks of her biceps, she benched some serious weight. "Do the guys give you a hard time?"

She cackled wickedly. "Not anymore! How 'bout you?"

Out of nowhere, I felt intimidated by her. I wished I had her steadfast confidence. "I've always had to prove myself at every new job," I said.

"Well, you don't have to prove yourself to me. Any woman that's been at it as long as you have must be able to do the work."

My self-doubt evaporated. She was right. Of course I could do this.

Before we started fire training, we began our physical training—a half-hour of calisthenics followed by a two-mile run. We then gathered in a meeting room. No hokey 1950s training movies here like I'd watched at

Florida. Twinges of anticipation accompanied the lectures about fire, fire, and more fire.

After work, we ran another two miles. Limping a little at the end of the run, I thought, *Dammit, why did you forget the knee braces? That was stupid.*

Friday I drove thirty miles down the winding mountain road, endured heavy Tucson traffic, ramped onto the Interstate south, and arrived home after eight, utterly exhausted. Monday morning, I left at four a.m. to make the return trip. This summer was going to be tougher than I'd thought.

I changed for P.T.s and the two-mile run, wearing elastic knee braces on both knees. Each time my foot hit the dirt, I felt sharp stabs, prompting me to focus harder on my mantra: *You can do this, and you will, you can do this, and you will.* Afterward, I joined Sharon and eighteen men, climbing into our crew bus to go stack slash, branches left from thinning operations, into piles for winter burns. On the short ride, I tuned out the lively conversations around me. With my eyes closed, I willed my ability to do my job, repeating my mantra over and over to make it happen.

That night, after our second two-mile run, I placed a heating pad first on one knee, then the other. In the morning, I pulled on the knee braces, convinced the support helped. With steely determination, I thought—*I can work through this.* Soon, it became—*I have to work through this.*

At the end of week four, Sharon approached me at the fire cache. "Boss wants to see you."

Unconcerned, I sat down in front of his desk. Avoiding eye contact, he pulled on his mustache, stalling. "Um, well, we've got a problem here," he finally said.

*What is he talking about?*

"I can tell your knees are bothering you. We need you in perfect health, and you're not."

My face burned—the weight in my chest, crushing. How did he know my knees hurt? Was it that obvious? I wanted to deny his accusations, but the words would not come.

"Look," he said, his voice less stern. "It makes sense your knees wore out after all this time fighting fires. But you'll have to quit, or I'll have to fire you for lying on your job application."

*Fire me? No!* Terror struck my soul. I could *not* let them fire me. I'd never been fired. Would I be fired? *Oh God, don't let him fire me.* My eyes brimmed with tears, my face burned with shame, as though he'd caught me stealing. *Had I lied? No!* I scrambled to think of a way to avoid making either choice, but I couldn't come up with anything. Silence permeated the room while he waited for me to respond. Finally, I gave in. I uttered the painful words: "I'll resign."

He threw up his hands, flinging himself back in his chair, startling me. "Heck, file a worker's comp claim. After all, you aren't the first person in this line of work to ruin their knees."

I stood up and stormed out of his office without looking back. No longer able to contain the rush of tears, I sobbed as I stuffed clothes into my duffle bag. The screen door opened, then slammed. Someone spoke, but the words didn't register.

Sharon raised her voice. "Linda! Why are you packing?"

Between sobs, I said, "They told me I had to quit, Sharon, so I did."

"What?" She paced, ranting. "They can't do this to you! It's not right. Why, I'll help you fight this, I will . . ."

Eyes swollen with tears, my throat closed so tight that it hurt to speak, I managed to tell her that there was nothing she could do.

She stared at me wretchedly. "I'm so very sorry. I really am."

Devastated, I loaded my car and left.

On the drive home, not yet grasping the full impact of what had just happened, in a trance of sorts, I wondered when I'd wake up from this horrible dream.

# THIRTY-NINE

*My Legs Are pinned under a tremendous, invisible weight, crushing my bones and tissue. I try to scream, but my voice won't work. Snatching a breath, I strain to call out, "Help!" Finally, I eek out a moan. Then, one much louder. I awaken in a deathly cold room of stark white.*

OVER A YEAR passed before the Worker's Compensation Program approved my knee surgery, allowing the doctor to remove the remnants of destroyed cartilage in both knees. When I awoke in the recovery room, I was in so much pain my moans turned into screams.

Joe stayed with me the entire first day while I lay with my legs immobilized in rigid braces, spacey from the morphine. Day two, late morning, a physical therapist steered my wheelchair down to the exercise room.

"We need to get you mobile," he said.

With considerable effort, I stood up from the wheelchair, and he supported me to the parallel bars to practice walking. Moments later, the crushing pain in my legs made me weak. I broke into a cold sweat, and fainted into his waiting arms. The next day we tried again. That time I managed two steps. Third day we graduated to crutches, where I managed to make three steps. I'd never felt so completely helpless, and hated every minute of it.

Seven days later, Dr. Percy, my orthopedic surgeon, decided I could go home. Terrified, I thought, *How can they send me home?* True, I finally could walk with crutches, but not very far. How would I manage? Would Joe even know how to take care of me? However, that didn't matter, the hospital wanted me out.

Joe had tossed an old mattress in the back of our pickup and tried to get me comfortable for the long ride in the late fall heat. I stared at the roof of the camper shell, sensing the stop-and-go of traffic, feeling the vibrations of the road and missing the air conditioning of my hospital room. *Where are we? Must be the Interstate now; no more traffic lights . . .*

Parked in our driveway, we discussed options to get me inside. Joe decided to carry me. Wrapping my arm around his neck, he placed his arms under my legs to lift, making them bend naturally. My blood-curdling scream startled him, and he put me down. I'd have to get in the house on my own power. When I reached the stairs, I set the crutches down and dragged myself up, one step at a time. After what felt like forever, I collapsed onto the couch, exhausted from the ordeal. One pain pill put me to sleep for the rest of the day.

Having been independent in the past, it was hard for me to depend on Joe for my every need. I felt guilty asking for help, so postponed asking until I desperately needed it, yet I seemed to always need it desperately.

When Monday rolled around, Joe had to go back to work. Now I had no choice but to manage by myself.

At lunchtime, I felt a bit hungry. Using my crutches as a hoist, I lowered my legs to the floor, and heaved myself up. The room spun as I waited for equilibrium, and then, one tiny step at a time, I maneuvered to the refrigerator. There, the dizziness reappeared, and fearing I'd collapse, I made my way back to the couch, hunger now gone. I slept away the afternoon.

Simply taking care of basic necessities filled my entire day. Personal hygiene took up most of the morning. At least the Velcro closures allowed me to remove the leg braces so I could bathe, although getting in and out of the tub proved quite challenging. By week two, I had a hard time securing the braces tightly enough to keep them from falling down. Four weeks later, I couldn't keep them up at all. *What's wrong with these things? Are they stretching out?* I stepped on the bathroom scale and stared in disbelief: I'd lost twenty pounds.

After six weeks, I was allowed to walk without the braces and to start physical therapy. Liberating! But my reflection in the mirror made me feel a little ill: my legs had thinned so much from atrophy, I wondered if I'd ever get those lost muscles back.

The physical therapist sent me home with some "easy" home exercises. *Easy for him to say,* I thought the second day, scooting onto the bed so I could let my legs hang over the edge. Fortified with a deep breath, I again tried to relax and let them fall naturally, but stretching the frozen muscles felt like they were tearing off the bone. Panting and sick to my stomach, I pulled my legs back onto the bed and sobbed. *I can't do this!* But I knew I had to; and I did, over and over again.

Instead of having Joe take a day off work to drive me forty miles to ride a stationary bike at therapy, I purchased one. Every day, I pedaled miles, keeping my legs flexible with less pain. A friend offered me a swim-pass to her apartment pool.

Unable to drive yet, on a chilly December day, Joe dropped me off at the heated outdoor pool. Slipping into the warm water gave me back some of my lost freedom as I swam back and forth for an hour. I almost felt normal, moving pain free, gliding effortlessly through the silky water. I decided to do this as often as possible.

We needed groceries, and although outings were hard for me, I insisted on accompanying Joe. At the grocery store, a woman in a pretty dress and a bounce in her step selected an item off the shelf. I stood in the aisle, using the grocery cart to hold myself upright, feeling ugly and crippled, eyes brimming with tears. *I used to walk like that, will I ever again?* Right now, I had to think about *how* to walk: *Lift leg, bend knee, step forward.* My doctor had told me I could return to work in six months. *Six months?* I'd be lucky if I walked normally in six months, much less hike again. For sure my firefighting days were over.

At last, in January, I regained enough flexibility to drive my truck's standard transmission. All I wanted to do was check the mail and pick up the newspaper at our convenience store down the road. Once behind the wheel, I had an odd, disorienting moment. Had I forgotten how to drive? None of the motions felt familiar. However, I managed, and soon parked in front of the store. I opened my door, extracted my crutches from behind the seat, and made my way to the entrance. Just as I reached the door, a man cut in front of me, and let the door shut in my face. My face burned with shame and anger—shame that my injury had made me reliant on others, and angry that many now treated me like I was invisible.

Another a whole year slipped away, with pain a daily reminder that I wasn't recovering the way both I and my doctor had planned. Afraid of addiction, and frankly never a pill believer, I had quit taking pain medication after the first day home.

"I don't want to mask the pain," I said to Joe, adamant. "I want it to go away."

At one follow-up visit, Dr. Percy suggested acupuncture. Game for anything, I went.

An oriental man of slight build explained that if the procedure could help, I'd know within two sessions. I climbed onto the exam table.

"This shouldn't hurt," the man said.

Each time he tapped a thin needle around my knee, I winced. After the needles were in place, he left the room. Afraid any movement would dislodge them, I stayed motionless, trying to focus on anything but the needles sticking up out of my skin.

When he finally removed the needles, I tried to stand, but my legs wobbled uselessly, like they were made of Jell-O.

The acupuncturist frowned. "This won't work for you, I'm sorry."

Joe carried me to the car, where I stared out the window on the drive home, feeling just that much more helpless than ever.

Alone, limping around, trying to stay busy, but hurting every minute, feeling lost and worthless—my thoughts turned dark. Who was I now that I couldn't do the work I loved? Filled with pain and resentment at the forced major life change, I withdrew from life, and slowly sank into a dark, deep hole.

My marriage also suffered.

Joe didn't know what to do to help me, and I didn't know what to ask for. We fought bitterly, especially when he got called to a fire. Those calls reminded me I'd never fight fires again. It didn't help that Joe rarely contacted me while he was gone, sometimes for as long as six weeks. Late at night, sick with worry, I envisioned him injured and maimed, or dead, never coming home again. Rational thinking? No, of course not. But I wasn't rational about anything anymore.

One night, the phone rang just after dinner, and Joe answered.

My stomach twisted and turned. *No! No, no, no . . . don't let this be a fire call. I can't take being alone again . . .*

"Okay, I'm on my way, " Joe said, hanging up.

"Please don't go," I said, pleading. "They won't miss you just this once." Tears streamed down my face. The phone rang again. I barricaded the phone with my body. "Please, don't answer it . . ."

Frustrated and angry, Joe ripped the phone from the wall, and threw it so hard at the closed bedroom door, it left a hole. Now hysterical, I sank to the floor. Joe marched into the bedroom, packed his fire gear, and left.

My meltdown continued throughout the night, followed by waves of guilt all the next day. I knew it wasn't fair to interfere with his job, but I couldn't seem to stop myself. *If only he understood how hard it is for me to see him go to fires when I can't go,* I thought. *That would make me feel better.* But would it? I wasn't sure anything would make me feel better. In fact, I believed I had nothing to live for. That night, I prayed I wouldn't wake up in the morning. *That will surely make Joe's life easier,* I thought viciously.

The telephone became a stealthy enemy. Each time it rang, my stomach turned over. Another fire call? When it was a fire call, I watched Joe pack, angry, resentful, and hurting.

Then, one horrible day, after Joe and I'd fought yet again, I blurted out, "I wish I was dead!" Which was quite true. I did.

Joe's face turned crimson, and he yelled, "The rifle's in my shop. Go for it!"

At that moment, I died inside. If he didn't care if I lived or died, why should I? Why couldn't he say things like: *I love you and don't want to lose you. Things will get better. You'll see.* But no, Joe never was good with words. When we'd met, I'd been attracted to his strong, silent-type personality. That very trait was now destroying us.

EIGHTEEN MONTHS AFTER surgery, I hobbled into the exam room for another progress evaluation.

"How's the pain level on a scale of one to ten?" Dr. Percy asked, pen poised over his clipboard.

"Nine," I said. I wanted to leave room for the really bad days.

He lowered the clipboard. "I think you're worse. We can try a second procedure . . ."

*More surgery? No!* I burst into hysterical tears, sobbing uncontrollably.

Eyes startled wide, Percy turned to his intern. "Get this woman on anti-depressants, now!" The intern sped out of the room. "I won't operate on you until we get your depression under control. I'll have my office recommend a counselor."

Several weeks later, Joe and I fought again, about what, I don't know. He sat in front of the TV, not wanting to deal with me any longer, and I opened the junk drawer in the kitchen. I removed a straight-edge razor blade from its box, and oddly calm, took it into the bathroom. There, I shut the door, and sat on the toilet seat. I began to sob—deep, guttural sobs that hurt my chest. I opened my hand and stared at the razor blade in its cardboard safety cover, then at my wrist. I wanted to slice my wrist open, end the emotional pain, but I couldn't make myself do it.

The bathroom door flew open. Joe stood in front of me with his hands on his hips.

"Give it to me, now."

I clenched the blade tighter and shook my head, no.

"I said give it to me!"

I handed the blade over and sobbed.

He sighed loudly and left me sitting there.

I wailed, rocking back and forth, until exhausted. Then I crawled into bed and slept for twelve hours to avoid thinking about what I almost did.

At my first counseling appointment, my therapist explained depression and a treatment plan. At the second one, he checked on my progress. "Has Joe locked up his guns, hidden razor blades, and removed all prescription drugs from the house?"

I nodded. At least Joe had taken my counselor's initial request seriously.

"Are you taking your meds? It's very important that you continue. We can talk about your feelings here, and we will, but you need more than just talk therapy. Okay?"

Again, I dissolved into floods of tears. Would I ever stop crying? Would I ever feel better? Although I was at my lowest weight since I was a teenager, I felt heavy, like I carried an additional twenty pounds.

"Do you realize this is not your fault? The injury? Joe's anger?" my counselor asked.

No, I didn't. I blamed myself for being unable to cope, for venting my mad frustration at Joe and for my body falling apart. But, talking did help. And soon, the weekly sessions became my lifeline.

# FORTY

GROGGY, I PEELED my eyes open to look around me. A steady hum from the machine sitting next to my hospital bed, the only sound. The room gradually came into focus: my legs were strapped to a machine, which slowly bent and straightened them. Minutes later, Dr. Percy and a group of residents stood by my bedside.

"My oldest living patient," Percy said, stone-faced, in the way of an introduction. A joke (at least I hoped so) I'd heard often since he first operated on me two years ago. Was that a good thing?

"You'll be out of here in no time," he added, glancing at me, then down to his clipboard. He was right, too. I left in just a few days.

Six months later, though, my knees still hurt. Incredibly discouraged, I couldn't believe I went through all that torture only to continue to suffer. Lost and still depressed, I sat in front of my counselor.

"I want my old life back!" I cried, frustrated tears again falling.

"What's holding you back?" he asked. "You could go to college, start a new career."

I dabbed a sodden tissue at my eyes. "I'll be thirty-four by the time I graduate."

"You'll be thirty-four in four years whether you go to college or not," he said with a grin.

I gave him a pained smile.

He suggested that I take a career test.

Hundreds of questions later, I held a computer printout of careers that might be a good fit for me. I smiled wryly when forestry technician (my firefighting classification) came up *below* sanitation engineer. Garbage man? *Oh, give me a break.* Fourth down on the list—landscape architect. The Forest Service often hired landscape architects—my heart lightened at the possible way back into the agency, where I longed to be. After two years in limbo, I'd finally found new direction and new hope.

That Christmas with my family, I announced my plan to enroll in the University of Arizona's landscape architecture program the next fall. Cheers and claps surprised me. I would be the first in my family to attend college.

Dr. Percy, in the meantime, had retired, and at my final appointment with his replacement, I lamented how I had no relief from daily pain. He heaved a sigh, and told me that maybe someday I would wake up and the pain would be gone. *Is he serious? That's it?* Annoyed by this cavalier remark, I figured I'd have to learn to live with pain the rest of my life. No big deal: I was used to it.


THE DECISION TO go to college was the easy part. But when I found out I had to take an entrance exam to get in, I worried. *Could I pass an entrance exam?* I decided I'd better take Algebra and English over the summer. I passed the exam. Now to fill out paperwork and register for classes.

"You're in the wrong building," the snarky woman snipped at me. "The department you want is in Student Services."

I stared at her in disbelief. I'd just come from Student Services—clear on the opposite side of campus. Emerging into the blistering July heat, my knees weak and throbbing, sweat pouring down my face, I trudged along, thinking, *What in the hell am I doing here?* Why *am I doing this?* Again at Student Services, I stood in yet another long line, where they told me I was in the wrong place, and directed me back to the Administration Department—the very building I'd just left. Furious, I limped across campus, cursing under my breath at my counselor: "Dammit! Look what you got me into!"

At last, though, I was down to my final task—buying textbooks. The minute I walked inside the campus bookstore, I felt something I hadn't felt for years: excitement. I scoured the shelves and lifted a hefty, oversized book filled with full-color photos. *This looks interesting . . . Landscape Architecture.* Then another one, with its distinctive new book smell . . . the cover crackled when I opened it. *This one's optional, but I really want it.* Loaded with more books than I could carry without discomfort didn't matter. I couldn't wait to get them all home so I could start reading.


MAY OF 1990: I graduated at the top of my class. Convinced that working for free would eventually pay off, I volunteered with the Coronado National Forest, full-time, in their landscape architecture department, commuting sixty miles per day. My hopes soared when they advertised a real, paying job in that very department. I applied, confident the position was mine.

Weeks later, on the phone with the Forest's HR department, I thought the voice on the other end must have called the wrong number. They'd given the job to someone else. Despite my degree, three months of volunteering and my on-the-job injury, they'd picked a man—a man with an undergraduate degree, *in English!* I'd sacrificed my knees and my health for the Forest Service, and they'd dumped me. I slammed down the phone and screamed at their indifference—*Damn you!*

Frustrated with the slow economy and no jobs, two years later I returned to the University for a masters degree in recreation planning. In my heart, I still wanted a Forest Service job, and maybe *this* degree would finally get me there. But, no. Instead, I found myself in the world of land development. Not quite working in nature, but it paid well. I advanced quickly in my new career, and within several years I held a high-paying position. Although my knees still gave me problems, I continued exercising, and graduated to hiking the gentle Nature Trail in Madera Canyon once a week.

Joe had never liked firefighting as much as I did, and when the Forest Service offered him a position in a different department, he accepted it. Settled into my new career, and with Joe's job no longer a source of contention between us, I thought our conflicts would end—that we would no longer fight.

I passed on the Forest Service party that Joe wanted to attend, not interested in socializing with people who didn't give a damn about me. Yes, I knew I disappointed him, but I thought he understood. He said he'd be home by eight. When I awoke at two a.m. and he wasn't home, I paced the house, worried sick that something bad had happened. Just then headlights swung into the driveway. I ran out, concerned. One look at him and my concern evaporated. Drunk to the point that he couldn't even stand, I raged at him for worrying me as well as for driving drunk. His eyes blazed, and he grabbed me by the throat, squeezing until I choked. Terrified, I pried his hands off my neck and ran into the house. Sinking to the floor, in between heaving sobs, I told the 911 operator what had happened. They said help was on the way. Joe stood over me for a moment, and then, resigned, calmly walked into the bedroom and lay down on the bed.

The next day he returned, angry at me because the sheriff's deputy had removed him from our home. He blamed me for setting him off in the first place. But this time, I refused to accept the blame.

"You must go to anger management counseling, or we're through," I said.

To my surprise, he went. After a few months, he invited me to attend a session with him.

"Joe has something he wants to say," his counselor said.

For the first time since Joe had told me to get his gun if I wanted to die, he took my hands, and apologized. "I'm sorry. I know that hurt you terribly. I didn't mean it."

Could I accept this? Deep down, I thought his apology had been offered way too late. How could I ever forget? However, he continued to see a counselor and made an effort to change, and that impressed me. For the first time, I didn't feel alone in wanting our marriage to work. Over the coming months, things between us improved. Encouraged, I hoped that all would continue to be good.

AS I DID every Saturday in cool weather, I buzzed up the Nature Trail, clearing my mind of work stresses. Just being here raised my spirits. I passed a family, and the father grinned at me, saying, "I'd recognize a power-hike anywhere."

I smiled. Moments later, his comment got me thinking. *Maybe this trail's getting too easy.*

A week later, I hiked five miles up a steeper trail with ease. Standing in Josephine Saddle, I read the junction sign: *Mt. Wrightson 2.5 miles.* Motivated, I decided next week I'd go to the top.

I left early. A little snow and ice challenged me on this cold and blustery day. When I reached the summit, my knees trembled from the precarious exposure. It'd been years since I'd stood on this volcanic pillar, with expansive views in every direction. I shed my daypack, huddled out of the wind as best I could and opened the old Army ammunition box to sign-in. With my frozen fingers grasping the pencil stub, I wrote:

*I never thought I'd ever hike again, much less make it to the top. But I'm here!*

Ecstatic, I jumped up and screamed, "Woo-hoo!" flailing my arms.

Seconds later another hiker joined me. Embarrassed, I wondered if he'd heard me. We exchanged greetings, hollering over the howling wind. He seemed friendly, so I yelled out the significance of my being there.

He yelled back, "Congratulations!"

Yes, indeed. I deserved congratulations.

Doors were now wide open. *I can hike anywhere I want!* I revisited every trail in the Santa Rita Mountains. Hiking connected me to my twenty-year-old self—the strong woman who used to be a firefighter. My favorite trail to Florida Saddle, a tough, steep, rocky trek, didn't offer views as grand as the trails to Mt. Wrightson, but here, Douglas firs reached their full potential, some so big it would take three people to wrap their arms around them. I greeted a familiar one and wrapped my arms around its ample girth. *Thanks for waiting.*

At the saddle, surrounded by these peaceful, majestic trees, I couldn't help but think about my summers of fire in these very mountains. Despite everything that happened to me: discrimination, knee injuries, painful surgery, and even more painful recovery—I had no regrets. I'd discovered that when you love what you do, it's not called work.

Someone asked me not too long ago if I missed firefighting. I'm not sure why I'd said "no," because as soon as they walked away, I thought, *of course I do*. My time as a firefighter will always be an important part of who I am. I still feel nostalgia for the camaraderie, the excitement, the glamour, the hard work—all of it. I love to tell fire stories to anyone who will listen.

On the news, I hear that another wildfire rages out of control—over a hundred thousand acres. Fires get so much bigger now. Glued to the screen, I can't look away. I hear that voice, feel that twinge, that says—

*I want to go.*

# EPILOGUE

IN APRIL OF 1987, Eric called, bearing sad news. Glenn had died in his sleep the day before, at the age of fifty-seven. I hung up the phone and stood in shock for a moment before it registered. *Glenn is gone.* Although I hadn't seen him since Joe and I moved from Madera, I felt a deep, profound loss. Tears coursed down my cheeks. How sad many people would never know that a great, humble man had just died way too young.

Also in the '80s, Mark and I became friends again. This was important to me. I never could stop caring about someone I used to love, and I appreciated that he forgave me for all that transpired between us.

My marriage to Joe continued to be a difficult and rock-filled road. However, committed to stay with him, I spent many hours in front of many marriage counselors—sometimes with him, sometimes without, trying to mend what I thought could be fixed if only I tried hard enough. But finally, after a twenty-three year marriage, I realized that Joe's violent, angry outbursts were not my fault, and that they were not going to end. This time, the major life change was my choice. Knowing it would not be easy, but knowing I couldn't live like that anymore—in 2004, I told him I wanted a divorce. He took this extremely hard, as I'd worried he would; but only once did he ask me if we could try again. When he did, I shook my head "no." I knew in my heart that I'd done everything in my power to make our relationship better, and "one more shot" wasn't going to make any difference. I didn't want to live my life wondering when he would punch another hole in the wall, or destroy yet one more inanimate object, or, worst of all, when he'd switch from hitting things to hitting me. I was tired of being treated like I wasn't important enough for him to change his behavior. *No more.*

Whoever said that divorce is more painful than losing your partner to death was right. It is excruciating. But after the post-divorce dust settled, Joe and I began talking weekly. I wanted to. I didn't hate him. We had so much history together. I wanted to keep him in my life—if he wanted to be there. Gradually, we established a friendship—far better than our marriage ever was. He showed me only his good side—the one I fell in love with.

Fast-forward three years: the economy collapsed, and my company laid me off. At the exact same time, my mom's health rapidly declined after a series of strokes.

On a drizzly, cold, grey February afternoon, the hospice facility called to warn me she might not make it until morning. I called Joe, sobbing, and delivered the sad news. An hour after I hung up, he knocked on my door. We sat together in my kitchen, heads hanging low, not feeling a need to say one single word. The phone rang.

"She's gone," my sister said. I hung up the receiver and turned to Joe. He gathered me into his arms and stroked my hair while I wailed in pure, deep, utter despair.

It took a year for the rawness of her passing to ease. At this writing it's been seven, and I still miss her every single day.

Over the next six years, Joe and I continued to exchange several phone calls a month, birthday lunches, holiday dinners—until the day he blindsided me, cutting off all communications because he found someone else. How had I missed this coming? What a stupid idiot I was, to think that it wouldn't happen, that he would always love me. Even worse, a few months before this I'd actually wondered if we would get back together. Is it selfish of me to be hurt that he's moved on? Maybe. I've quit trying to explain to friends why his ostracizing feels like he poured battery acid into my heart. If it's selfish to miss someone you've been close to for decades, then so be it. I'm selfish. But I do find myself again asking this question again: how do you extract someone from your heart after they are firmly embedded there? I still don't know, but I'm working on it—I have to. I have a life to live.

My decision to write this book came at a time when I needed to escape to the past, because the future looked so bleak. I thought it would help me to write about some of the best times of my life: the love and romance, fun, laughter . . . the challenging, but satisfying, work. It could boost my spirits. But it turned into much more.

Writing this book led me on a journey. I've been able to reflect on my fight to work in a field where I was not welcome, but how I never let that stop me from pursuing what I loved to do. I've reflected on past loves, and how many of those men still occupy a place in my heart, which makes me realize that I was, and still am, worth loving. I've reflected on losing my former career, finding a new one, then losing that one, too.

My friends say I'm amazingly strong and resilient—a true survivor. I protest—because many days I'm not feeling strong and wonder if my life will ever be better.

But you know what? There's a little voice inside that I've finally started to listen to: I've made it through some really tough times before—enough to test anyone to the brink of giving up. Can I do it again? Maybe I already am. Three years after the layoff, I reinvented my career. I started my own landscape design business and began teaching classes in desert plant care. It's wonderful to see my clients excited over my designs, and to see eager-to-learn faces in my classes. I should learn to trust what my friends say: I am strong enough. I will survive this tough time. Life will get better. And who knows, maybe I have room in my heart for one more love . . .

As the first woman firefighter at Florida, and among the first in the nation, I'd like to think that my perseverance and hard work made it easier for the women who followed me.

Back in the 1990s I'd read some encouraging news: some men consider women firefighters to be dedicated comrades and a team asset. My coworker Robert, at Florida Work Center, recognized that in 1976. Men work harder with women present on the crew, and women work even harder than the men in order to prove themselves (an inequality I still resent.) It's also theorized that men take unnecessary risks, ones that women wouldn't take. It is thought that the all-male Granite Mountain Hotshots, killed in the summer of 2013, left their safety zone feeling a need to reengage an active fire. Did they take an unnecessary risk? I wonder. No one will ever know what happened on that horrible day, because no one survived to tell the tale.

The reality? Discrimination is alive and well, and is perhaps one reason why only one-percent of all firefighting jobs are held by women. It's frustrating for me to see that the same outdated attitudes I faced over forty years ago still persist. The same sexist comments, the same disrespect, the same ostracizing. It's as though attitudes are frozen in place and time.

Should women be firefighters? Why not? Sure, dangerous work isn't for everyone. But if someone has what it takes, what difference does gender make? To this day, the all-woman Apache 8 crew are still highly revered elite wildland firefighters. I remember reading a short time ago that men have joined this crew. Now, isn't that an interesting twist?

The fact is that each individual contributes their own knowledge, skills, and abilities. If everyone in the crew had identical abilities, then it would have duplicate strengths and weaknesses, making the weaknesses more pronounced. It makes sense that a diverse crew would cover the spectrum of strengths, cover each other's weaknesses, and therefore be more complete. A fire crew is just that—a crew—a team, all working together for a common goal. And this goal is more readily achieved through the combined and varied strengths of all the members on that crew.

Linda Strader is a landscape architect in southern Arizona, the very same area where she became one of the first women on a Forest Service fire crew in 1976. Summers of Fire is a memoir based on her experiences not only working on fire crews, but how she had to find her courage and resiliency after losing her way. Her publishing history includes many web articles on her expertise of landscaping with desert plants. A local newspaper, the *Green Valley News*, printed an article about her firefighting adventures, which led the magazine, *Wildfire Today*, to publish an excerpt. The article generated interest in her speaking on this topic to several clubs, including the American Association of University Women.